Divine Discontent

Divine Discontent

The Religious Imagination of
W. E. B. Du Bois

JONATHON S. KAHN

OXFORD
UNIVERSITY PRESS

2009

OXFORD
UNIVERSITY PRESS

Oxford University Press, Inc., publishes works that further
Oxford University's objective of excellence
in research, scholarship, and education.

Oxford   New York
Auckland   Cape Town   Dar es Salaam   Hong Kong   Karachi
Kuala Lumpur   Madrid   Melbourne   Mexico City   Nairobi
New Delhi   Shanghai   Taipei   Toronto

With offices in
Argentina   Austria   Brazil   Chile   Czech Republic   France   Greece
Guatemala   Hungary   Italy   Japan   Poland   Portugal   Singapore
South Korea   Switzerland   Thailand   Turkey   Ukraine   Vietnam

Copyright © 2009 by Oxford University Press, Inc.

Published by Oxford University Press, Inc.
198 Madison Avenue, New York, New York 10016
www.oup.com

Oxford is a registered trademark of Oxford University Press

Library of Congress Cataloging-in-Publication Data

Kahn, Jonathon Samuel.
  Divine discontent : the religious imagination of
W. E. B. Du Bois / Jonathon S. Kahn.
    p. cm.
  Includes index.
  ISBN 978-0-19-530789-4
  1. Du Bois, W. E. B. (William Edward Burghardt), 1868–1963—Religion.
  2. Naturalism—Religious aspects. 3.   Pragmatism. 4.   Natural theology.
  5. African Americans—Religion. 6.   Race relations—Religious aspects—Christianity.
  7. United States—Race relations. I. Title.
  E185.97.D73K34 2009
  303.48'4092—dc22   2008050496

9 8 7 6 5 4 3 2 1

Printed in the United States of America
on acid-free paper

Acknowledgments

Of all Du Boisian virtues, this book is motivated most fully by piety. From piety, i've found, can come the motivation to pray, to give thanks, to engage in ritual and in social activism, and to love. This book represents my effort to track down the loyalties of my existence.

Du Bois issues many calls to piety to white America. They come through most clearly in the final paragraphs of *The Souls of Black Folk* where Du Bois asks, "Your country? How came it yours?" Du Bois demands that white America realize and acknowledge the ways in which the sources of this country's existence depend on the efforts and strivings of black folk. I am acutely conscious of these, never more so than in the community I live in in Harlem. I am constantly struck by the fact that never in the history of this country were black people welcomed into a white community as my neighbors have welcomed me into theirs. This, to me, is grace, and it produces a sense of gratitude that I carry with me daily.

This book, though written in some solitude, was hardly written alone. I would like to first thank my graduate school advisor, Wayne Proudfoot, who saw me through those years with constant conversation, attention, and friendship. I am forever grateful to Eddie Glaude, who in response to an unknown graduate student became the intellectual steward of this project; at some point while writing I realized that I was, in part, writing to him as a way of honoring the gifts of generosity and intellectual passion he showed me.

A community of scholars is responsible for this work. I'd like to thank Columbia University's Society of Fellows for two years' time to rethink and rewrite. Bob O'Meally welcomed me into the Center for Jazz Studies at Columbia, and the opportunity to construct a lecture series on jazz and religion shaped this work in unseen ways. Casey Blake encouraged me to seek publication sooner rather than later. Anthony Pinn and Edward Blum were vitally supportive. I appreciate Ted Trost's including me in the University of Alabama's conference on the African Diaspora and the study of religion. Thanks also go to Lauren Winner and Deak Nabers, whose readings of my work better enabled me to say what I meant. Matt Bagger deserves special mention—his close and pointed readings of my work forced me to sharpen my thinking. The same can be said for my colleagues at Vassar College, in particular Tyrone Simpson, Kiese Laymon, Eve Dunbar, Kristen Carter, Laura Yow, Candace Low, Quincy Mills, and Light Carryuo. I also deeply appreciated delivering a piece of this work in Vassar's Africana Studies annual lecture series. Special mention goes to my department at Vassar College: Marc Epstein, Rick Jarow, Lynn LiDonnici, Max Leeming, Larry Mamiya, Michael Walsh, and Judith Weisenfeld made me feel at home from the start and took the time to read parts of this work. I'd also like to acknowledge the fine eye of my student copyeditor, Aaron Naar.

I owe great thanks to my editor, Theo Calderara, whose steady hand pushed this project along and his assistant, Mariana Templin, who was attentive throughout.

Family and loved ones make life worth living. I was made by the love of my parents and sister. I owe much to Donald Marcuse, who helped me understand what possibility looks like.

Finally, tremendous, magical things have occurred since the start of this book. I met Nnenna Lynch, we married, and we learned love from each other. Her devotion and care pull me into life. Now our young son Ellis, who glimmers, is giving us love lessons anew. I am theirs. I dedicate this book to them.

An earlier version of chapter 1 was published as "The Pragmatic Religious Naturalism of W. E. B. Du Bois," in *The Souls of W. E. B. Du Bois: New Essays and Reflections*, edited by Jason R. Young and Edward J. Blum (Macon, GA: Mercer University Press, 2009).

Parts of chapter 2 appear as "Religion and the Binding of *The Souls of Black Folk*," in *The Journal of Philosophia Africana* (vol. 7, no. 2, August 2004).

An earlier version of the conclusion was published as "Toward a Tradition of African American Pragmatic Religious Naturalism," in *The African Diaspora and the Study of Religion*, edited by Theodore Trost (New York: Palgrave Macmillan, 2007).

Contents

Divine Discontent

Introduction: Divine Discontent as Religious Faith

I cannot promise you happiness always, but I can promise you *divine discontent* with the imperfect.

—W. E. B. Du Bois[1]

In 1940 W. E. B. Du Bois rose to the podium and delivered the commencement address at Wilberforce University, where forty-six years earlier he had assumed his first academic post. Du Bois, never known for his tact, announced himself to his audience as an "open and frank" critic of Wilberforce and, true to his word, then launched into an address that surely scorched his audience's ears. He began bluntly: "One searches almost in vain for tangible evidence of scientific work done by Wilberforce professors and graduates.... You have not produced great scholars or scientists, great technicians nor great thinkers, and yet there is no earthly reason why you should have not done this."[2] As hard as this must have been to hear, his remarks on the place of Christianity at Wilberforce, founded in the mid-nineteenth century by the great AME bishop, Daniel Payne, and directed by the African Methodist Episcopal Church, surely cut the deepest:

> I have noted in your president's report the insistence that
> Wilberforce University is a Christian institution. This is
> an old note.... It was a matter of emphasis when I was here
> near a half century ago and it did not impress me because
> it was all too evident that what most people at Wilberforce
> called Christianity was as childish belief in fairy tales, a

word-of-mouth adherence to dogma, and a certain sectarian exclu-
siveness. It often seemed to me when I was here a miserable apprehension of the teaching of Christ.... Frankly, I have never found
at Wilberforce University any outstanding evidence of this kind of
Christianity.[3]

To us and certainly to his Wilberforce patrons, the irreligion in these words—
his unvarnished anticlericalism, his suspicion of religious dogma, his rage at
what he saw as black Christianity's hypocrisy and betrayal of its central cause
of helping the poor and disenfranchised—is deafening. The causticity of his
irreligion is hardly surprising or anomalous. Throughout his career, Du Bois's
irreligious voice thundered against whatever he considered religious betrayal
and treachery. The Wilberforce talk gives expression to a representative strain
of Du Boisian discontent with religion and divinity, as well as the moral and
political dispositions to which he saw them leading. Du Bois held aspects of
African American religion, in particular the black church, in opprobrium.[4] In
his most famous text, *The Souls of Black Folk*, Du Bois, in cadences that portend
a young Malcolm X, reproved African American religion for having sent black
folk "wooing false gods and invoking false means of salvation, and at times
has even seemed to make them ashamed of themselves."[5] He lambasted the
black church as "pathetically timid" and "stand[ing] on the side of wealth and
power."[6] Of course, Du Bois did not reserve his lashings for his own community. He saw nothing but moral failure and rank hypocrisy in white Christian
America's unwillingness to "prayerfully inculcate, love and justice for our fellow men, but on the contrary the treatment of the poor, the unfortunate, and
the black within our borders is almost a national crime."[7] At the end of his life,
as his Marxist commitments became more explicit, Du Bois extolled the Soviet
Union for having the "courage to stop" "allow[ing] children to learn tales and
so called religious truth.... One can hardly exaggerate the moral disaster of
this custom."[8] In short, Du Bois's discontent with the divine was acute.

Irreligious sentiments like these make it easy to understand why the last
fifty years of Du Bois studies have been dominated by readings that either
ignore Du Bois's relationship to religion or pronounce him a foe of religious
faith after finding his irreligion simply self-evident. Adolph Reed's major
work on Du Bois effectively silences his use of religious language by stating
that it is limited to an "occasional use of biblical metaphor."[9] Prominent critic
Cornel West finds in Du Bois's encounters with religion the hostile mien of
an Enlightenment *philosophe*, distant from the religious folkways of black
America.[10] But no text is more persuasive or influential than David Levering
Lewis's Pulitzer Prize–winning, two-volume biography of Du Bois. Lewis gives

short shrift to the topic of Du Bois and religion, flatly pronouncing him a "serene agnostic" who, as an undergraduate at Fisk, decisively discarded "the familiar architecture" of his youth, his Congregationalist religious faith. Lewis writes that "he calmly adjusted, outwardly at least, to the departure of another central force in his life...his religious faith shriveled in the hot breath of hypocrisy and intolerance."[11] In fact, Lewis implies that the unexpected commercial success of *Darkwater,* which "sounds the emotional depth of a whole people," occurs only *in spite of its* "hieratic language" and its "trances, Gnostic visions, dark nights of the soul and...other intensely religious moments that are surprising at first to see in an agnostic and publicly restrained Du Bois."[12]

My hope in writing this book is to contest this normative view of Du Bois as one-sidedly hostile to religion, as uninterested in religion and its rhetoric, concepts, narratives, and practices, and most important, as bereft of something recognizable as religious faith. Indeed, I believe Lewis has it exactly backward Du Bois achieves the strong emotional and popular hold on his readership in writings such as *Darkwater* and, more significantly, *Souls* on the strength of his use of religious vocabulary. There is much evidence that black America responded to Du Bois's writings precisely because it heard a prophetic voice of deep religiosity. We would do well to listen to historian and editor of Du Bois's work Herbert Aptheker, who cautions against mistaking Du Bois's anticlericalism or even his doubts about normative Christian supernatural commitments for total irreligion: "The impression exists that Dr. Du Bois was areligious or even antireligious. The facts are otherwise."[13] These "facts" deserve greater attention.

If we are open to the religious timbre of Du Bois's writings, we will find his use of religious modalities hiding in plain sight. If in breaths Du Bois sounded deeply irreligious depths, expressing for example genuine doubt about the existence of God, in other breaths, indeed, at times in the next breath, he expressed deep devotional desires. (As we will see in a moment, the Wilberforce speech is just such an example.) From his epoch-making *Souls,* to his neglected *Prayers for Dark People,* to *Darkwater* and his largely unstudied series of parables that depict the lynching of an African American Christ, Du Bois was unable to keep his hands off religion's resources. His work is a rich world of sermonic essays, jeremiads, biblical rhetoric, and prayers, all of which are devoted to the overarching goal of fighting for the spiritual, political, and social conditions of those who "live within the Veil." In a word, Du Bois's corpus is thoroughly inhabited by religious resources and modalities. This book is devoted to listening to and analyzing this Du Bois in order to determine what sorts of religious oils his writings are dipped in. *Pace* Lewis, there was nothing serene, shriveled, or withered about Du Bois's relationship to religion. The error that

Lewis and others make is to assume that Du Bois's hostility toward the corruption and hypocrisy he sees in religious institutions represents irreligion *in toto*. When accounts of the religious in Du Bois are limited to his rejection of religious convention, they reveal little about Du Bois and more about their authors' impoverished understanding of the nature of religion.

My claim for Du Bois's religiosity goes beyond acknowledging that Du Bois the sociologist and historian, in texts like *The Philadelphia Negro* and *The Negro Church*, recognized and researched the centrality of religion to the creation, politics, and survival of African American life. My deeper claim is that Du Bois's writings exhibit a spiritual life of their own—that in light of his vast and powerfully engaged uses of religious modalities, a portion of Du Bois's work expresses a deep religiosity or religious sensibility. That sensibility cannot be reduced to an Enlightenment embrace of morality. Against a Kantian ethos, Du Bois insists on including in the the resolutions of the Eighth Conference for the Study of the Negro Problems (held at Atlanta University), that "religion of mere reason and morality will not alone supply the dynamic of spiritual inspiration and sacrifice."[14] Religion needs to do more. It provides the political bravery and the courage to seek the greater moral good; it provides the good with its vigor, its captivating qualities, and its ability to ensoul, which is to say to sustain people through tragedy and suffering. In those same Atlanta conference resolutions, Du Bois writes, "We need, then, first the strengthening of ideals of life and living; of reverent faith in the ultimate triumph of the good and of hope in human justice and growth."[15] At its heart, this study is committed to two tasks: tracking down what Du Bois means by reverent faith and showing how his own writing embodies it. Du Bois's use of religious modalities turn his works into religious resources that fortify the varieties of work he wants to accomplish in the world: political protest, social uplift, the honoring of one's ancestors, the development of moral ideals, and even the carving out of time for personal reflection. These are the efforts of Du Bois's reverent faith.

Du Bois expresses a similar notion in the closing moments of his central chapter of *Souls*, "Of the Faith of the Fathers." There he announces a "seeking in the great night a new religious ideal."[16] Like the phrase "reverent faith," this mention of a "religious ideal" is, too, a cryptic and abbreviated line, one that he does not explicate further in systematic detail. Yet, both of these early turn-of-the-century pronouncements of religious desire arc deep into the heart of his corpus. Critics may protest that Du Bois's use of religious modalities is more apparent at the beginning of his career. It is true that in 1903 he stands in *Souls* like Moses "peering from this high Pisgah, between Philistine and Amalekite, we sight the Promised land."[17] Yet as late as the 1950s, Du Bois was trying to salvage a vision of God. For example, in a poem written in 1952, when his Marxism is typically thought to be resolute, Du Bois exhorts, "Save the tattered shreds of God!"[18] In between we find a diverse and eclectic variety of appeals to religion; by 1920, with his growing internationalism, Du Bois nods toward Buddhism and Islam: "So sit we all as one....The Buddha walks with Christ! And Al-Koran and Bible both be holy!"[19] The activity of Du Bois's religious imagination—his invocations of biblical language, his depictions of a black Christ, his prayers and jeremiads, and his repeated return to slave spirituals as a form of spiritual renewal—needs to be understood as a lifelong effort to imagine, fashion, and embody a reverent faith or a new religious ideal.

How to fathom Du Bois's efforts? What kind of religious ideal is he after? What does he revere, and to what is he faithful? What is certain is that his religious sensibilities do not make for straightforward reading. His is a cross-hatched religious sensibility. Du Bois himself uttered perhaps no truer words of self-description than when declaring himself a religious heterodox: "I do not subscribe to ordinary Christian doctrine."[20] Indeed, twenty or so years after he wrote his palimpsest, *Prayers for Dark People*, Du Bois questions the very idea of prayer: "I do not believe in prayer. I do not believe that there is a personal conscious King of the world who will, upon fitting petition from me, change the course of world events to suit my needs or wishes."[21] As late as 1939, Du Bois can be heard, on the one hand, professing his belief in "the Father Almighty, Maker of Heaven and earth; and in Work, his only Son our Lord; who was conceived by Human Vision, born of the Virgin Need, suffered under Poverty; was crucified, died and buried,"[22] and, on the other hand, casting doubt on that very creed: "I do not believe in the miraculous birth and the miracles of the Christ of the Christians."[23] Du Bois seems Christian but only to a point; as not only a ready user of the language of divinity and the Bible but also a deep skeptic of supernatural truths, he is both suspicious of ecclesiastical convention and institutions and sympathetic to the African American religious tradition.

Du Bois's religiosity exists and thrives without normative bulwarks of religiosity. In fact, his protests and admonitions against religious institutions and what he understood as a banal theological hope for divine intervention were often framed and adorned with a host of religious modalities. In other words, a crucial characteristic of Du Bois's irreligion is that it often gives expression to his religious longings. At these moments, his irreligion itself turns religious. Du Bois's speech at Wilberforce, in fact, exemplifies this dynamic, for Du Bois follows his unvarnished brickbats with a Christian vision of his own cobbling. He insists that "Christianity means sympathy; the realization of what it costs a human being to live and support a family in decency....Christianity means unselfishnesss; the willingness to forego in part one's personal advantage and give up some personal desires for the sake of a larger end which will be for the advantage of a greater number of people."[24] In this account of Christian sacrifice, Du Bois urges Wilberforce to reform itself *religiously*, and yet religion in Du Bois's key seems to hold the supernatural at arm's length. He finishes his speech by proclaiming a vision of godliness in what becomes one of his mantras: "Love is God and Work is His Prophet." And in his last word, with a biblical line that appears repeatedly in his work, Du Bois consecrates this vision with a moment of biblical prophetic flourish from Isaiah: "Awake, awake, put on thy strength; O, Zion, put on thy beautiful robe."[25] The pattern of the Wilberforce speech—scathing irreligion followed by an emphasis on Christian virtues such as love, sacrifice, and work—runs through his writings. The result is a religious disposition that is synonymous with social criticism of this-worldly conditions and concerns.

It is here that I turn to the epigraph that heads this chapter and from which I draw the title of this book: "I cannot promise you happiness always, but I can promise you divine discontent with the imperfect." I submit that we hear the key phrase, "divine discontent," not as Du Boisian disgust and rejection of religion. It is misread as flatly or vituperatively irreligious—as though Du Bois warns or threatens against divinity and religion. Instead, we should hear in "divine discontent" a promise, a covenant, and an urging toward a state of dissatisfaction with politics and society. Du Boisian discontent is a religious sensibility and a spiritual achievement.[26] "Divinity"—religious language, ideas, narratives, virtues—becomes in Du Bois's hands a tool to express discontent. His uses of religion do not distract from the imperfect but focus attention ever more intently on the imperfect and on what exists in order to transform it into a worldly ideal. Divine discontent is an accomplished state that Du Bois seeks. His divine discontent becomes a state of grace.

Consider, for example, the following passage from *Souls:* "Some day the Awakening will come, when the pent-up vigor of ten million souls shall sweep irresistibly toward the Goal, out of the Valley of the Shadow of Death, where all that makes life worth living—Liberty, Justice, and Right—is marked for 'White People Only.'"[27] In this moment of religiously imbued social criticism we find the pattern of Du Bois's religious ideal and reverent faith—his divine discontent. His focus is on this world and not on the supernatural. Du Bois brings the eschaton down to earth, which is where ideals must be made to live and flourish. Here he constructively relies on religious images and notions as levers for fashioning political sensibilities, deploying "divinity"—religious language, ideas, and form—to *give expression* to his discontent. Through religious language, Du Bois draws attention to political and social disquietude. Religion serves as an agitating agent; it enables him to imagine ideals but only by evincing and articulating the imperfect more clearly. Ideals for Du Bois are dialectically grounded in unflinching acknowledgment of limitations and infirmities. Arnold Rampersad speaks of the "instability of his religion" and urges us not to "deny its vitality or scope."[28] He is exactly right to point out its eclecticism (though he does not go beyond these few words). My suggestion is that Du Bois's religious spirit is rooted in its peripatetic instability. Du Bois's idiosyncratic use of religious vocabulary produces a reverent form of discontent that comes from critical questioning, from challenging dogma, and from attempting to tie tradition to future demands. This is the promise of divine discontent.

I do not want to give the impression that I am the first to alight upon the notion that Du Bois's relationship to religion matters. In this respect, my work builds on other remarks that have intuited the importance of this connection. Langston Hughes's famous association, "my earliest memories of written words are those of Du Bois and the Bible," and Rampersad's more recent claim that "[a]mong black intellectuals, above all, *The Souls of Black Folk* became a kind of *sacred* book"[29] speak to the type of religious ethos of Du Bois's work that I suggest accounts for its preeminent place in black American life and letters. Aptheker notes that "[t]he language of the Hebrew Prophets permeates Du Bois' speeches and writing; their major lesson—let justice prevail though the heavens fail—was a fundamental theme in his long and fabulous life."[30] Yet, Aptheker's remarks do not go much beyond this.[31]

In truth, there are only two substantial and sustained writings on Du Bois and religion. The first is Manning Marable's 1985 essay, "The Black Faith of W. E. B. Du Bois," which is notable for its ear for the richness of Du Bois's use of religious vocabulary. The second is Edward J. Blum's *W. E. B. Du Bois: American Prophet,* which was published in 2007 and represents the first full-length text on Du Bois's engagements with religion. In a certain respect, Blum's Du Bois embodies a more resounding and abounding version of Marable's claim of Du Bois as a "passionate convert to the black version of Christianity."[32] Blum, too, turns Du Bois into a Christian by placing him in Gayraud Wilmore's narrative of radical black Christianity. While there is much to recommend Blum's text, the echo in Blum of Marable's language of "conversion" to Christianity overlooks what is fundamental and distinct about Du Bois's religious sensibilities.[33] Du Bois did not accept or abide by the doctrines, beliefs, and practices of an already-established religious tradition, institution, or way of life. It is ill fitting to describe Du Bois unproblematically as a Christian. His heterodoxy runs too deep, and throughout his life he chafed against the label "Christian."

To Blum's credit (and unlike Marable), Blum is all too aware of Du Bois's heterodoxy. For example, Blum acknowledges that Du Bois's Christ parables eschew resurrection scenes and are scrubbed clean of supernaturalisms. The problem is that Blum does not capitalize on insights like these and do more with the religious Du Bois who cannot be comfortably suited into his Sunday best. The most we get is this suggestive line: "Minimizing the supernal elements of the Bible did not necessarily position Du Bois in the agnostic or secularist camp. Rather, it showed that he was a religious modernist."[34] What does it mean to be a religious modernist? How is this category compatible with Christianity, and how does it fit into African American religious thought? Blum does not pursue these threads. Moreover, when he falls back on seeing Du Bois as a part of a normative tradition of black Christian thought, he does not capture the way Du Bois complicates categories not only of "the religious" and "the secular" but also of African American religious thought. Doing this complicating work is a major goal of this text.

Finally, in this book I understand my work as putting aside the biographer's desire to definitively determine how Du Bois understood his own religiosity. I want to dispense with the need to positively establish whether Du Bois thought of himself as a theist, deist, agnostic, or atheist (and the evidence is mixed on this). Instead, I focus on how Du Bois adopts and adapts the language and resources of religion in his work. My primary interest is not in crawling inside Du Bois's head to ascertain what he believed. Rather, I want to characterize the sort of sensibility that Du Bois creates textually through his varied uses of the religious modalities. In addition, I want to characterize this sensibility and explain what these varied uses of religious vocabulary were good for. What sort of ends and purposes do his uses effect? What does religious language enable him to do?[35] My answers to these questions engage philosophical, literary, and political sources, not historical ones. I ask now for the reader's forgiveness if, when speaking to these questions, I sometimes slip and make what sounds like a claim about Du Bois himself. The slippage is merely rhetorical. I make no pretense of understanding what the "great man" himself believed. I am after the sensibilities, ends, and actions to which the "great man's" writings about religion appeal.

Five Theses on Du Bois's Religious Imagination

At the heart of this book are the following five claims about Du Bois's religious imagination:

1. Du Bois's religious voice is decidedly antimetaphysical. Poignantly, Du Bois is not interested in the essence or real nature of God, nor

does he believe that God's will forms the superstructure that sustains the history and fate of the world. Indeed, Du Bois often marshals religion in order to challenge Christological explanations in which God intervenes in world events and functions to confirm a divine economy. For Du Bois, these sorts of explanations represent "the temptation in the wilderness," and he mocked and reviled religious folk who saw the world in these terms: "Must not God himself and his angels come and come quickly to settle this awful problem of color and race?...He stared at the devil. The devil was a priest in robe and mitre chanting long prayers."[36] Like Nietzsche, a certain type of God—imperious, authoritative, historically determinative—is dead for Du Bois.[37] In short, the terminus of religious devotion for Du Bois is not in establishing a metaphysics of the divine, what Clifford Geertz calls "an authoritative conception of the overall shape of reality."[38] Repeatedly Du Bois begs off a foundational metaphysics: "Our whole basis of knowledge is so relative and contingent that when we get to argue concerning ultimate reality and the real essence of life and the past and the future, we seem to be talking without real data and getting nowhere."[39] When Du Bois speaks religiously—when he uses God talk, when he prays, when he refers to the Christ—it is not to confirm the existence of a supernatural divine order.

2. Du Bois deploys religious vocabularies in order to craft a moral and political sensibility attuned to the finite needs of selves and communities (most often black selves and communities, but not exclusively) struggling against concrete social and political realities. As I said earlier, Du Bois uses religion to pull the eschaton down to earth. For Du Bois, religion is (or can be made to be) essential to life only if it is reworked to help minister to human finitude. Concerns such as rights, education, and historical self-understanding are at times religious concerns for Du Bois. Here is a characteristic sentiment: "Christianity for black men started with the right to vote, and nothing less."[40] Religious formulations are also valuable in that they are tools for philosophical reflection on the conditions of human finitude: "The true joy of living dwells in that Higher Life, that sitting above both sunshine and shadows, that values them at their worth and strives to wind them to his will. In that higher life, my friends, there are three things: Work, and Love and Sacrifice—these three—but the greatest of these is Sacrifice."[41] Do not be fooled by Du Bois's idealistic rhetoric: The higher life is clearly moored in earthly acts: work, love, and doing

without for the sake of others. The focus of the higher life is on the earthly conditions of "living" and the hard-fought efforts needed to secure its goods. Salvation exists for Du Bois, but its dimensions are human.

3. Religious vocabularies enable Du Bois to craft ends that appear to sit in tension with one another. On the one hand, Du Bois uses religious modalities to argue for black people as a fundamental, irreplaceable part of the larger American nation; in this there is an integrationist force to his use of religious vocabulary. On the other hand, Du Bois uses religion to fashion a sense of black peoplehood central to his conception of black American identity. Religion enables Du Bois to bind black people—through hope, love, and at times reprimand. In other words, religious modalities allow him to chart a taut and dialectical path between a unifying account of American democracy that includes black and white together and an account of black identity with an integrity of its own, Du Bois's version of a "nation within a nation."

4. Three interrelated religious virtues dominate Du Bois's religious discourse: piety, jeremiadic protest, and sacrifice. All three virtues are the crucial instances in which Du Bois revises normative Christian notions.

5. In light of the way he uses and approaches religion, Du Bois needs to be understood as an African American pragmatic religious naturalist. By this I mean that, like Du Bois, the American tradition of pragmatic religious naturalism, which runs through William James, George Santayana, and John Dewey, seeks religion without metaphysical foundations. The central complications of Du Bois's religious register—tension between religious disbelief and devotion, refusal to attribute earthly events to divine metaphysics, construction of identity, peoplehood, and nation from the lived exigencies of race and not racial essences, as well as pursuit of an earthly form of human salvation rooted in human relations rather than antecedent realties— mirror basic pragmatist commitments. Moreover, they set Du Bois outside of normative black Christianity. At the same time, the sources on which Du Bois draws in fashioning this heterodox religiosity are African American. The existentialism of the slave spirituals, the protestations of the African American jeremiad, and a preacher's facility with biblical rhetoric and interpretation compose his religious voice. Du Bois's faith is most certainly black.

My claim is that Du Bois drinks fully from both streams—from pragmatist and African American traditions. In drawing on these two traditions—in creating a race-imbued pragmatic religious naturalism—Du Bois transforms both the American philosophical tradition and African American religious thought. By using pragmatist tools—by embracing religious resources without metaphysical commitments and by using these resources to address the realities of race—Du Bois creates a new black faith: a radical version of pragmatic religious naturalism that displays a grasp of the sociopolitical implications of pragmatist thought that is more powerful than the pragmatists themselves. Du Bois inaugurates a line of African American pragmatic religious naturalism.

What exactly is pragmatic religious naturalism, and why is it relevant to reading Du Bois on religion? I admit that the category of pragmatic religious naturalism sounds decidedly recondite, perhaps more abstruse than profound. I also admit that it is possible to accept the validity of seeing Du Bois's engagements with religious vocabulary as antimetaphysical, as rooted in social conditions, and as striving for both a specific black identity and a place in the larger American nation (theses 1–3) without necessarily seeing him as a pragmatic religious naturalist. Nonetheless, it is precisely these characteristics that make Du Bois a pragmatic religious naturalist. Pragmatic religious naturalists subvert traditional religious metaphysics of ultimate truth and foundational beliefs while holding tight to religious stories, moods, symbols, rhetoric, and moral values because they are links to the past, because they are powerful tools and narratives for shaping and envisioning life, and because they can allow for a type of spirituality that emphasizes the fallibility, fragility, and power of the human-made ties that bind us and make us dependent on each other. Santayana writes: "Religions will thus be better or worse, never true or false."[42] Pragmatic religious naturalists use religion for ends that have to do with exploring the angled perplexities of human finitude and not the wholeness of godly infinity. Pragmatic religious naturalists conceive of religion as funding the deepest sources of ourselves, while insisting that those sources get their depth from linguistic and historical webs of meaning. We would be remiss in not seeing that Du Bois's religious voice follows these lights.

My placing of Du Bois in pragmatist waters follows the work of Cornel West, George Hutchinson, Ross Posnock, and Paul Taylor.[43] Furthermore, my insistence on seeing Du Bois as part of a tradition of African American pragmatism and religion follows the path set by Eddie Glaude and Beth Eddy, who have begun the work of showing the ways in which pragmatic religious naturalism resides at the crossroads of religion, politics, and identity in black American rhetoric.[44] Of course, there are also the often-quoted lines from Du Bois in which he aligned himself, albeit quite generally, with James's pragmatism.[45]

However, my reasons for bringing the category of pragmatic religious naturalism to bear are not rooted in Du Bois's remarkable biographical proximity to the early pragmatists at Harvard.[46] Instead, I do so because pragmatic religious naturalism is textually apposite—because it is a frame through which Du Bois's disjunctive, intemperate, and quixotic religious voice can be made to congeal. I insist on Du Bois's pragmatic religious naturalism because it captures the eclectic, disjunctive, and dynamic religious voice that exists in Du Bois's texts. Here I am following a crucial essay by Taylor, who defends Du Bois's pragmatism solely on the basis that thinking of Du Bois as a pragmatist throws new light onto Du Bois's writings and thereby allows us to evince aspects of his work that have been neglected and overlooked.[47]

In the same way, I invoke pragmatic religious naturalism because it alerts us to Du Bois's uses of religion. Pragmatic religious naturalism, because it allows for religion without metaphysical commitments, enables us to see Du Bois's uses of religion as legitimately religious. The vocabulary of pragmatic religious naturalism frees us from shoehorning Du Bois into ready-made Christian constructions and allows us to imagine Du Bois as practicing what might be understood as an original black American faith—one that pays homage to African American Christian pasts but radically reconfigures them for an ecumenical future. Pragmatic religious naturalism corrects Lewis's failure of imagination in seeing Du Bois's "indifference to the hypothesis of an interactive supreme being as to be indistinguishable from atheism."[48]

What emerges is a slightly antinomian and deeply devotional religious imagination that Du Bois uses to endow his world with meaning. Du Bois's black faith—his African American pragmatic religious naturalism—imagines grace and sacredness rooted in the work and efforts that humans effect collectively. Salvation—whether in the form of racial reconciliation or African Americans ministering to their own needs—is necessarily a precarious and fragile construction that must be tended to in light of human hands, human standards, and human limitations. Du Bois's black faith eschews the certainty and pretense of true belief and uses indeterminacy and impertinence to fund his most important spiritual strivings. With it, he is able to express an appropriate sense of hope that acknowledges the hardships faced by black people. He turns critical thinking into a form of religious practice. He expresses his love for black people while (or even through) constantly interrogating that love. He speaks a prophetic language of sacrifice and the jeremiad that seeks concrete redemption in the here and now while forgoing promises of otherworldly divine promise; in this Du Bois reshapes American democracy by disrupting the very ideas of the American consensus and divine guarantee and presenting a dialectical account of American unity that allows for a black nation responsive to its own pressing need and interests. Finally, as I argue in my conclusion, Du Bois stands at the head of a rich and complex twentieth-century tradition of African American pragmatic religious naturalists: Zora Neale Hurston, Ralph Ellison, and James Baldwin all belong. Like Du Bois, they, too, reject conventional theological and institutional religious strictures. They also use God talk not to talk about true belief but to unsettle or destabilize conventional loyalties to race, nation, and religion.

It is possible, if we are so inclined, as I am, to look to Du Bois and the African American pragmatic religious naturalists who follow him for hope in this modern age, where religious dogma and theological certitude can dominate our political discourse. The lasting legacy of Du Bois's black faith, his divine discontent, is the way he uses religion to introduce indeterminacy and impertinence without relinquishing religion's power to inspire, motivate, and vivify. Uncertainty and ambivalence do not drain religion of its galvanizing powers. Du Bois and the tradition of African American pragmatic religious naturalism respond to Weberian disenchantment by reenchanting the world with a religious disposition that thrives on criticism, protest, uncertainties, irony, and a deep wonder at the human condition of mutual dependence. Du Bois provides religious rejuvenation that relies on critical energies. The United States today would do well to adapt this combination of critical faith, devotion, and reverence, along with progressive politics, for the challenges we collectively face in the twenty-first century. The sacred, by my lights, lies in these hills. My hope is that this work on Du Bois better equips us in our contemporary world to explore them.

Some Final Brush Clearing: Are Du Bois's Uses of Religious Modalities Really Religious?

What does it mean to call Du Bois's heterodox engagements with religion religious? Is there a notion of religion that is applicable to and survives Du Bois's types of irreligion: his heated anticlericalism and skepticism of the supernatural?

Current critic Jeffrey Stout argues not only that the term *religion* survives the absence of these two characteristics but also that there exists a strong tradition of nineteenth- and twentieth-century American religious voices who, though critical of religious dogma and unassailable truth, are not pejoratively dismissive of religion *in toto*. Stout argues for a "neglected tradition" of religious

ethicists who have operated "outside of institutional settings in which cleri-
sies, ecclesial or academic, exercise power."[49] These critics have persisted with
and relied on religious attitudes, dispositions, and ideals in order to meet the
democratic demands of political and social pluralism. In conceiving of this tradition of religious ethics, Stout casts a wide net: Emerson, Whitman, Thoreau,
Margaret Fuller, John Dewey, Kenneth Burke, Ralph Ellison, and Wendell
Berry all belong. He does not mention Du Bois in this tradition of modern religious ethical discourse, but it is the central conviction of my work that Du Bois
belongs.[50] "It would be foolish," Stout writes, "to construe either the *arguments*
these authors produce or the *authors* themselves as nonreligious...simply
because they are not tied to a religion—which is to say an institutional setting
officially designated as religious."[51] For these writers, there remains, as ever,
the need for notions of the good and virtuous forms of communal practice. For
these writers, certain aspects of religion, when distanced from its normative
institutions and normative metaphysical claims, emerge as critical and vibrant
resources for imagining democracy.

When Stout says that it would be "foolish" to try to deny the terms *religion*
and *religious* to figures like Du Bois, I take him to be saying the following about
the category of religion. "Religion" has no fundamental essence or essential
definition. Since its inception, religious studies has struggled mightily to produce a stable, single definition, and these efforts, though they have led to
enormous insight into the workings of aspects of religious life, have failed.
Religion is a manufactured category, built for certain contexts and for certain
purposes.[52] Acknowledging this does not mean that we should no longer use
"religion" and "religious." By all means, we should continue to use the terms,
but we need to be explicit about which questions about the nature of religion
they are really about. They are not about determining a definitive account of
religion. Instead, questions such as "What does that *remark* have to do with
religion?" are better understood as questions about the sets of interests and
commitments that constitute a context in which religion comes to mean one
thing rather than another.[53] Our answers to these questions will always tell us
about the grammatical conditions in which we live.

So let me tell you what I mean when I call Du Bois's uses of religious
vocabulary religious. I am not assuming an essence of religion. What I mean is
that his uses of the modalities of religion are religious in that they bear enough
similarity to other language uses, ideas, and narratives that we already agree
upon as representative of religion. When Du Bois talks—as you will see—in
the language of the Bible or about the virtues of sacrifice or in the tones of
the American jeremiad—he is drawing on recognizably religious contexts:
American and black American forms of Christianity. Moreover, when we read

Zora Neale Hurston on the "characteristics of Negro expression," we learn that African American rhetoric has long been marked by an inventiveness that defies normative boundaries.[54] Religion in the African American tradition has never lived solely in the church; it has always spilled out into the streets and public political contexts. Thus, even though Du Bois's use of religious rhetoric is distinct and heterodox, it is sufficiently in touch with the larger religious tradition to allow us to think of his engagement with religious vocabulary as religious itself.

Wittgenstein called this line of reasoning a "family resemblance," and he insisted that all attempts to define anything necessarily follows this logic: "Why do we call something a 'number'? Well, perhaps because it has a direct-relationship with several things that have hitherto been called number; and this can be said to give it an indirect relationship to other things we call the same name. And we extend our concept of number as in spinning a thread we twist fibre on fibre. And the strength of the thread does not reside in the fact that some one fibre runs through its whole length, but in the overlapping of many fibres."[55] The central idea here is that concepts are discursive, not essential. Concepts are tools; by pointing out the connections words have to other words and contexts, we indicate that they either illuminate matters or they do not. Wittgenstein suggests that the use of the concept of religion rests solely on the idea that pointing out family resemblances amounts to something that makes sense to others. The *plausibility* of a family resemblance is what matters most, where plausibility is a matter of social reception and acceptance. Most important, this situates arguments over the concept of the religious in the appropriate arena: Religion becomes a cultural and contextual conversation.[56] The strength in this, as Wittgenstein suggests, is in the way that defining religion becomes an interdependent affair—a pluralistic practice of interpretation.[57]

What I am counting on is this: that enough readers will be convinced that even though Du Bois does not readily believe in a normative Christian God or belong to a Christian church, his substantial borrowings from these contexts should count not simply as interesting but also as religious. The very nature of Du Bois's religion—an unsystematic, improvisational borrowing from religious contexts while both skeptical and critical of those very same contexts—speaks to the dynamic nature of African American and American religion. Rafts of scholars of religion—no more so than in our modern moment—have told us that the boundary between the secular and religious has long been permeable, flexible, and dynamic.[58] Du Bois is an overlooked example of this unsteady dynamic, and part of the fruits of puzzling over the religious Du Bois is his emergence as a rich and overlooked example of the intertwined complexities of the religious and the secular in American culture. In fact,

Edward Blum is on exactly the right track by suggesting that "the irreligious Du Bois...is a mythical construction that serves the purposes of the secularized academy far more than elucidates the ideas and beliefs of Du Bois."[59] Those purposes have been to construct "religion" as diametrically opposed to the "secular." Du Bois confounds this distinction; with Du Bois we can begin to see the way the secular and the religious are porous and intertwined.

Is it not the case that many of us today find ourselves echoing Du Bois's disposition: skeptical about religious dogma but drawn, no matter what, to the power of religious narratives, concepts, and practices? When we are unwilling to consider Du Bois "religious," I think we have revealed an intense Protestant bias toward insisting that religion is synonymous with belief in supernatural divinity. The only reason I see to deny the concept of religion to Du Bois is to make a polemical point about the necessity of denominational supernaturalism to religion. However, if we do not feel the need to make this polemical point—which I do not—then lots of other typical religious concerns emerge in Du Bois's work. These include, for example, the use of biblical rhetoric and narrative to give priority to questions of justice and one's obligations to one's neighbor; the self-conscious creation of moments of giving thanks; and the development of habits and virtues that acknowledge dependencies on things bigger than oneself.

One might object that this study of Du Bois is simply a study in rhetoric—an examination of the ways and ends for which Du Bois deploys religious symbols, language, and forms. I object to the idea that his rhetoric is "mere" if what is meant by this phrase is meaningless language. I equally object to the idea that Du Bois's use of the language of religion is merely contrived and strategic—as though Du Bois did not "believe" in invocations of religious modalities and instead turned to them purely to appeal (read: manipulate) to an African American and a larger American audience, for whom religion was deeply important. Not only do those views minimize the abundance of religious symbols in Du Bois's corpus, but they also more basically mischaracterize the function of language. All language is strategic—it is designed to communicate. All strategic language is substantive; it works to shape and motivate human identity, politics, culture, and ethics. If we are narrowly focused on figuring out the deep beliefs at the bottom of language, we will miss the real work that language does with or without (mostly without!) deep agreement on belief.

In this I follow Kenneth Burke, for whom "the subject of religion falls under the head of *rhetoric* in the sense that rhetoric is the art of *persuasion*, and religious cosmogonies are designed, in the last analysis, as exceptionally thoroughgoing modes of persuasion."[60] On this view, the question of Du Bois's "substantive" uses of religious language becomes a matter not of ferreting out his deepest and truest beliefs about religion but of characterizing and analyzing what the language is persuasive of. Here again Burke is helpful in that his interest is "not directly with man's relationship to god, but rather with his relationship to the *word* 'God.' "[61] In this statement, Burke, I believe, is severing the normative obligation to take that use of the word *God* to reflect commitments about who God is and what God's nature might be. Why should we assume that God talk is religious only when it is understood as having a theological importance? What if we understand religious language not as expressive of the deepest substratum of reality but, as Sally McFague urges, as metaphorical, "constantly speaking about the great unknowns, mortality, love, fear, joy, guilt, hope, and so on."[62] Understanding religious language as metaphorical and not symbolic of fixed realities shifts our focus to the effects of that language: "Good metaphors shock, they bring unlikes together, they upset conventions, they involve tension, and they are implicitly revolutionary.... In this regard, one could characterize symbolic...thinking as priestly and metaphorical thinking as prophetic."[63] Du Bois is just this sort of metaphorical prophet. As we will see, he uses the language of religion not to reflect on God's nature but to urge changes in this-worldly realities such as justice, mortality, love, guilt, and hope—though always shaped by the circumpressure of politics and race.

For my purposes, not a great deal would be changed if a historian were to discover a hidden document in which Du Bois admits that he turned to religion purely as an artifice in order to appeal, say, to the readers of *The Crisis,* the NAACP newspaper he stewarded, in which so many of his religious invocations appeared, or to white America writ large. Du Bois would still have left behind a universe of religious rhetoric that played on black Americans' and white Americans' relationship with the word *God.* This would still require interpretation by scholars of religion.

I

What Is Pragmatic Religious Naturalism, and What Does It Have to Do with Du Bois?

Since religion is dead, religion is everywhere. Religion was once an affair of the church; it is now in the streets, in each man's heart. Once there were priests; now every man's a priest.

—Richard Wright, *The Outsider* (1953)[1]

And all that I really have been trying to say is that a certain group that I know and to which I belong...bears in its bosom just now the spiritual hope of this land *because of the persons who compose it and not by divine command.*

—W. E. B. Du Bois, *Dusk of Dawn* (1940)[2]

Matthew Towns, the African American protagonist in Du Bois's novel *Dark Princess* (originally published in 1928), finds himself in a clandestine political meeting in Germany, seated around a table with an eclectic array of "the Darker World."[3] They represent the elite from China, India, Japan, and Egypt, all devoted to the question of how to wrest power and culture from white imperial hands. This meeting of supposed activists has never had an African American or a black African in its circle, and the conversation turns uncomfortable when one of the Japanese participants explains this exclusion: "But for us here and for the larger company we represent, there is a deeper question—that of the ability, qualifications, and real possibilities of the black race in Africa or elsewhere."[4] So this group asks Towns—who has left the United States after he was denied admission to medical school because of his race—for evidence of his race's cultural or political achievements.

Towns becomes apoplectic, and he summons this response:

> The blood rushed to Matthew's face. He threw back his head and
> closed his eyes, and with the movement he heard again the Great
> Song. He saw his father in the old log church by the river, leading
> the moaning singers in the Great Song of Emancipation. Clearly,
> plainly he heard that mighty voice and saw the rhythmic swing and
> beat of the thick brown arm...and suddenly Mathew found himself
> singing. His voice full, untrained but mellow, quivered down the
> first plaintive bar:
>> "When Israel was in Egypt land—"
> Then it gathered depth:
>> "Let my people go!"[5]

The Negro spiritual "Go Down, Moses" spills from Towns's mouth; it is Towns's evidence of black American excellence. It is not too much to suggest that here Towns functions as Du Bois's mouthpiece. Du Bois thought similarly of black spirituals, that they represent true cultural excellence, what he called "The Gift of the Spirit," "the peculiar spiritual quality which the Negro has injected into American life and civilization."[6]

It is crucial to realize the grounds on which Towns and Du Bois bring this slave spiritual forth. Towns is not making a theological claim. He does not sing "Go Down, Moses" to say that black "abilities," "qualifications," and "possibilities" are personified by a strong relationship with God; he does not offer an example of African American spirituality in order to say that African Americans' recognition of God's reality stands as black America's greatest accomplishment or contribution. What stands out in Towns's singing is the intimate intersection of memory, struggle against crushing existential conditions, and political liberation. Towns performs this song because its spiritual excellence is a form of democratic excellence. As Towns has it, the continuing legacy of songs like "Go Down, Moses"—songs of deep memory and resolve in a long religious tradition from slavery to freedom—is "teaching the world one thing...and that is, the ability and capacity for culture is not the hereditary monopoly of the few, but the widespread possibility for the majority of mankind if they only have a decent chance in life."[7] Democratic excellence here is not only embodied by forms of social activism but is also found in acts of memory—in the very notion of communal solidarity earned by efforts for communal memory.

Very clearly, the temporal realm of Towns's rendition is this-worldly. The terms of this form of spiritual excellence are those of human finitude, not an otherworldly conception of the afterlife. They acknowledge the virtue of demanding justice now, honor a tradition of fighting for justice, and, finally, conceive of the members of that tradition as making up a "people." The religious sensibility—the gift of the spirit—of this passage is *constituted* by these virtues. To be religious by this account—to moan with the singers and beat one's arms in a backwoods church—is inseparable from an exhortation to construct a democratic existence in which the common man resists and triumphs in dignity. Du Bois expresses this same religious sentiment in *Prayers for Dark People:* "Herein alone do we approach our Creator when we stretch our arms with toil, and strain with eye and ear and brain to catch the thought and do the deed and create the things that make life worth living."[8] Godliness is in the acting and the straining for earthly improvement. What sort of vocabulary is this? What sort of precedents do we have for this type of religious sensibility—where God the Creator is inextricably an expression of critical thinking and of a critical review of the way human existence is rooted in our mutual dependence on each other's lives, resources, and histories?

The obvious answer is the nineteenth-century tradition of black religion and black radicalism, to borrow a phrase by Gayraud Wilmore, which runs from Richard Allen through David Walker and Sojourner Truth.[9] This tradition of black religion is, of course, a Christian tradition. And Du Bois's appropriation of slave religion's Moses in the voice of Towns—or elsewhere in Du Bois's portrayal's of a black Christ in his short story "Jesus Christ in Texas"—makes it only logical to assimilate Du Bois in a tradition of politically radical black Christianity. As I mentioned earlier, this is exactly what both Manning Marable and Edward Blum do in their works. For example, Marable writes: "The soul of Du Bois confronting the black world had no choice except to embrace black Christianity."[10]

Nonetheless, to my mind, this overstates the case. Beyond the difficulties of actually identifying the definitive black version of Christianity,[11] Marable's language of "embrace" and "conversion to" Christianity—and the echo of this in Blum's work in his claim that Du Bois "conceived of a new Christianity"[12]— mutes what is distinct about Du Bois's religious sensibilities: Du Bois self-consciously held at arm's length normative religious doctrines and practices. In fact, he was often quick to reject them outright. What certainly is true is that he drew intimately on black Christian resources. Yet there is something discomfiting about describing Du Bois as a *convert* to black Christianity. His heterodoxy runs too deep. Consider, for example, his doubt about the very idea of an afterlife: "My thought on personal immortality is easily explained. I do not know. I do not see how any one could know."[13] In an Easter prayer from *The Crisis*, Du Bois insists that the "King of glory" is "the Friend who is no impossible god or simpering angel, but human like us, hungry as we are and disappointed; who smokes and drinks with us and walks beneath the stars."[14] This sort of base language is startling and exceedingly unusual for the early twentieth century. Moreover, for Du Bois, God is not omnipotent and did not self-reveal by intervening in history. To be sure, Du Bois's God was black: "I am carving the God in night / I am painting Hell in white."[15] Yet, it is important to note that Du Bois the poet says *he's* carving God; what is more, by locating God's agency in a human act of creation, Du Bois overturns the Christian supernatural God of revelation. Du Bois embraced a spirituality inspired by the power of human efforts rather than the supernatural. In *Darkwater*, Du Bois even writes of a mortal god: "Help us, O Human God! in this Thy Truce, To make Humanity divine!"[16] Sentiments like this, which expose a deep skepticism of the Christian supernatural God of revelation, establish considerable critical distance between Du Bois and any number of normative versions of Christianity, black or white, of his time. Indeed, to most African American Christians, his agnosticism and doubting of the supernatural deity would have been blasphemous.

The dialectical tension here is thick. Du Bois clearly roots his religious faith in black religious history and its resources.[17] On the other hand, Du Bois purposely distances himself from the normative tradition of African American Christianity. These are the two truths of the relationship of Du Bois's religious voice to African American Christianity. Du Bois's faith is a black faith that emerges out of the skein of black American Christianity. At the same time, Du Bois establishes the blackness of his religious voice as much in its criticisms and revisions of traditional African American formulations.[18] Marable's insistence on Du Bois's black faith is exactly right. Nonetheless, his claim that Du Bois builds it solely by embracing African American Christian traditions ultimately does not do justice to the complexity of that faith. Forcing a conversion to Christianity on Du Bois misses the centrality of this dialectical tension. An important distinction must be made: Du Bois did not accept and convert to the conventions of African American Christianity as much as he drew on, adapted, and altered that tradition by his own lights.

The result was a race-imbued religious vision galvanized by African American religious traditions, yet very much pushing beyond its boundaries. We have to confront the fact that Du Bois creates a type of black religion that is openly hesitant or ambivalent about calling itself traditionally Christian. His radicalness is in his revisionary swerve, his refusal to either convert to or rebel fully against black Christianity.[19] This is the complexity we need to wrestle with.

To do justice to this complexity, the central claim of this chapter is that Du Bois creates his particular black faith by reaching for the philosophical tradition of American pragmatism and, more specifically, pragmatic religious naturalism as it runs through James, Dewey, and Santayana. As we will see, the essential dilemma of the pragmatic religious naturalists is this: How can religion continue to meet what Williams James called life's "religious demand"[20]— the gap between the suffering and brutishness in human natural life and the deep human desire for a sense of well-being and accomplishment—when it is no longer equipped with an a priori supernatural foundation? Pragmatic religious naturalism represents a religious response to James's 1895 question, "Is life worth living?" when we can no longer rely on supernatural skyhooks but only on the finite means that humans have within their grasp.[21] The pragmatist response is this: Life, indeed, is worth living, and religion not only can help but may also be essential to constructing worthwhile lives—but only if our understanding of what religion is, how it works, and what sorts of purposes it serves are reworked to reflect the limits of human finitude.

If the phrase "making life worth living" sounds familiar, it is because I have already cited Du Bois's use of it a couple of times. It is a favorite phrase of his, and he used it throughout his career. Given the complexities of Du Bois's religious voice—particularly his hostility to metaphysics and his focus on human finitude—it is well worth our while to consider the ways in which we might understand Du Bois as a pragmatist and a pragmatic religious naturalist, for it is when we begin to see Du Bois's engagements with religion along pragmatist lines that we can fully appreciate the way in which his religious voice represents a moment of radical creation in black religious faith. As a pragmatic bricoleur, he transformed the African American religious tradition in pragmatic religious naturalistic ways to produce a distinctive black faith: African American pragmatic religious naturalism.

This is important. There is no way of understanding Du Bois's pragmatic religious naturalism as anything other than black, despite its debts to thinkers who are white. To think otherwise—to suggest that to place Du Bois in relationship with American pragmatism is to separate him from black America— represents a misunderstanding of the dynamics of race in the United States. To do so would only confirm the ways that "studies of the (white) American cultural nationalists and pragmatists of the early twentieth century have almost entirely ignored African American writing, thus comporting with the conventional differentiation of American from African American culture, the exclusion of blackness from definitions of Americanness."[22] In my view, Du Bois's drawing on the rhetoric, tropes, and categories of larger American philosophical discourse simply ratifies what Ralph Ellison sublimely argues later in the twentieth century: that America is a much "darker" notional place than it acknowledges.[23] To say this is to suggest that American pragmatism must also be considered an African American tradition. In turn, Du Bois transforms American pragmatism in speaking to the exigencies of race.

These convictions vivify this chapter's exploration of pragmatism, religious naturalism, and its Du Boisian trajectories. The time I spend in discussing James, Dewey, and Santayana *for the purposes of understanding Du Bois* needs to be understood as nothing less than the recovery of African American philosophical and religious tracks. In the end, Du Bois's black religious faith resides squarely in his pragmatic and naturalistic transformations of black American religious vocabulary. The objectives of this chapter are to introduce the reader to pragmatism and pragmatic religious naturalism with the aim of better "catching the shadows" of Du Bois's African American religious register.[24]

Du Bois's Pragmatism Reconsidered

But if a man do not speak from *within the veil,* where the word is one with that it tells of, let him lowly confess it.

—Ralph Waldo Emerson[25]

In *The Souls of Black Folk,* W. E. B. Du Bois begins with what has become his clarion call to racial consciousness: "The problem of the Twentieth Century is the problem of the color-line."[26] This line, of course, has achieved iconic status in American life and letters, and its status is well deserved: Du Bois's sentence is prophetic both in its prescience and as a statement of one of modernity's crucial moral and spiritual dilemmas.

Yet sometimes when a line becomes a proverb or a truism, it becomes harder to hear its subtler cadences. In this way, rarely is any attention paid to the philosophical importance of Du Bois's use of the word "problem" to characterize the color line—he even goes so far as to repeat the word in the single phrase. When one turns the page to the opening paragraphs of "Our Spiritual Strivings," it becomes even clearer that the language of problems dominates the start of *Souls.* Twice in the chapter's opening paragraph Du Bois repeats this question: "How does it feel to be a problem?" Indeed, it becomes evident that "being a problem," "a strange experience,—particularly even for one who has never been anything else,"[27] represents the birth of Du Bois's language of identity and selfhood. For it is by seeing himself "through the revelation of the other world" and painfully acknowledging "this sense of always looking at oneself through the eyes of others, of measuring one's soul by the tape of a world that looks on in amused contempt and pity"[28] that Du Bois constructs the constituent terms that make identity possible in *Souls*. Of course, this is the birth of Du Bois's now epochal notion of "double consciousness," which is born from this very dynamic, that is, from problematizing one's social station. The notion that problems generated Du Bois's life mission guides him throughout his career. He writes at age seventy-two: "My life had its significance and its only deep significance because it was part of a Problem.... My living gains its importance from the problems and not the problems from me."[29]

Is there any special significance in Du Bois's choosing this specific language, the language of problems? I contend that the question of Du Bois's pragmatism and, by extension, the question of his pragmatic religious naturalism begins here with the idea of making and solving problems. Pragmatism properly understood is first a theory and a method of *problematizing*.[30] Dewey describes pragmatism as "necessarily alert for problems; every new question is an opportunity for future experimental inquiries—for effecting more directed change."[31] This is a wonderful description. It indicates how pragmatists construct problems: empirically, out of "the things of the environment experienced in our everyday life, with things we see, handle, use, enjoy and suffer from."[32] Moreover, it indicates how pragmatists use problems as tools and instruments for shaping and affecting the concrete terms of human experience. Pragmatism, as James tells us, cannot survive without problems: "It appears less as a solution, then, as a program for more work, and more particularly as an indication of the ways in which existing realities can be *changed*."[33]

My point here is not to turn Du Bois seamlessly into a Jamesian or Deweyan pragmatist. In fact, I see myself in agreement with Shamoon Zamir, the best critical opponent of Du Bois-as-pragmatist, who observes that "*Souls* [does not] reveal an emotional tenor or intellectual orientation that can be termed *unproblematically* Jamesian."[34] Yet, I am not sure why the standard for thinking about Du Bois's connections to James or another pragmatist has to be unproblematical. The question we should be asking about Du Bois's pragmatism or his relationship to James's thought is not whether Du Bois is unproblematically a pragmatist. The question is whether he can be plausibly thought of as *problematically* a pragmatist in that he adapts and extends a Jamesian radical empiricism to moral, social, and political questions about race and power in American life, issues and concerns that James and the rest of the pragmatists were largely deaf to.[35] Thus, I can agree with Zamir, as well as with Robert Gooding-Williams, that James and pragmatism writ large lack a coherent and sustained history of truly politically progressive and socially active politics.[36] It is true that James and the rest of the pragmatists never transformed a philosophical theory of action into trenchant forms of political activism. As James Kloppenberg tells us, the politics of early pragmatism, with its emphasis on individual will and responsibility, "were problematical because they neglected the persistence of power."[37]

At the same time, it is a matter of bad faith to deny the ways in which the pragmatists did develop crucial philosophical and theoretical perspectives that were geared for and aimed at social and political conditions. In its ideal form, James's famous notion of "radical empiricism" *"does full justice to conjunctive relations,"* which is to say that it does not "exclude . . . any element that is directly experienced."[38] James's radical empiricism insists that, to the degree we can answer any questions—of philosophy, selfhood, or politics—we must draw on practical activity and experience. As Kloppenberg writes of James: "Through his radical empiricism and his pragmatism he helped to nurture the seeds of a new political sensibility, which reached fruition in the writings of John Dewey and other like-minded radicals between 1890 and 1920, by insisting that knowledge begins in the uncertainty of immediate experience and that all ideas must remain subject to continuous testing in social practice."[39] Nor should we ignore the bearing James's model of the self has for Du Bois. James presents a model of selfhood in which the very sense of who we are takes shape only by understanding ourselves in relation to others; selfhood "is an affair of relations, it falls *outside, not inside, the single experience considered, and can always be particularized and defined.*"[40] James insists that the self—in fact, a single person's multiple selves—develops from perspicacious social vision and analysis: "Properly speaking, *a man has as many social selves as there are individuals who recognize him* and carry an image of him in their mind."[41]

Indeed, James announced that the standard to hold American philosophers to centers around social and political activism: "His books upon ethics, therefore, so far as they truly touch the moral life, must more and more ally themselves with a literature which is confessedly tentative and suggestive rather than dogmatic,—I mean with novels and dramas of the deeper sort, with sermons, with books on statecraft and philanthropy and social and economic reform."[42] In many respects, Du Bois is the American critic who best fulfills James's standard. *Souls* stands as an exemplary text—with its literary essays on the divided self, the relationship between material conditions and social mores, the tensions between individual and communal will, and a political liberalism that is itself critical of the liberal tradition. Of course, this only throws into stark relief the way in which James himself failed to live up to his own standard. He may have described the self as "a kaleidoscope revolving at a uniform rate, although the figures are always rearranging themselves."[43]

In actual fact, James did not succeed in producing accounts of selfhood that were sensitive to the sorts of social and political factors that create such kaleidoscopic effects. Du Bois does what James does not: He constructs a kaleidoscopic model of identity to elaborate the social and political ambiguities of black existence. In Du Bois, critical intellection leads to analysis of material conditions. In giving pragmatism the political traction and social vision that James lacked, Du Bois seems to have a more powerful grasp on Jamesian thought than James did. In doing this, he stands as an exemplar of pragmatic excellence that James never achieved.

Nowhere is Du Bois's pragmatic empiricism more evident than in his famous constructions of double consciousness and the veil. Both of these emerge from his early experiences with racism, "this sense of always looking at one's self through the eyes of others, of measuring one's soul by the tape of a world that looks on in amused contempt and pity." Undeniably, both double consciousness and the veil are burdens and hardships that involve "a painful self-consciousness, an almost morbid sense of personality and a moral hesitancy which is fatal to self confidence."[44]

Yet, Du Bois's veil and double consciousness are glossed too quickly and superficially if taken as grievous laments. To be sure, Du Boisian double consciousness is a burden, but it is one that Du Bois pragmatically transforms by embracing a notion of selfhood that thrives on decoding and understanding the social, political, and historical nature of the gaze of the white other. In other words, Du Bois's model for self-realization is rooted in his ability to perceive the terms by which he is understood to be a problem. For Du Bois, these terms are to be engaged and wrestled with, not shunned.[45] The result is a protean self, a divided self, whose double consciousness renders it sensitive to ambiguity and conflict. While at times Du Bois describes double consciousness as a hindrance, in the fullness of *Souls* he transforms it into an achievement of critical consciousness. In his hands, double consciousness represents a program for widening the lens of raced experience and for making manifest the "buried many things" and "the strange meaning of being black here in the dawning of the Twentieth Century."[46] The Du Boisian African American self is riven on *the strength of realizing its complex social positioning*. Toni Morrison writes of double consciousness: "W. E. B. Du Bois's observation about double consciousness is a strategy, not a prophecy or a cure."[47] This is an insight of a pragmatist sort: Double consciousness and Du Bois's great metaphor of the veil represent pragmatist tools for thinking critically about African American existence in light of a relentlessly metastasizing American racism. In effect, Du Bois turns the double consciousness problematic into a call for agency:

> It changed the child of Emancipation to the youth with dawning
> self-consciousness, self-realization, self-respect. In those somber
> forests of his striving his own soul rose before him, and he saw
> himself,—darkly as through a veil; and yet he saw in himself some
> faint revelation of his power, of his mission. He began to have a dim
> feeling that, to attain his place in the world, he must be himself, and
> not another. For the first time he sought to analyze the burden he
> bore upon his back, that dead-weight of social degradation partially
> masked behind a half-named Negro problem.[48]

In turn, seeing darkly through a veil is Du Bois's most important tool against what he calls "a conspiracy of silence...almost everyone seems to forget and ignore the darker half of the land, until the astonished visitor is inclined to ask if after all there *is* any problem here."[49] Indeed, double consciousness is what allows him "[s]lowly but surely...to catch the shadows of the color-line";[50] its fundamental drive is this worldly "careful inquiry...to listen to all the evidence."[51]

This is not to say that the double consciousness of Du Bois's veil provides immediately for crystal-clear social vision. Indeed, his veil fits into pragmatism's efforts "to recover *pragmata*," the unpredictable, "unsettled circumstances" that mark humankind's ethical life.[52] Ross Posnock is absolutely right to observe that Du Bois picks up James's efforts to deliberately introduce vagueness as a "condition of perception" in order to "blur divisions, and grant respect to the intricacy of the black experience."[53] Du Bois explicitly says as much in the forethought to *Souls*: "I have sought to sketch, in vague, uncertain outline, the spiritual world in which ten thousand thousand Americans live and strive."[54] Nonetheless, it is important not to overstate matters. Du Bois's veil is not a technique of the vague for the sake of vagueness.[55] *Souls* is a literary crucible in which Du Bois refashions and converts the vague and the strange into sharply detailed sketches of the diversity of raced living. For him, "the strange meaning of being black" is not something to be dodged. Strangeness is the stuff of insight in *Souls*. The veil is the tool he uses in order to provide greater vision and the critical ability to analyze a wide range of experience; its revelatory powers prompt and demand human archival work. Seeing darkly through a veil is to track down the historical and concrete social conditions that make up the problems of race. Seeing darkly allows him and his readers to see that a problem exists.[56]

In turn, Du Boisian double consciousness neither attempts to name a transcendent, extrasocial self nor becomes solely an account of feeling divided and torn by the torsion of standing socially. The Du Boisian self, born of double consciousness and the veil, is an affair of human contingencies, sensitive to ambiguity and conflict, and ultimately an achievement of black critical consciousness: "Yet there was among us but a half-awakened common consciousness, sprung from common joy and grief, at burial, birth, or wedding; from a common hardship in poverty, poor land, and low wages; and above all, from the sight of the Veil that hung between us and Opportunity. All this caused us to think some thoughts together; but these, when ripe for speech, were spoken in various languages."[57] This is a remarkable pragmatist's account of selfhood and its uses. It is crucial to see how Du Bois defines and constructs racial identity empirically and stereoscopically. What he yearns for in this passage is an empowering form of race consciousness that draws from African American memory and history. With James, it refuses a metaphysical "inside" or "aboriginal stuff" as identity's core and conceives of the self as "an affair of relations." With Dewey, ideal selves "are not made out of imaginary stuff. They are made out of the hard stuff of the world of physical and social experience.... The new vision does not arise out of nothing, but emerges through seeing, in terms of possibilities, that is, of imagination, old things in new relations serving a new end which the new end aids in creating."[58]

Who black people are is rooted in a collection of common experiences that are at once deeply personal and circumscribed by the politics of race. Black folk share certain experiences of oppression and suffering, as well as the cultural, existential, and intellectual common ground of surviving these experiences. At the same time, there are differences in translation, and *Souls* also remains sensitive to differences among members of the black community—spoken in various languages. Du Bois does not shun these variations but insists that they are also constitutive of blackness. Double consciousness is an expansive construct that does not name a deep metaphysical or noumenal racial substance that sits behind the world of appearances. Double consciousness instead is an interpretative lens that makes apparent the dense, contested, yet integral skein of social, cultural, and political allegiances that make up Du Bois's understanding of blackness and the black community. It is on these terms—as a method to construct and analyze the problems of race—that Du Bois's veil and double consciousness can be understood as radically innovative techniques in pragmatic radical empiricism.

This account of Du Bois's pragmatic antiessentialist rendering of race runs in the face of Anthony Appiah's now canonical portrayal of Du Bois as a racial essentialist.[59] Appiah's evidence for this claim resides entirely in Du Bois's "Conservation of Races" (1897), in which Du Bois conceives of an essential, even mystical, "common blood" blackness, "a vast historic race that from the very dawn of creation has slept, but half awakening in the dark forests of its African fatherland."[60] To be sure, this is the language of racial essentialism. However, a preponderance of evidence suggests that Du Bois spent the rest of his career, in effect, correcting the essentialism of that very early essay and conceiving of race not as an ontological but as a pragmatic social reality.[61] Consider Du Bois's account of race in *Darkwater* (1920): "There are no races, in the sense of great, separate, pure breeds of men, differing in attainment, development and capacity. There are great groups,—now with a common history, now with common interests, now with common ancestry, more and more common experience and present interests."[62] The notion that race, when subject to these sorts of contingencies, constantly shifts follows him throughout his later career: "[Race] had as I have tried to show all sorts of illogical trends and irreconcilable tendencies. Perhaps it is wrong to speak of it at all as a 'concept' rather than as a group of contradictory forces, facts and tendencies."[63]

Nowhere is this constructivist view of race more vividly and powerfully expressed than in a 1928 exchange of letters between Du Bois and Ronald Barton, a high-school sophomore who objects to the use of "Negro" in *The Crisis*: "The word 'Negro,' or 'nigger,' is a white man's word to make us feel inferior." "[B]y the time I am a man," Barton hoped, "this word, 'Negro,' will be abolished."[64] Du Bois responds by defending the name "Negro," and it is nothing less than a classic pragmatist's lesson in the nature of language—on how words get their meaning and what language is good for. Du Bois writes: "Names are only conventional signs for identifying things. Things are the reality that counts.... Names are not merely matters of thought and reason; they are growths and habits."[65] In calling words "growths," "habits," and "conventional signs," Du Bois insists that they gain their significance from the social contexts in which they are used. As James writes, "All human thinking gets discursified; we exchange ideas; we lend and borrow verifications, get them from one another by means of social intercourse."[66]

Thus, the name "Negro" stands as a marker of a people's specific history and experiential struggle with American racism: "But...what word shall we use when we want to talk about those descendants of dark slaves who are largely excluded still from full American citizenship and from complete social privilege with white folk?" Here, "Negro" does not speak of an ontological or atemporal racial essence—there is no distinct and stable Negro substance. Instead, it refers entirely to the history of sufferings and strivings of a people with a common social experience. It is a word for remembering ancestors and creating community.[67] Moreover, Du Bois also sees the word "Negro" as necessary to daily practices of dealing with the present and imagining the future: "Here is Something that...we Negroes could not live without talking about. In that case, we need a name for it, do we not? In order to talk logically and easily and be understood...And then, too, without the word that means Us, where are all those spiritual ideals, those inner bonds, those group ideals and forward strivings of this mighty army of 12 millions?"[68]

For Du Bois, the word "Negro" is a critical tool for African American living. As a word that means "Us," it creates a sense of solidarity and moral obligation necessary for practically effecting and bringing about hoped-for realities.[69] Du Bois uses "Negro" to look backward and to express loyalty to generations of black folk, and he uses it as a term to look forward for action now and tomorrow.[70] Questions of identity—who we are—reside in "talking about," with the way we use language to relate history to futurity and with how talk about the past affects current and future experience and activities. In short, Du Bois considers the name "Negro" for the work—moral, social, cultural—that it can be made to do. His criterion for continuing to use race-specific language—the "conservation" of race—precisely follows James's assertion that words "can always be brought down to some particular consequence, in our future practical experience."[71] Race "exists" for Du Bois as all truths exist for pragmatists: as socially powerful conventions that have undeniable material effects. In this, Du Bois's pragmatism is on full display for all to behold.

An Anatomy of Pragmatic Religious Naturalism

For Du Bois and the pragmatists, religion is a problem. For both, ambivalence reigns. For the pragmatists the problem begins with a profound naturalistic realization. Pragmatic religious naturalists cannot abide a religious supernaturalism based on unempirical assertion or ecclesiastic dogma. For them, there is no empirical evidence of the existence of metaphysical realities and divine undergirdings, and there is no reason to trust religious tradition's assertions on this matter. James writes: "The visible surfaces of heaven and earth refuse to be brought into any intelligible unity at all."[72] All that pragmatic religious naturalists have to go on are normative commitments in critical thinking, rational persuasion, and historical reflection.

At the same time, in a way that may strike many moderns as familiar, pragmatic religious naturalists find that admitting doubts about God's existence and church authority does not relieve them of James's "religious demand"—the sense that we belong to something larger than ourselves, the sense of moral justice, and the need, when justice fails, for well-being and consolation in a world suffused with suffering and brutishness. Even without a metaphysically robust God, we humans still find ourselves wanting to make the world live up to a heavenly ideal. Pragmatic religious naturalism, according to Henry Levinson, its best critic, springs from this pinch.[73] In describing James's ambivalent relationship to religion, Levinson invokes Matthew Arnold's characterization of the nineteenth-century pinch between modernity and religion: "One is, that man cannot do without it: the other, that they cannot do with it as it is."[74] Supernatural religion can no longer be accepted. Yet, the human needs, which religion meets, persist. In turn, religion must be reconceived without recourse to a supernatural foundation. How do we answer life's religious demand for meaning when we can no longer clearly discern a divine, underpinning reality? This is the galvanizing question of pragmatic religious naturalism.

Du Bois, too, is caught in the same bind—he cannot do with religion as it is, and he cannot do without it. Again and again, Du Bois doubts and disrupts supernatural complacencies: "I may say frankly that I am unable to follow the reasoning of people who use the word 'spirit' and 'spiritual' in a technical religious sense…in a vague attempt to reassure humanity, because reason and logic seemed to have failed."[75] In the fashion of pragmatic religious naturalism, any knowledge available to Du Bois comes solely from terms that reflect the immanent and conditioned nature of human life. At the same time, his famous language of "soul" and the "spiritual strivings" shows he cannot do without religion. Like Matthew Towns's singing of "Go Down, Moses," Du Bois uses religion and its modalities to draw from the reality of black experience in order to envision, demand, and call us to a world in which justice, right, sympathy, solidarity, and memory matter: a new religious ideal in this great night. Santayana would perfectly understand this Du Boisian turn in which religion "remains an imaginative achievement, a symbolic representation of moral reality which may have a most important function in vitalising the mind and in transmitting, by way of parables, the lessons of experience."[76]

Du Bois needs to be placed in conversation with this tradition of religious thought. To do so, I now address the work of James, Dewey, and Santayana. The attention I pay to these three thinkers may seem slightly digressive, but I think it is worthwhile. It builds a base vocabulary of pragmatic religious naturalism that will be deeply edifying once we turn directly to Du Bois. I also take some care to distinguish between the pragmatic religious naturalisms of James, Dewey, and Santayana, each of whom responds to the dilemma of the movement in distinct ways. In addition, these distinctions will be helpful for discerning more precisely Du Bois's specific version of pragmatic religious naturalism.

Pragmatic religious naturalism begins in skepticism: skepticism of supernatural explanations, metaphysical realities, and ecclesiastical dogma. It is not necessarily the case that pragmatic religious naturalists are certain that things such as supernatural bodies do not exist. James's *Varieties of Religious Experience* does not dismiss this question and even concludes that the belief in a "wider world of being than that of our every-day consciousness" is warranted.[77] However, the pragmatists agree on the futility of securing epistemic certainty about foundational supernatural or metaphysical truths.[78] How does religion confirm deep epistemic realities such as supernatural foundations? How does it allow us to make contact with the divine reality? How can we know that our lives receive divine sanction? For pragmatic religious naturalists, all of these questions, questions that ask for epistemological certainty, are exercises in futility. Religion simply cannot provide this type of foundational knowledge.

What, then, does religion provide if not antecedent truths? What are its sources of knowledge if not supernatural ones? And what is its value if it does not disclose the nature of the really real? Santayana writes the following in *Reason in Religion,* his great exposition of pragmatic religious naturalism: "For this human dust lives; this misery and crime are dark in contrast to an imagined excellence; they are lighted up by a prospect of good. Man is not adorable, but he adores, and the object of his adoration may be discovered within him and elicited from his own soul."[79] For pragmatic religious naturalists, religion remains a site of grandeur, wonder, and stirring visions of ideal forms of life, but the source of its power is immanent to human life itself: "Whatever makes life worth living is to be found 'in the world of matter and history.' We can account naturalistically—materially and historically—for parts of spiritual life that matter to us, even though spiritual life has traditionally (and mistakenly) depended on a supernatural or metaphysical explanation."[80] If pragmatic religious naturalists had calling cards, some version of this would be printed on them because it captures not only central tenets of pragmatic religious naturalism but its audacity as well. We are alone in our human dust, in its contingency and finitude, and who we are is forever mediated by contingent terms of our own making. James writes: "For pluralistic pragmatism, truth grows up inside of all the finite experiences.... Nothing outside of the flux secures the issue of it. It can hope for salvation only from its own intrinsic promises and potencies."[81] This focus on finitude yields a concomitant focus on mortality and death. Levinson claims that pragmatic religious naturalists are "death-haunted creatures" precisely because they cannot find succor in metaphysical assurances of life after death:[82] Death is not "turn[ed] into life, evil into good, absurdity into comprehension; it does not eradicate pain."[83]

Here, too, is the audacity of pragmatic religious naturalism. How can anything redemptive and inspirational be found in death? Levinson asks: "But what sort of spiritual triumph is a live option for somebody who claims that the denial of death is a lie and that providence is not simply improbable or unreasonable, but not even alluring?"[84] Pragmatic religious naturalists think that religion naturalistically conceived—without supernatural foundations and surviving only on human dust—does not sap religion of its power and strength of necessity. Human finitude—its lengths and limits—possesses the power to inspire. Phrased slightly differently, pragmatic religious naturalism suggests that it is possible to conceive of religion as rooted in the finitude and natural limits of human existence and yet still meet James's religious demand for higher ideals. Without deep epistemic certainty, religion can still impart a sense of goodness and deep consolation because it provides imaginative and symbolic worlds for humans to live in—worlds that induce emotional and moral dispositions and shape patterns of behavior that allow humans to gain purchase on life as it is mortally lived. Santayana writes: "The only truth of religion comes from its interpretation of life, from its symbolic rendering of that moral experience which it springs out of and which it seeks to elucidate.... Whatever is serious in religion, whatever is bound up in morality and fate, is contained in those plain experiences of dependence and affinity to that on which we depend."[85] Pragmatic religious naturalists remain enthralled by religious resources—stories, experiences, moral concepts and virtues, prayers, songs, and rituals—because they represent instances, opportunities, and modes for creating, in Dewey's words, "an effective realization of the sweep and depth of the implications of natural human relations...more intense realization of the value that inheres in the actual conditions of human beings with one another."[86] Pragmatic religious naturalism is itself religious in creating inspiring visions of the good and ideal modes of living from empirical conditions of existence.

This combination of the ideal and the real is deeply emblematic of pragmatic religious naturalism. James writes, "I offer this oddly-named thing pragmatism as a philosophy that can satisfy both demands. It can remain religious like the rationalisms, but at the same time, like the empiricisms, it can preserve the richest intimacy with facts."[87] Ideals play, as James says, a "re-directing function,"[88] where their power resides ultimately in their effectiveness as a tool for humans to shape meaning and spur action: "But the only force of appeal to *us*, which either a living God or an abstract ideal order can wield, is found in the 'everlasting ruby vaults' of our own human hearts, as they happen to beat responsive and not irresponsive to the claim. So far as they do feel it when made by a living consciousness, it is life answering to life."[89]

Again, the origin of these ideals is not in an antecedent reality or a static, nonhuman essence. Ideals emerge from "the richest intimacy with facts," that is, from the efforts and experiences of men and women who, in living flawed and imperiled lives, are nonetheless able to imagine standards to which they insist on aspiring to.[90] Religion becomes, in Dewey's words, "an idealizing imagination that has laid hold of natural goods," where the "aims and ideals that move us are generated through imagination. But they are not made out of imaginary stuff. They are made out of the hard stuff of the world of physical and social experience."[91] Thus, a version of salvation persists: It is framed by values and ideals that represent not an antecedent reality but the sense of possibility in the efforts of humans to render their imaginations real. This sense of salvation is in Dewey's call for a "pragmatism which shall be empirically idealistic, proclaiming the essential connexion of intelligence with the unachieved future—with the possibilities of transfiguration."[92] Santayana spins a naturalistic idealism of his own: "The dignity of religion lies precisely in its ideal adequacy, in its fit rendering of the meanings and values of life, in its anticipation of perfection.... Its function... is to draw from reality materials for an image of that ideal to which reality ought to conform, and to make us citizens, by anticipation, in the world we crave."[93]

It is here that pragmatism and pragmatic religious naturalism can begin to sound a tad too optimistic, romantic, and even Pollyannaish. This emphasis on religion as a source of new progressive ideals and possibilities seems to proceed all too swimmingly. Indeed, James himself proclaims that pragmatism is at heart melioristic: "It is clear that pragmatism must incline toward meliorism."[94] However, it is crucial that we understand what James meant by meliorism and distinguish it from the common understanding of meliorism as the belief in society's innate, inexorable tendency toward improvement. James's meliorism—or Dewey's and Santayana's—holds no such belief. In fact, James goes to great efforts to distinguish between optimism and meliorism. Optimism "would be the doctrine that thinks the world's salvation inevitable," which James strongly denounces in the face of the world's irrefragable hardships as a form of "ethical indifference."[95] In contrast, meliorism is properly understood as hope held in full recognition of the factors that make this world a vulnerable and tragic place: "Doesn't the fact of 'no' stand at the very core of life? Doesn't the very 'seriousness' that we attribute to life mean that ineluctable noes and losses form a part of it, that there are genuine sacrifices somewhere, and that something permanently drastic and bitter always remains at the bottom of its cup?"[96] Pragmatic meliorism is hopeful in girding itself for real battle with factors and forces that make the universe a serious place of real loss: "He is willing to live on a scheme of uncertified possibilities which he trusts; *willing to pay with his own person, if need be,* for the realization of the ideals which he frames."[97] As James says, pragmatic meliorism "treats salvation as neither inevitable nor impossible. It treats it as a possibility, which becomes more and more of a probability the more numerous the actual conditions of salvation become."[98] The hope of these ideals is born of strife and striving.

Here is where I want to begin distinguishing between the pragmatic religious naturalists, splitting James off from Dewey and Santayana. While it is true that, for James, religion is constructed out of natural goods—"Every religious phenomenon has its history and its derivation from natural antecedents"[99]—he never really develops a thick description of the sources of these natural goods on which we depend. Are they social, historical, political, biological, or cultural? In *Varieties* James retreats behind his famously individualistic and protestant definition of religion as *"the feelings, acts, and experiences of individual men in their solitude, so far as they apprehend themselves to stand in relation to whatever they may consider the divine."*[100] Furthermore, in so doing, he in effect gives up on deeply pursuing potential naturalistic sources of religious life. He is content in the *Varieties* to relegate these natural sources to a vague margin or periphery of which "the subject does not guess the source, and which therefore, take[s] for him the form of unaccountable impulses."[101] From this follows James's interest in mystics, ascetics, and saints. Religion becomes reduced to solitary, mysterious experience "that occurs outside cultural life," and in this sense James reneges on his own naturalism.[102]

The pragmatic religious naturalism of Santayana and Dewey stands in stark contrast to James's withdrawal into solitude. For Santayana and Dewey, this represents a callow distortion of the most crucial insight of their interpretation of the religious life. When religion is understood naturalistically, we come dramatically face-to-face with the fact that we live lives that are dependent on the efforts, histories, insights, and practices of those around us. Religion consists of human natural relations and not solitary encounters with the divine, which presents us with the possibility of "opening up a vista in which human prosperity will appear in its conditioned existence."[103] When Santayana describes religion as "an imaginative achievement" and "a part of experience itself, a mass of sentiments and ideas," he is speaking of religion as a collective endeavor.[104] Santayana is firm on this: Even when in private prayer, religious folk are relying on their communities. Santayana's spiritual person should never "forget the infinite animal and vulgar life...which palpitates with joy and sorrows, and makes after all the bulk of moral values in this democratic world."[105] Dewey is of the same mind: Religion, when conceived in light of natural finitude, speaks of human interconnection and mutual dependence. Religion, once emancipated from supernaturalism impresses upon us the reality of having "grown up in the matrix of human relations."[106]

From here, with this great deal in common, Santayana and Dewey part ways, for if both conceive of religion as a function of communal natural dependencies, each emphasizes different types of communities and dependencies, and the effect creates two distinct visions of the religious life. For Dewey, realizing natural dependences means shedding religious traditions and institutions: "Religions now prevent, because of their weight of historic encumbrances, the religious quality of experience from coming to consciousness and finding the expression that is appropriate to present conditions, intellectual and moral." Only then can we free what he calls the core "religious quality of experience," which for Dewey is represented by a critical intelligence in the pursuit of democratic social action: "There is such a thing as faith in intelligence becoming religious in quality."[107] This is the heart of Dewey's religious faith, his cardinal connection between intelligent criticism and the ability to actualize human social strivings and moral ideals: "One of the few experiments in the attachment of emotion to ends that mankind has not tried is that of devotion, so intense as to be religious, to intelligence as a force in social action."[108] Dewey, in essence, dissolves any tension between religion as a solitary practice and a form of social activism; for him, religion is socially relevant; otherwise, it is not religion at all. As Levinson writes: "For Dewey, spiritual life and citizenship are not only inseparable; they are identical. The political task in democracy is a divine process; it is, he asserts, participation 'in God.'"[109]

In contrast to Dewey's beliefs, Santayana's faith nurtures a complex tension between religious practice as social activism and what one might describe as a contemplative activism: "For Santayana...spiritual life and citizenship are intertwined as parts of a form of life; but spirituality requires *time out* from political deliberation and social work."[110] Humans have a need to pursue interests that are not explicitly activist in nature and that require time alone: Contemplation, intellectual study, and the appreciation of art are all good examples. This time apart is not time outside of human nature, nor does it represent a fantasy about escaping human finitude or society. It is instead a superlative spiritual perspective that comes from contemplatively realizing the depth of our debt to the efforts of others. Santayana strikingly describes religion as "a conscious impotence...an avowed perplexity."[111] By this he does not mean that religion renders its practitioners ineffectual and incapable but that, at its best, religion induces in us a heightened sense of the way we rely on natural things rather than ourselves for meaning: "Impotence has a more positive side.... We recognize our dependence on external powers."[112] These external powers are not supernatural but are what he calls natural dependencies, which represent the ways that humans have come to rely on and collaborate with each other in confronting the impotence of radical finitude. By learning to recognize, cherish, and even celebrate those natural dependencies, Santayana finds in religion a way to imbue the prosaic conditions of living with profound dignity, that is, to "love life in the consciousness of impotence."[113]

Religion helps us do this by instructing on the sorts of commitments and obligations that make up community and family; Santayana is for conserving those institutions and practices that instruct us well. At the same time, he is well aware that these same codified natural dependencies can prejudice us against people and ways of life outside the natural dependencies we identify with: "It is spiritual practice or aesthetic discipline that lets people distance themselves from socially funded moral propriety and national arrogance and get critical leverage on such limitations and pretensions."[114] Thus Santayana, unlike Dewey, both embraces and critically distances himself from external powers like family, community, and traditional religious practices. His religion is audacious in its dialectical engagement with tradition, history, and community. Where for Dewey these are only "historic encumbrances" that can be traded in wholesale for new natural dependences that support desired political ends, for Santayana no such trade-in is possible. History and tradition are inherited trusts that, if we honestly acknowledge the natural sources on which we depend, cannot be evaded. They can be dialectically wrestled with only from within and with the practices and standards that this tradition offers. The critical stance of Santayana's religion is deeply imminent.

Is Du Bois a Pragmatic Religious Naturalist?

—If we destroy reason and religion and do not rebuild, help us, O God, to realize how heavy is our responsibility and how great the cost.

—W. E. B. Du Bois[115]

My account of pragmatic religious naturalism has highlighted four central characteristics: (1) skepticism of supernatural revelation; (2) the conception of religion's powers as coming from human trust; (3) the belief that religion's genius lies in its pairing of the real with the ideal; and (4) a resulting meliorism in which hopefulness emerges only from a frank confrontation with real struggle and loss. James, Dewey, and Santayana differ importantly on how they express, arrange, and understand the implications of these. Nonetheless, they hold all four in common.

Is Du Bois a pragmatic religious naturalist? The signs are all there. His religious register dramatically exhibits all four qualities, and the rest of this book can be seen as one large effort to explicate them. I hope to show not simply that these four key characteristics of pragmatic religious naturalism animate Du Bois's religious voice but also that the distinctive ways Du Bois expresses them distinguishes him from James, Dewey, and Santayana and marks his pragmatic religious naturalism as a black faith. This, of course, cannot be done in one breath. Rather, it unfolds over the following chapters' treatment of *Souls* and the moral virtues of piety, sacrifice, and jeremiadic expression. In all, we will find the four key qualities of pragmatic religious naturalism.

In the remainder of this chapter I begin this process by giving an essayistic account of Du Bois's adherence to the four key qualities of pragmatic religious naturalism. In fact, his antisupernaturalism is not hard to find. Here again is another example of Du Bois's skepticism of supernatural revelation: "I cannot believe that any chosen body of people or special organization of mankind has received a direct revelation of ultimate truth.... It may well be that God has revealed ultimate knowledge to babes and sucklings, but that is no reason why I, one who does not believe in this miracle, should surrender to infants the guidance of my mind and effort."[116] With this emphasis on his own powers of intellection, Du Bois makes clear that religious life for him has essentially nothing to do with giving witness to God's supervening strength. Sounding basic pragmatist principles, Du Bois makes clear in a passage on immortality that knowledge is contextual and forever in flux:

> My thought on personal immortality is easily explained. I do not
> know. I do not see how any one could know. Our whole basis of
> knowledge is so relative and contingent that when we get to argue
> concerning ultimate reality and the real essence of life and the past
> and the future, we seem to be talking without real data and getting
> nowhere. I have every respect for people who believe in future life,
> but I cannot accept their belief or their wish as knowledge.[117]

Nor does religion have to do with discovering God's nature; religion for Du Bois does not ultimately promise an esoteric or gnostic form of knowledge.[118] In effect, he disdained forms of religion that claimed metaphysical or institutional authority:

> Ask any thorough churchman today and he will tell you, not that
> the object of the church is to get men to do right and make the

majority of mankind happy, but rather that the whole duty of man is to "believe in the Lord Jesus Christ and be saved"; or to believe "that God is God and Mohammed is his prophet"; or to believe in the "one Holy and Catholic church," infallible and omniscient; or to keep the tomb of one's grandfather intact and his ideas undisputed.[119]

For religion to speak to Du Bois, it must follow the light of empiricism: "No light of faith, no matter how kindly and beneficent, can in a world of reason guide human beings to truth unless it is continually tested by pragmatic fact."[120] Expressing a naturalism very much like James's, Du Bois is agnostic on God's existence, and these uncertainties provide no cause for further faith or belief: "I did not rule out the possibility of some God also influencing and directing human action and natural law. However, I see no evidence of such divine guidance. I did see evidence of the decisive action of human beings."[121] Du Bois shifts the epistemic value of God from the nature of the divine existence to the notion of God as a force to reframe and refocus our energy on the deep marrow of human finitude: "Let us learn quickly in our youth, O Father, that in the very doing, the honest humble and determined striving, lies the realness of things, the great glory of life."[122] Or consider the following stark moment in which Du Bois combines an invocation of God with a resolute, even harrowing vision of human morality: "We thank Thee, O Lord, for the gift of Death—for the great silence that follows the jarring noises of the world—the rest is Peace."[123]

The juxtaposition of religion, death, and finitude persuasively evokes Levinson's description of pragmatic religious naturalists as "death haunted creatures": thoroughly mortal beings whose religion refuses transcendence and the supernatural for natural finitude. Du Bois, for his sake, finds death and its finality utterly irresistible: "Woe to the man, who, with the revelation of the world once before him, as it stands before you now, has let it fade and whiten into common day—life is death."[124] In turn, Du Bois understands religion—its prayers, language, and moral values—as tools to focus worldly energies for this-worldly ends: "The prayer of our souls in this night is a petition for persistence; not for the one good deed, or single thought, but deed on deed, and thought on thought, until day calling unto day shall make a life worth living."[125] There again is the pragmatist's call to faith, challenging us to conceive of what makes life worth living. As we will see again and again, Du Bois's religious rhetoric undercuts supernatural powers in order to extol the strength of human interdependence.

Further, Du Bois's insistent pairing of the real and the ideal is unmistakable. In language that resounds with James's pragmatism, Du Bois embraces what pragmatists see as the felicitous tension between the ideal and the real: "To make here in human education that ever necessary combination of the permanent and the contingent—of the ideal and the practical in workable equilibrium—has been there, as it ever must be in every age and place, a matter of infinite experiment and frequent mistakes."[126] This becomes a religious technique for Du Bois: setting up an ideal as a way of spurring concrete analysis and action. The passage I cite in the introduction as the quintessential example of Du Bois's religious ideal stands as a dynamic example of the way he interweaves ideals and political exigencies: "Some day the Awakening will come, when the pent up vigor of ten million souls shall sweep irresistibly toward the Goal, out of the Valley of the Shadow of Death, where all that makes life worth living—Liberty, Justice, and Right—is marked 'For White People Only.' "[127] Du Bois's rarified moral, intellectual, and spiritual ideals are strategic frames he uses for locating the right sorts of contingent struggles worth pursuing. His use of ideals such as liberty and justice are not *idealist* in the philosophical sense of the term.[128] Thus, when Du Bois envisions how liberty and justice might reign, he looks not to the forms or behind the transient world of appearances but to human capacities and sensibilities: "Only by a union of intelligence and sympathy...shall justice and right triumph."[129] It stands to reason that when Du Bois asks, "Wither, then, is the new-world quest of Goodness and Beauty and Truth gone glimmering?"[130] his response is to provide a concrete program for the right to vote, civic equality, and an education broad enough to address the nature and importance of democratic ideals. "Christianity for black men started with the right to vote, and nothing less."[131]

Du Bois's meliorism emerges from this juxtaposition of the real and the ideal, from the consistent link he draws between the struggle and striving and the possible ideals that make life worth living: "Freedom, too, the long-sought, we still seek,—the freedom of life and limb, the freedom to work and think, the freedom to love and aspire."[132] What distinguishes Du Bois's meliorism from that of James and the rest of the pragmatists is the critical sharpness in Du Bois's account of the stubborn persistence of real difficulties and real pain. His meliorism is seething and scathing. There is no teleological rationalization of today's suffering in Du Bois's religious ideal. He concludes the penultimate essay of *Darkwater*, "Beauty and Death," by resoundingly denouncing the sort of Panglossian visions that hope against hope for messianic bliss on earth: "So strong is the spell of beauty that there are those who, contradicting their own knowledge and experience, try to say that all is beauty. They are called optimists, and they lie. All is not beauty. Ugliness and hate and ill are here with all their contradiction and illogic; they will always be here—perhaps, God send, with lessened volume and force, but here and eternal."[133]

Indeed, Du Bois comes to define beauty and by extension the ideals of justice by their perishability and by the fact that both beauty and justice are necessarily contingent on the finite natural world: "There is something in Beauty that demands an end.... Beauty must be complete—whether it be a field of poppies or a great life,—it must end, and the End is part of the triumph of Beauty.... It is always new and strange. It is the reasonable thing. Its end is Death—the sweet silence of perfection."[134] The heart of Du Bois's religious imagination is this dramatic tension. For him, the ideal must be joined to and lived in full light of the bitter realities of finitude. Dealing with the exigencies of race—which means not only facing the bitter bare facts but also lighting and charting a path of inspiration out of deprivation, cruelty, and a poverty of sympathy—requires tying the one to the other. Beauty is contingent on death; the ideal is dependent on and resides in the lives of the finite.

Nowhere are these tensions more viscerally apparent than in his account of his son Burghardt's birth and death in *Souls*. Burghardt's birth occasioned in Du Bois a mixed sensation, one of honor and dignity, joined by a good deal of wariness and foreboding: "Within the Veil was he born; said I," Du Bois writes in *Souls:* "and there within shall he live,—a Negro and a Negro's son. Holding that little head—ah, bitterly!—the unbowed pride of a hunted race, clinging with that tiny dimpled hand—ah, wearily!—to a *hope not hopeless but unhopeful,* and seeing with those bright wondering eyes that peer into my soul a land whose freedom is to us a mockery and whose liberty a lie."[135] And on his young son's premature death, Du Bois tries, it is true, to assuage his grief by imagining his young son sleeping "above the Veil": "Better far this nameless void...than a sea of sorrow for you."[136] Cornel West denounces this as a form of "glib theodicy" that is characteristic of Du Bois's refusal to "linger with the sheer tragedy of his son's death."[137] Yet West fails to note that Du Bois immediately and emphatically retreats from this soothing vision: "Idle words, he might have borne his burden more bravely than we." With this, Du Bois's elegy loses its escapism and expresses an angry hope, a melioristic sense of possibility that is acutely sensitive to tragic loss.

I have found the phrase "a hope not hopeless but unhopeful" to be deeply valuable in thinking about Du Boisian meliorism. The repetition of the word "hope" speaks to the importance of the notion of promise, opportunity, and possibility in the text. Above all, *Souls* represents Du Bois's commitment "to bring this hope to fruition."[138] At the same time, Du Bois constantly depicts hopes dashed and speaks explicitly in terms of the sense of hopelessness that American racism breeds. Even in *Souls*—before his Marxism is full bodied—Du Bois harbors no illusions about the prospects for racial harmony, justice, or simple notions of progress. He denounces the concept of culture— "The price of culture is a Lie"[139]—and shows the exact shambles of American civilization: "the ridicule and systematic humiliation, the distortion of fact and wanton license of fancy, the cynical ignoring of the better and the boisterous welcoming of the worse, the all-pervading desire to inculcate disdain for every-thing black, from Toussaint to the devil,—before this there rises a sickening despair that would disarm and discourage any nation."[140] He constantly depicts hopes dashed—"Is this the life you grudge us, O knightly America"—and refers repeatedly to the bodily stakes, "the dull red hideousness of Georgia," of being African American.[141] He diagnoses racism's stubborn resistance to moral progress and insists that the color line will forever circumscribe his life: "I shall die in my bonds."[142] His confrontation with the impossibility of ideals and the brutal forms of resistance they necessarily meet gives Du Bois's melio-rism a sense of the tragic.

Yet, hope persists. Du Bois, while fully committed to depicting the noes and losses of black American life, does not turn his back on the promise of action and even the hopeful, hard-fought promise of progress. His pervad-ing pessimism is constantly cut by the tonic of the prospect of fighting and struggling for the ideals to which he is committed. This admixture defines American life for Du Bois: "It is a land of rapid contrasts and of curiously min-gled hope and pain."[143] Thus, he persists in framing "the spiritual strivings of the freedmen's sons" in terms of "the name of this land of their fathers' fathers, and in the name of human opportunity."[144] He holds fast to "the sover-eign human soul that seeks to know itself and the world about it; that seeks a freedom for expansion and self-development."[145] At one point he describes the slave spiritual "Wrestlin' Jacob" as "a paean of hopeful strife," and there is no more apt description of Du Bois's meliorism.[146]

Du Bois has no easy answer for his melioristic question, "How shall man measure Progress there where the dark-faced Josie lies?"[147] His religious response, as we will see over the course of the following chapters, neither denounces progress as an utter chimera nor points assuredly to its obvious manifestations. Progress, rendered by Du Bois in the terms of pragmatic reli-gious naturalism, is better understood as a form of critical intelligence that acknowledges the bitterness and seriousness at the heart of life but unfailingly finds redemptive moments in its radical humanness. Such a moment comes at the end of "Of the Coming of John" in *Souls,* when John and his sister speak of the life-threatening stakes of a Deweyan sort of critical intelligence:

"John," she said, "does it make every one—unhappy when they study and learn lots of things?" He paused and smiled. "I am afraid it does," he said. "And John, are you glad you studied?" "Yes," came the answer, slowly but positively. She watched the flickering lights upon the sea, and said thoughtfully. "I wish I was unhappy,—and—and," putting both arms about his neck, "I think I am, a little, John."[148]

Here Du Bois's hope is not hopeless but unhopeful. John, as readers of the story know, ends up being lynched for defending his sister from being raped. Later I show how Du Bois also turns John into a Christ figure. What is important to see is that Du Bois makes sure to affirm a dawning self-consciousness—a black consciousness—fueled by hope's bitter confrontation with the social, political, and historical conditions of deprivation and dispossession.

Hope follows work, conflict, and confrontation, and thus hope is always born of the complexity of strife: "I know there are those who envisage a beauty eternal. But I cannot.... Ugliness to me is eternal, not in the essence but in its incompleteness; but its eternity does not daunt me, for its eternal unful-fillment is a cause of joy."[149] It is this pragmatic understanding of ideals as products of struggles with social complexities that makes for moral and spiri-tual renewal. Du Bois expresses this notion as follows: "Religion is necessary either as a solvent or a salve."[150] That is, as a solvent, religion is capable of viti-ating other dynamics: breaking down prejudice and injustice, expressing the dissatisfactions of the social critic. As a salve, religion—at times in response to its own dissolving properties—solidifies by constructing salubrious visions, ideals, and hopes. Here we confront the heart of Du Bois's divine discontent, when critical intelligence emerges from religious vocabularies to itself become religious. Nowhere is this more apparent than the vibrant and resounding pas-sage, even prayer, of divine discontent with which Du Bois closes his 1945 work, Color and Democracy:

> There has been a surfeit of creed, dogma, and priestly assumption to bridle the intelligence of men; there has been enough of the aimless arrogance of science used to heal and kill, destroy and build. The day has dawned when above a wounded, tired earth unselfish sacrifice, without sin and hell, may join through technique, shorn of ruthless greed, and make a new religion, one with knowledge, to shout from old hills of heaven: Go down, Moses! [a musical bar from the slave spiritual follows][151]

The thoroughgoing pragmatic religious naturalism of this passage is remark-able. Du Bois bristles against ecclesiastic arrogance; at the same time, he is aware of the technological and rational hubris that falsely insists that instru-mental reason can adequately govern human affairs. He clearly believes that humans need something more to inspire them to work and care for the good of each other. This more, however, is not a Jamesian "More" beyond human ken. Du Bois's "new religion" decidedly does not search for a metaphysical supernaturalism. It is without "sin and hell"; both represent the type of supernatural fears and threats that churchly authorities use to exact obedience from their congregants. In place of fear and obedience, Du Bois finds the More within human reach: intelligence, empirical technique, and historical trusts. He insists that these must be joined to certain religious virtues. Sacrifice, as we will soon see, is a central Du Boisian virtue, a religious technique transformed by naturalistic intelligence. Here, in this passage, there is true virtue in turning for inspiration and guidance to the creative spirit of the sorrow songs. Like Dewey, Du Bois seeks to release the devotional quality of religious experience by detaching it from the worship of an antecedent realm of Being and applying it to the values and goods immanent in human-natural relations. Like Santayana, Du Bois understands that, to effect this, the critical technique to learn is not Deweyan surgery, which attempts to excise the devotional quality from its historical context, but the technique of religious practice itself. Sacrifice, the jeremiad, prayer, religious song, and religious rhetorical exhortation all persist as essential techniques for developing critical intellection, and this distinguishes Du Bois's black faith—his African American, pragmatic religious naturalism—from the likes of James, Dewey, and Santayana.

In the next chapter we will see that Du Bois's black faith—his African American, pragmatic religious naturalism—and the way in which it contrasts with that of his pragmatist colleagues is most evident in his greatest text, *The Souls of Black Folk*. *Souls* is galvanized by the techniques of pragmatic religious naturalism, which characterize Du Bois's divine discontent. I also see it as an inaugural moment of a distinctly African American form of pragmatic religious naturalism. By embracing African American religious resources without metaphysical commitments and by using them to address the realities of race, *Souls* initiates a rich, complex, and diverse twentieth-century tradition of African American religious naturalism that runs through Zora Neale Hurston, Ralph Ellison, James Baldwin, and Cornel West. The next chapter, however, stays close to *Souls* alone. By so doing we become intimate with Du Bois's specific form of African American pragmatic religious naturalism and the way his combination of progressive politics and attention to historical tradition differentiates his version from the larger pragmatist tradition.

2

Pragmatic Religious Naturalism and the Binding of *The Souls of Black Folk*

In 1902 the McClurg Company approached W. E. B. Du Bois with an offer to publish his set of essays on race and America, which had appeared over the years in popular periodicals. From the start, Du Bois resisted.[1] He worried about the viability of collections of essays; he believed that piecemeal essays did not hang together coherently; and he was initially convinced that his disparate writings (what he later calls his "fugitive pieces") would suffer from inconstancy.[2] Ultimately, Du Bois agreed to publish the collection of his writings under one critical condition: that he add five original pieces, essays we might reasonably assume he believed would provide greater clarity and congruence to the text as a whole. These essays, along with revisions of his previously published work, compose *The Souls of Black Folk,* a triumphant and unique example of the Platonic axiom that the whole is greater than the sum of its parts.[3]

What sorts of essays did Du Bois add? What revisions did he make to his previous work? And what relevance do they have to making sense of *Souls* as a whole? Largely overlooked in a century's worth of study of *Souls* is the importance of religion and the role it plays in Du Bois's fashioning a single text from his wide-ranging essays.[4] Of the five new essays Du Bois wrote for the collection, four of them contain clear religious cores. "Of the Sorrow Songs" is Du Bois's tour de force exposition of slave spirituals; "Of Alexander Crummell" is a narrative of pious indebtedness to this conflicted African American religious figure; "Of the Passing of the First-Born" is, as Arnold

Rampersad suggests, an elegy to Du Bois's infant son. Rampersad describes it as "anti-Christian, a bitter parody of the Christian elegy,"[5] yet to my mind the chapter works more as an angry, politically engaged jeremiad on race relations. Finally, "Of the Coming of John" is a parable that pivots on the triangular confrontation between the secular black protagonist, John; the Southern church of his rural community; and the town's white racist power structure; it is a confrontation that results in John's being lynched, transforming him into a figure of Christ-like sacrifice.

This is not all. Du Bois also newly wrote the "After-Thought," which borrows the language and cadence of religious prayer, including the curious but distinctly Du Boisian juxtaposition between God and people: "Hear my cry, O God the Reader."[6] His "Forethought" announces that *Souls* intends to capture an elusive but also religious aspect of African American life: "I have sought here to sketch, in vague, uncertain outline, the spiritual world in which ten thousand Americans live and strive."[7] The pairing in this sentence of "spiritual" and "strive" refers to the most prominent and important revision he makes of his original essays. Du Bois changes the title of the opening essay from "Strivings of the Negro People," as it appears in the 1897 *Atlantic Monthly*, to "Of Our *Spiritual* Strivings,"[8] and with this addition of the word "spiritual," Du Bois decisively places the wide range of black America's political, social, and individual hopes and ideals into a religious frame. Du Bois further wraps *Souls* in a religious ethos by placing musical bars of slave spirituals at the head of each chapter. The effect is that each one begins with a prayerful consecration; the worlds of African American consciousness follow from sorrow songs. Du Bois also changes the title of the essay "The Religion of the American Negro" to "Of the Faith of the Fathers," signaling a less impersonal relationship and an increasingly deeper identification with African American religion. Finally, the title he chooses should not go without notice: *The Souls of Black Folk* is an assertion of African American soulfulness, an assertion that resounds as a historical critique of the way white Christianity's dithering about the souls of black folk was actively complicit with slavery and white supremacy. In this, he signals that religious notions, too, are battlegrounds of American racism.

The overarching argument of this chapter runs as follows: Du Bois uses the modalities of African American religion—its language, songs, concepts, and narratives—along with his explicit discursive writings about religion, to create, stitch, and bind *Souls* as a single, cohesive, and indeed sermonic and religious text. To do this, he employs African American religious sources as a pragmatic religious naturalist. He understands religion as a naturalistic practice, as a historical product of human interpretation, and as the efforts of historically situated actors—"indeed the siftings of centuries."[9] Furthermore, the

shape of those efforts and siftings reflects the intentions and interests of neither God nor an underlying historical spirit but rather the human resolve to
survive and flourish by finite means within human grasp. At the end of "Of
the Faith of the Fathers," Du Bois provides us with an inestimable description
of religion, which, he states, is nothing more or less than "simply the writhing
of the age translated into black."[10] For Du Bois, the age's writhings have every-
thing to do with history, community, society, politics, and, of course, race.

In turn, Du Bois takes the religious products of these writhings—soul,
black American spiritual strivings, the spirituals, and, as we will see, the veil
itself—and crafts a religious sensibility of his own that yearns to meet the
finite needs of black selves and black communities struggling to make lives
worth living. In *Souls,* Du Bois renders "religious heart-searching," "intense
ethical ferment," and "intellectual unrest" as the crucial nexus of African
American life.[11]

Herbert Aptheker is exactly right in thinking of *Souls* as a sermon: "From
that book's title to its last page, one may consider *Souls* a kind of sermon in
prose."[12] Du Bois explicates the complexities of this nexus to fashion a text
that itself stands as an example of the "new religious ideal" that he seeks. In
this light, as a type of religious performance, *Souls* should be seen as a spiritual manual. Of spiritual manuals, Wayne Proudfoot writes: "These guides,
whether written or transmitted orally by a spiritual adviser, are designed for
self-examination. They are aids for moral self-scrutiny, and they help to dispel illusion, unmask self-deception, and to distinguish the genuine from the
counterfeit."[13] Like Nietzsche, Du Bois uses historical criticism to initiate a radical course of self-examination for the sake of reorienting self-understanding.
Like Kierkegaard, he uses "language to arouse, provoke, and seduce the com-
placent reader."[14] Yet Du Bois's ends are radically different from Nietzsche's
immoralism or Kierkegaard's teleological suspension of the ethical. *Souls*
embodies a religious ideal in which religious language thrives on political
activism, in which "deep religious feeling" is enlisted for critical and intelligent engagement with the history, rights, and ideals of the American republic,
and finally in which reflection on and with religious resources leads to a deep
sense of appreciation of black American ancestors. The result is a work that
stands as the inaugural text of an African American pragmatic religious naturalism that stands distinct from the work of James, Dewey and Santayana.

In this chapter I focus on the way that Du Bois brokers an interaction
between the religious and this-worldly politics and activism in *Souls.* I show the
way he builds his political critical consciousness—his epoch-making notion of
"double consciousness" itself—from religious reflection. (In the next chapter I
focus more on a critical result of this consciousness: the virtue of appreciating

ancestors. Pragmatic religious naturalists call this piety.) In his chapter on African American religion Du Bois explicitly says that it is *part of the world* that "must perpetually discuss the 'Negro Problem,'—must live, move, and have their being in it, and interpret all else in its light or darkness.... With this come, too, peculiar problems of their inner life,—of the status of women, the maintenance of Home, the training of children, the accumulation of wealth."[15] As we will see, Du Bois does not believe that, historically, African American religion has responded well to these problems; his criticisms are scathing. Yet insofar as *Souls* itself does religious work, it should be seen as just such an attempt to make Du Bois's religion speak of the complexities and finite conditions of the world, of which religion is a part.

Religious Experience and Double Consciousness

Robert Stepto asks what I see as the most incisive question in all of the scholarly literature about *Souls* and religion: "A compelling question here is why, of all his previous essays, Du Bois chose 'The Religion of the American Negro' to be the catalyst for the 'Veil' section of his book."[16] It is a critical observation in that it proposes a link not simply between religion and those "voices from within the veil." Stepto, however, never answers his own question. In fact, not only does he not answer it, but he also goes on to undermine it. For in the next moments, he effectively sunders religion and its practices from this-worldly social and political concerns:

> Du Bois's sustained evocation of the spiritual world of a race...is
> the *volume's narrative creation beyond historiography;* thus Du Bois's
> fashioning of a *self beyond history*...necessarily involves the assumption of a spiritual posture in a spiritual space.... Obviously a discussion of religious principles and practices directly impels further explorations of a race's spiritual world, but Du Bois has other intentions as well.[17]

These other intentions are political and activist in nature, and for Stepto, because they occur within time and for finite goals, they stand over and against Du Bois's spirituality. It is precisely these suggestions—that Du Bois sunders religion, its principles, and its practices from the worldly; that his account of religion moves beyond history; and that Du Bois uses "spiritual" to refer to metaphysics and not worldly conditions—with which I take issue.

From Harold Bloom we have learned that from strong misreadings come insights compelling and percipient, and Stepto's suggestion of a connection between the veil, double consciousness, and religion is of this sort.[18] For if we understand the veil as a tool for political and social consciousness and we understand religion as connected to worldly politics, we are left with something promising: the evocative suggestion that religion is generative of a perspicacious, veiled double consciousness. To answer Stepto's question, the reason Du Bois uses religion as the catalyst for the veil section of *Souls* is that religion is the matrix out of which a critical double consciousness arises. On a closer textual look, this basic connection holds up, for nowhere in *Souls* does Du Bois refer to the development of a double consciousness with more detail and complexity than in his account of religion, "Of the Faith of the Fathers." The rhetoric of doubleness suffuses this narrative of African American religious development, including the famous passage, at once plaintive, defiant, scathing, and proud, in which Du Bois recounts the way the uncertainty of historical contingencies has affected religious mind-sets:

> The worlds within and without the Veil of Color are changing, and
> changing rapidly, but not at the same rate, not in the same way;
> and this must produce a peculiar wrenching of the soul, a peculiar
> sense of doubt and bewilderment. Such a double life, with double
> thoughts, double duties, and double social classes, must give rise to
> double words and double ideals, and tempt the mind to pretence or
> revolt, to hypocrisy or to radicalism.

There is certainly a lament and a severe critique of religion in these words; religion is clearly far from the source of all that is sweet and light for Du Bois. However, the initial emphasis must be on the way Du Bois depicts African American religion as the primary historical crucible in which the details, difficulties, and debates of living and seeing doubly develop. Du Bois locates the "double life every American Negro must live" in his genealogy of religion. He makes it unambiguously clear that the multiplicities of the religious world reflect the complexities of the finite conditions to which they are responses: "The worlds within and without the Veil of Color are changing, and changing rapidly, but not at the same rate, not in the same way." In response to Stepto, it is precisely *because* Du Bois understands religion as the primary African American moral, political, historical, and aesthetic response to time-bounded complexities of race—because "religious heart-searching," "intense ethical ferment," and "intellectual unrest" form the crucial nexus of African American life—that he chooses religion as the leaven for double consciousness and for *Souls* itself.[19]

The question is whether Du Bois wants to embrace and extol the type of double consciousness that is enmeshed in religion. His account of what it is to live with the "double words" and "double ideals" of religion makes it seem that this synonymy is in fact deeply problematic and perhaps for the worse. The type of double consciousness Du Bois describes as produced by religion seems responsible for harmful and debilitating effects on black Americans: "From this must arise a painful self-consciousness, an almost morbid sense of personality and a moral hesitancy which is fatal to self-confidence."[20] In fact, religion appears guilty of a welter of moral confusions and intemperances. Indeed, "Of the Faith of the Fathers" functions, at least in part, as a stinging and upbraiding social critique of the sorts of moral perspectives that have emerged from religious practices, leaders, and institutional structures. That narrative, far from triumphant, laudatory, and liberating, is pocked by religion's ethical and moral missteps. On the one hand, he speaks of religion as a doctrine of submission and fatalism: "The Negro, losing the joy of this world, eagerly seized upon the offered conceptions of the next: the avenging Spirit of the Lord enjoining patience in this world, under sorrow and tribulation until the Great Day when He should lead His dark children home,—this became his comforting dream."[21] On the other hand, as social conditions change and the potential for emancipation appears more plausible, religion foments political and social rebellion—yet Du Bois describes the revolutionary religious response as having lost track of what is truly sacred: "Freedom became to him a real thing and not a dream. His religion became darker and more intense, and into his ethics crept a note of revenge, into his songs a day of reckoning close at hand . . . and his religion, instead of worship, is a complaint and a curse, a wail rather than a hope, a sneer rather than a faith."[22] For Du Bois, both stances—acceptance of worldly impotence and wild ragings against social and political structure—are lamentable: "Thus we have two great and hardly reconcilable streams of thought and ethical strivings; the danger of one lies in anarchy, that of the other in hypocrisy. The one type of Negro stands almost ready to curse God and die; and the other is too often found a traitor to right and a coward before force."[23] The commonality, as Du Bois sees it, in these religious responses is their excessiveness, an inability to modulate in the light of what he admits are extreme social forces: "What wonder that every tendency is to excess,—radical complaint, radical remedies, bitter denunciation or angry silence."[24]

Thus, while it may be true that Du Bois depicts African American consciousness developing out of religious context—"Whither went his longings and strivings, and wherefore were his heart-burnings and disappointments? Answers to such questions can only come from a study of Negro religion as a development."[25]—his stridently dichotomous account of African American religious life should be cause for pause. Eddie Glaude notes that Du Bois's characterizations of black religious ethical life are extreme and tend toward the reductive: "Sometimes ideal types are useful. They help us organize a crowded conceptual terrain. They tidy things up for us. But sometimes, ideal types can be too successful; they make things too neat for us. As such, we lose sight of the messiness of human action, the ambiguity that surrounds the moments that concern us most."[26] For Glaude, there is a way in which Du Bois's double life, marked by such extreme moral poles, suggests a divided state of the "psychic torment of black individuals" rather than the subtlety and tolerance of ambiguity, which is required to "account for the tortuous relation of African Americans to American culture: their lingering sense of being in but not of a nation ambivalent about its own identity."[27] For Glaude, ambiguity and ambivalence are not paralyzing inner flaws but "analytic tools" used by black America for a sharp and perspicacious vision of complex American social, political, and cultural landscapes. A sense of ambivalence and ambiguity is the outcome of cultural criticism sensitive to multiple social realities and political complexities; it arises through seeing America well. It is on these grounds that Glaude "prefer[s] the phrase 'structure of ambivalence' to Du Bois's use of 'double life.'"[28] This suggests that the idea of doubleness as Du Bois develops it in relation to religion seems more like a failure of critical thinking than a frame or a prompt for it. How can religion or double consciousness be thought of as a critical black consciousness when Du Bois depicts it as a contradiction and a source of moral myopia?

What is more, this is not all that is contestable, problematic, and even unlovely about Du Bois's depiction of African American religion. "Of the Faith of the Fathers" begins with his notorious account of attending his first "Southern Negro revival." His description of that backwoods shout appears to confirm a type of racial primitivism of black Americans as somehow preternaturally religious: "The Negro has been pointed out many times as a religious animal,—a being of that deep emotional nature which turns instinctively toward the supernatural."[29] Du Bois's infamous portrait of the revival reads as follows:

> A sort of suppressed terror hung in the air and seemed to seize
> us,—a pythian madness, a demoniac possession, that lent terrible
> reality to song and word. The black and massive form of the preacher
> swayed and quivered as the words crowded to his lips and flew at
> us in singular eloquence. The people moaned and fluttered, and
> then the gaunt-cheeked brown woman beside me suddenly leaped
> straight into the air and shrieked like a lost soul, while round about
> came wail and groan and outcry.... Those who have not witnessed

the frenzy of a Negro revival in the untouched backwoods of the
South can but dimly realize the religious feeling of the slave; as
described, such scenes appear grotesque and funny, but as seen they
are awful.[30]

In describing his sensation and shock at this "mass of black folk" participating
in "a scene of human passion such as I had never conceived before,"[31] Du Bois
marks a distance, certain and uncertain, between himself and the souls of
black folk. This passage leads Cornel West to upbraid Du Bois by claiming
that he found it "difficult not to view common black folk as some degraded
'other' or 'alien.'...In short, a black ritualistic explosion of energy frightened
this black rationalist. It did so not simply because the folk seem so coarse and
uncouth, but also because they are out of control, overpowered by something
bigger than themselves."[32] Shamoon Zamir sees in this passage "the same
exoticism that led the white middle-class reading public at the turn of the century to seek out works that revealed how 'the other half' lived."[33] Theologian
JoAnne Marie Terrell sees the scene as Du Bois's "derid[ing] the Africanism
of 'shouting' among black Christians" and as proclaiming the "inferiority of
African tribal religions and African retentions."[34] The common thread is clear
enough: Du Bois's description seems to resist sensitive political and social
analysis and instead appears to trade in racist images of atavistic and tremendous passions.

There is, then, cause for regarding Du Bois's chapter on religion with cir-
cumspection and distrust. Yet, to claim that he sees religion *only* as a source
of moral misdirection or primitive mysticism is to ignore the narrative development of the chapter. "Of the Faith of the Fathers" contains an embedded
counternarrative that understands religion, with its other-worldly rhetoric,
experiences, and encounters with the Divine, as an interpretable social affair.
This is Du Bois's radical empiricism, and unlike James, Du Bois roots experience in material, social, and political matrixes. As the chapter develops, black
folk and black religious life appear less as lurid exotica and more as critical
historical agents grappling with the extreme social conditions that mark "the
peculiar circumstances of the black man's environment."[35] The putative "religious nature" of African Americans more or less vanishes as Du Bois presents religion as a form of response to the complexities of being black in the
American republic: "The question now is, What have been the successive steps
of this social history and what are the present tendencies? First, we must realize that no such institution as the Negro church could rear itself without definite historical foundations."[36] He goes on to make the case that the lineage of

black leadership begins with the African "Priest or Medicine-man"[37] and continues with the African American preacher. Indeed, Du Bois's account of the development of the black preacher represents one of his most richly rendered social histories. The spiritual space occupied by the preacher is definitively worldly and social space:

> He appeared early on the plantation and found his function as the healer of the sick, the interpreter of the Unknown, the comforter of the sorrowing, the supernatural avenger of wrong, and the one who rudely but picturesquely expressed the longing, disappointment, and resentment of a stolen and oppressed people. Thus, as bard, physician, judge, and priest, within the narrow limits allowed by the slave system, rose the Negro preacher, and under him the first Afro-American institution, the Negro church.[38]

The preacher's spiritual posture is hardly beyond history but is itself a temporal posture for aiding and addressing the contingencies of African American selfhood. Here, too, Du Bois's secular chapter on the leadership of Booker T. Washington becomes a continuation of the historical role of the preacher: articulating the longing, addressing the unknown, and providing both succor and self-determination, which are essential for spiritual well-being.

Consider, too, this brief but vital account of religious song: "Sprung from the African forests, where its counterpart can still be heard, it was adapted, changed, and intensified by the tragic soul-life of the slave, until, under the stress of law and whip, it became the one true expression of a people's sorrow, despair, and hope."[39] The connection Du Bois draws between soul and the real-world social and physical forces of law and whip should not go unnoticed. In religious song Du Bois sees artifacts and expressions of contingent and variable social forces and not a reductionist and deterministic view of racial essence. Religious song is for Du Bois the crucial site of knowledge making. He depicts this very dynamic in a scene in "The Sorrow Songs." Du Bois's recollection of his grandmother teaching children an African spiritual stands, in essence, as an ancestral, epistemological scene:

> The songs are indeed the siftings of centuries; the music is far more ancient than the words, and in it we can trace here and there signs of development. My grandfather's grandmother was seized by an evil Dutch trader two centuries ago; and coming to the valleys of the Hudson and Housatonic, black, little, and lithe, she shivered and shrank in the harsh north winds, looked longingly at the hills and

often crooned a heathen melody to the child between her knees, thus:

> Do bana coba, gene me, gene me!
> Do bana coba, gene me, gene me!
> Ben d'nuli, nuli, nuli, nuli, ben d' le.

The child sang it to his children and they to their children's children, and so two hundred years it has travelled [sic] down to us and we sing it to our children, knowing as little as our fathers what its words mean, but knowing well the meaning of its music.[40]

The scene, as I say, is epistemological: It speaks of a broad historical development in the creation of knowledge and meaning. Moreover, it raises the crucial tensions and complexity of this process. Du Bois at once portrays himself as intimate and estranged, one for whom the roots of religious song are both understood and not: "They [the songs] came out of the South unknown to me, one by one, and yet at once I knew them as of me and mine."[41] The words, of course, he literally does not understand; yet he is able to make them into knowledge by recognizing religious song as a form of African American historical consciousness, the critical part of which is the tension between known and unknown. It is a tension that turns efficacious for Du Bois when those gaps between known and unknown become prompts or spurs for historical understanding, for taking something that appears mysterious and opaque and accounting for it in terms of the social and historical complexities of being black in America: This is the "meaning" of the music. Du Bois's further placement of the spirituals at the head of each chapter—without lyrics, in Western musical code, which does not give voice to the social context of songs—serves as a dramatic recurrence or reiteration of this epistemological crisis at the heart of *Souls* and, in turn, positions religious song at the center of "travelling down" and "knowing well" African American meaning and consciousness.

In a very real way, this is the drama of *Souls* writ large. Nowhere is this tension between the known and the unknown more central than in his accounts of black American religious life. In this way, the "pythian madness" of Du Bois's account of the religious shout represents this critical tension between the foreign and the familiar. Du Bois's account of religion begins with a wild, seemingly unaccountable scene of uncertainty but then moves toward tracking down and creating narratives that help explain this same scene in contingent terms. If anything, Du Bois *demystifies* the pythian madness to which he is initially attracted by coming to understand how these responses are rooted in naturalized religious practices for dealing with the worldly conditions of American blackness. Critic Cynthia Schrager understands this "mystical" scene "in the realm of esoteric, occult knowledge...deliberately presented as resistant to meaning" and providing "access to an unseen spiritual world that eludes realist representation."[42] For Schrager, Du Bois's mystical discourse is laden with a radical politics: "The discursive register of the spiritual is attractive to Du Bois precisely because it permits the expression of his profound discomfort with the contradictions and tensions of the methodologies of positivist science, particularly in the discourse of race."[43] Yet arguing this ignores the way the fullness of Du Bois's account works not to deny but to bring historical and sociological clarity to the scene. Schrager's attempt to embrace and revalue the category of discourse that West and Zamir disdain may have value as a political project, but all three share a common blindness that reduces and limits Du Bois's account of religion to that initial scene. Yet "Of the Faith of the Fathers" only begins there, and its substantial work is in tracking down and creating historical narratives that help explain it. The sensational aspects of that opening scene ultimately work not only in the service of portraying not only the communal context of African American religious experience but also in the way that communal and individual religious experience are interrelated and mutually influential. The "frenzy" turns into a rendering of religion as the place where the community—black folk—conducts moral, aesthetic, and civic business.[44]

Glaude's early cautionary words about Du Bois's apparent lack of ambiguity in his description of religious life are relevant here. In a certain sense, Glaude is right: Du Bois's emphasis on the religious extremes of radicalism and hypocrisy lacks subtlety. However, might it also be possible to see within those extremes the sort of ambiguity Glaude calls for? I would like to call on a line of Du Bois's that Glaude touches on but does not linger over: "Between the two extreme types of ethical attitude which I have sought to make clear wavers the mass of the millions of Negroes, North and South; *and their religious life and activity partake of this social conflict within their ranks.*"[45] Glaude cites only the first part of this line and interprets its use of "wavering" as Du Bois's saying that the masses of black folk themselves oscillate wildly from extreme to extreme, moving "from pretence to revolt, from hypocrisy to radicalism and back again."[46] But stressing the second half of the passage produces a different, viable reading. Du Bois's emphasis on the religious life of the masses of black folk as *participating in* social conflict suggests not a morally peripatetic folk but one involved and engaged in mediating the tensions created by the extremes. In other words, it is not that the preponderance of black folk is extreme; it is more that the extremes coexist within the preponderance of black folk. What

Du Bois depicts in the masses of black folk are souls that have historically been accustomed to *living with* conflict and ambiguity in religion's competing ethical and moral visions: "Feeling deeply and keenly the tendencies and opportunities of the age in which they live, their souls are bitter at the fate which drops the Veil between; and the very fact that this bitterness is natural and justifiable only serves to intensify it and make it more maddening."[47]

On this view, the religious life of African Americans comes to represent not simply extreme moral boundaries but also the reality that they live with a complex of moral perspectives. Religion is *about* lived social conflict for Du Bois, and it is not incidental that some of his most eloquent statements on lived social conflict emerge from his enumeration of the treacherous terrain of religious life:

> In some such doubtful words and phrases can one perhaps most clearly picture the peculiar ethical paradox that faces the Negro to-day and is tingeing and changing his religious life. Feeling that his rights and his dearest ideals are being trampled upon, that the public conscience is ever more deaf to his righteous appeal, and that all the reactionary forces of prejudice, greed, and revenge are daily gaining new strength and fresh allies, the Negro faces no enviable dilemma.[48]

Here, at the end of Du Bois's account of religion, we find no scenes of either "exotic" emotional release or unadulterated religious radicalism or religious fatalism. Instead, Du Bois presents the religious dilemma—indeed, the religious project—of trying to negotiate, sort through, and struggle with the competing extremes, ambiguities, and doubleness of the age.[49] To reiterate the earlier point, for Du Bois, African American religious life *partakes* of social conflict; ethics of revenge, hope, despair, endurance, and determination are products of contingent historical complexities and not atavistic, mystic, inborn impulse. As the historical locus of doubts, strivings, virtue, and vice, religion, in essence, has long been the important hermeneutic frame for the writhings of the age. By the end of the chapter, the question that Du Bois raises is whether or how religion is now going to address these writhings for today and tomorrow.

Religious Tradition and Political Progress in "Of the Coming of John"

How can African American religion continue to serve as a resource for assembling a political and moral vision for surviving and thriving in a racist

America? To what degree can religion negotiate the compound political crises of the modern age? These are the questions that sit at the heart of Du Bois's short parable, "Of the Coming of John." Consistently overlooked in the critical literature is the confrontation John has in church with his community after returning home from the North. What is more, to my mind this conflict—what John says and how his community responds—stands as a nodal point, which, if writ large, dramatizes the larger issue of religion and modernity at stake in *Souls*.

John, having been sent north by his community to acquire an education, returns home after seven years, ready to teach what he has learned. In church, John is reintroduced to the community by three preachers and is initially hailed and welcomed: "The house was crowded to overflowing." Yet John immediately strikes both the preachers and the community as deeply changed. His cool demeanor unnerves the preachers; no one catches the spirit; the community is set on edge: "This silent, cold man,—was this John? Where was his smile and hearty hand-grasp? ' 'Peared kind o' down in the mouf,' said the Methodist preacher thoughtfully. 'Seemed monstus stuck up,' complained a Baptist sister."[50] John takes the pulpit and offers a classic Enlightenment program of science and industrial progress while diminishing the importance of religious life, which is loyal to tradition, ancient texts, and local practices. The community's response to John is vehement and furious:

> A painful hush seized that crowded mass. Little had they understood of what he said, for he spoke an unknown tongue, save the last word about baptism; that they knew, and they sat very still while the clock ticked. Then at last a low suppressed snarl came from the Amen corner, and an old bent man arose, walked over the seats, and climbed straight up into the pulpit. He was wrinkled and black, with scant gray and tufted hair; his voice and hands shook as with palsy; but on his face lay the intense rapt look of the religious fanatic. He seized the Bible with his rough, huge hands; twice he raised it inarticulate, and then fairly burst into words, with rude and awful eloquence. He quivered, swayed, and bent; then rose aloft in perfect majesty, till the people moaned and wept, wailed and shouted, and a wild shrieking arose from the corners where all the pent-up feeling of the hour gathered itself and rushed into the air. John never knew clearly what the old man said; he only felt himself held up to scorn and scathing denunciation for trampling on the true Religion, and he realized with amazement that all unknowingly he had put rough, rude hands

on something this little world held sacred. He arose silently, and passed out into the night.[51]

It is this passage, I suspect, that leads Wilson Moses to see little but Du Bois's animus against religion in "John."[52] And yet, what I think is momentous here is the way in which Du Bois crafts this passage not to validate Enlightenment liberalism over religion but *to portray, develop, and complicate the live, pressing, and relevant uncertainties and ambiguities between the two.* He refrains from resolving matters in favor of an Enlightenment view. John emerges from his encounter with the church elder chastened, questioning for the first time the liberal truths of positivistic analysis he has learned up North. What I hear in the old man's rebellion is a distinct type of religious wisdom that insists that religion has long been this community's resource for addressing the very exigencies—brotherhood, education, charity, spread of wealth and work, and, not least of all, race relations—that John raises. In the "eloquence" and "majesty" of the old man's words, in the way they vivify the community, and in the way a notion of sacredness emerges from the religious doings of this community, John is forced to acknowledge the relevance of a religious conceptual scheme. Religion perdures: The community has long used it for ballast, and its historic place will not be vitiated by Enlightenment logic.

I do not want to overstate matters here. I am not saying that in this scene Du Bois is fully renouncing scientific and rationalist thinking and uncritically embracing and finding salvation in a religious worldview. It is not that the community does not want to hear John's progressive message; after all, they had sent him North for the purpose of garnering new knowledge, and they welcomed him home hoping that he could change their lives. Nonetheless, by situating John's speech in the church, depicting preachers as the translating medium for his message, and in essence surrounding him with a religious ethos, Du Bois demonstrates the way in which this community is going to hear that message only through a religious context. To this end, it should not be lost on us that the church elder's protest issues in a scene of communal solidarity. In this community, social ethics and religious ethics work hand in hand.

At the end of this scene Du Bois leaves his readers with a pressing dilemma. John's core project—updating moral and social life in light of changing political and personal desires and aspirations—remains essential. However, this community, this people—his people—cannot live without religion. For them, it is far too rich a source of interpretive tools for understanding human virtues and vices, achievements and failings. At the same time, the church elder is all protest and no prospective vision: There is nothing in what he says that will help to mobilize the town for desegregation or political representation. Du Bois expresses this same ambivalence about the black church in the 1903 sociological monograph, *The Negro Church:* "It must not be inferred from all of this that the Negro is hypocritical or irreligious. His church is, to be sure, a social institution first, and religious afterwards, but nevertheless, its religious activity is wide and sincere. In direct moral teaching and setting moral standards for the people, however, the church is timid, and naturally so, for its constitution is democracy tempered by custom."[53] The questions that emerge in *The Negro Church,* as well as in *Souls,* are of how to adjust, adapt, and integrate projects of democratic radicalism with the religious wellsprings that African Americans have historically relied upon in dealing with social problems.

Du Bois provides no pat answer here. In the end John is lynched for killing his adversarial doppelgänger in the story, the white John, who attempts to rape his sister. John refuses to abide by the tradition of Jim Crow, and in this he commits a seemingly secular revolt. Yet, in the final portrayal of John gazing out to the sea, Du Bois mirrors the close of the previous chapter on Alexander Crummell, in which Du Bois imagines Crummell "a King—a dark pierced Jew" applauding earthly moral and spiritual strivings.[54] In other words, Du Bois intentionally refashions John into a Christ figure; in this moment, his revolt against Jim Crow feels a good deal less secular. In this final action, Du Bois mirrors the pressing dilemma between religion and modernity that he depicts in the church.

It is possible that Du Bois is suggesting that any attempt to marry religion with changing political contingencies simply ends in violence and death. I think this is too simple. Instead, I believe Du Bois presents here a tension between a certainty and an uncertainty: the certainty that figures like John are needed to marry and transform religious virtues, sensibilities, and traditions for modern political problems, and the real uncertainty of how to achieve this and whether it can be done without enormous loss. In the next section I argue that Du Bois's sensitivity to this tension is the crucial characteristic of his pragmatic religious naturalism that differentiates him from James, Dewey, and Santayana. Du Bois provides no answers to this here or elsewhere. It is enough that he demands that we face the problematic.

Finally, should we not recognize the prescience in Du Bois's church scene? For fifty years later, the churches of Baton Rouge, Montgomery, Birmingham, and Greenwood, religious practitioners, led by the Northern-educated Dr. Martin Luther King Jr., flew into action and mobilized African Americans, who had long been chafing against Jim Crow and the color line that hemmed in them and theirs.

Souls and Spiritual Strivings: A Path between
Dewey and Santayana

At this point, we can definitely say that Du Bois leaves James's pragmatic religious naturalism behind. Recall that James understood religion as a solitary experiential practice. Du Bois, however, is far too committed to the black community and its critical place in shaping black religiosity. For Du Bois, there is no religion separate from communal settings, and this is true for him despite his hostility toward church institutions. One way of reading Du Bois's engagements with black religion in *Souls* is to reclaim black communal religiosity from the four walls of the church. His recuperation of the sorrow songs is an excellent example of this logic. Du Bois conceives of them as religious cultural products that reflect a human and not an institutional wisdom: "In these songs, I have said, the slave spoke to the world....The words that are left to us are not without interest, and, cleared of evident dross, they conceal much of real poetry and meaning beneath conventional theology and unmeaning rhapsody."[55]

Matters become more interesting and complicated when we ask whose pragmatic religious naturalism Du Bois's resembles more—Dewey's or Santayana's? On the surface, there is an obvious answer: *Souls* sits in the powerful stream of Deweyan thought, which links religious devotion to democratic social activism. This undoubtedly has merit. Du Bois's religious commitment to action and tasks is most clearly expressed in his gospel of work, which in the course of his life became part of his creed: "There is no God but Love and Work is His prophet—help us to realize this truth, O Father...filled with the glory of our Life-Work. God is Love and Work is His Revelation."[56] At the same time, we cannot forget the degree to which Dewey disdains religious traditions by wanting "whatever is basically religious in experience...the opportunity to express itself free from all historic encumbrances."[57] This desire to begin completely anew with utter disregard for tradition is not Du Bois's path. In Dewey, when it comes to religion, we find a desire to cut cleanly through historical knots. In *Souls* we find a historical consciousness that insists that innovation can fruitfully come only from tough dialectical work with African American religious history and ritual.

It is on these terms that we find the unexpected. In important ways *Souls* speaks to Santayana's sensitivity to religion because it portrays religion as a historical trust that gives us the coordinates of our existence and deserves our debt and gratitude. I suggest that *Souls* cuts an innovative path between the pragmatic religious naturalism of Dewey and Santayana and urges a type of social activism that is anchored by an appreciation of African American history and ritual. It is precisely this combination of progressive politics with critical historical reflection and appreciation of tradition that best characterizes Du Bois's distinctive form of pragmatic religious naturalism.

Nowhere is this form of pragmatic religious naturalism better seen than in Du Bois's uses of the language of "souls" and "spiritual strivings." What does he mean by each? What do souls strive for, and what aspect of their strivings is spiritual? It is remarkable how difficult these questions are to answer without pragmatic religious naturalism as a frame. There is nothing normative about Du Bois's renderings of soul. It is easy to miss in his peripatetic uses the way in which he refuses the notion of soul shared by both Augustine and Plato: soul as a metaphysical substance that lies outside of time and human experience.[58] Soul for Du Bois does not sit behind the realm of appearances and is not grounded in the firmament of the really real. In fact, he constructs the souls of black folk entirely out of the desires, efforts, practices, and accomplishments of African American life as it is lived. By my lights, the closest Du Bois ever gets to giving an account of what he means by soul is this: "the thought and feeling, the thousand and one little actions which go to make up life. In any community or nation it is these little things which are the most elusive to grasp and yet most essential to any clear conception of the group life taken as a whole."[59] Soul, then, is clearly a communally dependent category. For example, Du Bois speaks of the "soul-life of the land," the "soul-beauty of the race," and "soul-hunger."[60] Soul is an account of what a collection of souls have: the parts of communal identity that emerge in moments of struggle. In this fashion, soul refers to the values, ideals, and sufferings that give black life its forms of dignity. Years later, Ralph Ellison describes soul as "that quality of Negro American style" that "announces the presence of creative struggle against the realities of existence."[61] It is a pragmatic religious naturalistic construction that is clearly Du Boisian.

The relationship between soul and spiritual strivings is a symbiotic one. Soul is required for spiritual strivings; spiritual strivings produce soul. It is impossible to separate them: "and the spiritual striving of the freedmen's sons is the travail of souls whose burden is almost beyond the measure of their strength."[62] What is absolutely the case, though, is that, in Du Bois's hands, the spirit strives for concrete action and results. Later in his career, thirty years after writing *Souls*, Du Bois makes explicit the political and social traction he gives "spiritual strivings":

I may say frankly that I am unable to follow the reasoning of people who use the word "spirit" and "spiritual" in a technical religious

sense. It is true that after any great world calamity, when people
have suffered widely, there is a tendency to relapse into superstition,
obscurantism, and the formal religion of creeds in a vague attempt
to reassure humanity, because reason and logic seemed to have
failed. This instead of being a spiritual "awakening," is to my mind,
an evidence of ignorance and discouragement.

On the other hand, among some people, there comes in time of
stress and depression, an increase of determination to plan and work
for better conditions. This is not usually called a "spiritual" awakening, but it is apt to be condemned by the ignorant as "radicalism" and
an "attack" upon the established order. It is, however a manifestation
of the spirit in the highest sense and something of this I seem to see
beginning today.[63]

There is, then, a necessary connection between soul, spiritual strivings, and
activist politics. Soul and spiritual strivings are tools for effecting social justice. Ralph Luker's magisterial account of race and the social gospel movement
at the turn of the century gives credence to Dwight Hopkins's characterization
of Du Bois as a social gospeller: "One did not carry out and witness to the
good solely out of a secular motivation, without spiritual foundation. On the
contrary, the habit of giving of oneself for the sake of the community had a
profound sacred meaning. Self-transformation was tied to social transformation toward equality and democracy; this was the touchstone of a spirituality
of social justice struggle."[64] Though Hopkins barely mentions *Souls* at all, it is
a text that is certainly committed to a religious ethic of social justice in which
moral and economic improvement carries a spiritual dimension. Consider, for
example, Du Bois's warnings against the "Mammonism of America" in his
account of the industrial development of the South and the unequal distribu-
tion of goods and services; or his prefacing the chapter "Of the Black Belt,"
an account of land and place and the work needed to develop both, with a
biblical passage from "The Song of Solomon" that ties blackness to the challenges of being "the keeper of the vineyard"; or the conclusion of his exhorta-
tive narrative on the importance of education, "Of the Training of Black Men,"
which places African Americans on a biblical stage: "Peering from this high
Pisgah, between Philistine and Amalekite, we sight the Promised Land."[65]
Finally, in the text's penultimate paragraph, Du Bois invokes the history of
African American religion, in particular the legacy of religious song for the
this-worldly purpose of claiming ownership of the national rights, good, and
opportunities America afforded only its white citizens. His emphasis here on
action, on doing, and on work as forms of striving is an undeniable form of

social gospel:

> Your country? How came it yours?... Around us the history of the
> land has centred for thrice a hundred years, out of the nation's heart
> we have called all that was best to throttle and subdue all the worst;
> fire and blood, prayer and sacrifice, have billowed over this people,
> and they have found peace only in the altars of the God of Right. Nor
> has our gift of the Spirit been merely passive. Actively we have woven
> ourselves with the very warp and woof of this nation,—we fought
> their battles, shared their sorrow, mingled our blood with theirs, and
> generation after generation have pleaded with a headstrong, care-
> less people to despise not Justice, Mercy and Truth, lest the nation
> be smitten with a curse. Our song, our toil, our cheer, and warning
> have been given to this nation in blood-brotherhood.... Is not this
> work and striving? Would America have been America without her
> Negro people?[66]

The power of the activist thrust of this passage is palpable. At the same
time, we cannot be blinded by it. It is crucial to see that work, action, and direct
political intervention do not exhaust the politics of this passage. Du Bois's
call in the preceding excerpt is not only for material social justice but also
for the emergence of a sophisticated historical consciousness. His speaking of
the breadth of contributions of African Americans to life in the United States
needs to be understood as replacing a dominant American narrative of spiritual exceptionalism and triumphalism. (Here is where I separate Du Bois from
the social gospel; Luker's account makes it clear that the social gospel cannot
help but re-create an American exceptionalism.) In Du Bois's hands, America
becomes godly for its debts to black struggles and accomplishments and not
for the ascendancy of its Christian mission. In this way, he cannot "do with"
the normative American account of soul and spirituality for the way in which
Christian metaphysics has historically been used to exclude black America from
the "soul-life of the nation." In contrast, through the sense of soul and spiritual
strivings in black America's struggle, Du Bois reconstructs the "soul-life" of
the nation around historical and experiential narratives of black Americans. In
this way, I have come to think of *Souls* as a Nietzschean genealogy without the
Nietzschean foul air. *Souls* evinces a deep suspicion of America that breaks the
standard pedigree of U.S. history and introduces African Americans as a disjunctive source of American excellence.[67] This form of critical contemplation
is itself a crucial type of spiritual striving.

This is to say that the vocabulary of religion provides a vocabulary for
reinterpreting the very nature of the United States. Historical reflection that

joins religious discourse to historical insight in order to unveil the rich bed of African American contributions is the primary spiritual striving of *Souls*. Santayana defines spirituality as "liv[ing] in the presence of the ideal...for the sake of a true and ultimate good."[68] On these terms, the Du Boisian reinterpretation of the claim of black Americans to their own history and to America writ large is the great spiritual accomplishment of his pragmatic religious naturalism. *One of the deep spiritual strivings of* Souls *is the striving to interpret.* Reinterpretation fulfills James's criteria as a religious need: It provides deep consolation in uncovering the historical strands of black accomplishment. In fact, Du Bois's essay on Booker T. Washington is more powerfully read as an account of the importance of criticism, deliberation, and persuasion to the spiritual health of a people than as a social policy critique of Washington's program:

> But the hushing of the criticism of honest opponents is a dangerous thing. It leads some of the best of the critics to unfortunate silence and paralysis of effort, and others to burst into speech so passionately and intemperately as to lose listeners.... Honest and earnest criticism from those whose interests are most nearly touched,—criticism of writers by readers, of government by those governed, of leaders by those led,—this is the soul of democracy and the safeguard of modern society.[69]

In *Souls,* religious devotion to intelligence is not exhausted by the call to social action. Democracy for Du Bois not only is about right action but also represents the spiritualizing of intellection.

There is an undeniable Deweyan quality to Du Bois's demand for critical intelligence. As the previous chapter points out, for Dewey intelligence is "inherently involved in action," and "there is such a thing as faith in intelligence becoming religious in quality."[70] Du Bois's own religious devotion to intelligence certainly issues the same call: "We are groping for *light, movement, strength, decision, deeds!*"[71] However, Du Bois is also consistently devoted to directing his intelligence to a sympathetic (if critical) review of age-old African American trusts. In a passage that Dewey could never have written, Du Bois makes clear that he can never lead African American religious life behind: "These are the days and this is rightly the place of criticism and searching—of insistent questioning of old beliefs and old ways and old deeds; of quick recognition of error and superstition.... Make us ever mindful of the solemnness of world-old things, of the rightness of the old homely ways."[72] This prayer captures the spiritual strivings of *Souls* both in its having no truck with idols and in its insistence on searching retrospectively for wisdom. The same ethos yields Du Bois's appreciation of "The Sorrow Songs," which he calls "the spiritual heritage of the nation."[73]

Indeed, Du Bois is ever suspicious of America's demands for "progress." There is a side of *Souls* that is deeply meditative, repeatedly stressing the importance of "a union of intelligence and sympathy" and "the chance to soar in the dim blue air above the smoke."[74] *Souls* performs and engenders the sanctity of critical contemplation as a good in itself—or at least as a complement to direct political praxis. Spiritual strivings, in the tradition of Santayana's religious naturalism, do symbolic work, which is to say the real work of helping humans express, clarify, and figure out their natural dependencies. Rushing headlong into action is not always the best solution; sometimes what is required is suspicion of the terms of deeds, movements, and progress. In *Souls,* prayers for action sit side by side with prayers for suspicion, prayers for criticism, and prayers of appreciation. Together, Du Bois uses these to open up imaginative vistas for African Americans (and perhaps white Americans so inclined) to do the symbolic work of expressing and clarifying the natural dependencies on which black Americans rely.

In this light, it is helpful to see *Souls* as riven by the "contrary but not contradictory" tensions of "self-assertion" and "contemplation" that occupy Santayana.[75] Santayana writes: "In rational prayer the soul may be said to accomplish three things important to its welfare: it withdraws within itself and defines its good, it accommodates itself to destiny, and it grows like the ideal which it conceives."[76] It is not a stretch to say that Du Bois uses the spiritual strivings of the souls of black folk as a Santayana-like spiritual prayer: "The spiritual man should be quite at home in a world made to be used." However, where Santayana conceives of withdrawal into the self as initiating breaks from society—"His unworldliness is true knowledge of the world"[77]—Du Bois's spiritual strivings are nothing if not socially responsible. Du Bois's shifting veil shows that, to be black in America is always, even in moments of free play, to remain immersed in the social markers of race. His "withdrawal" is into the recesses of black American experience to find the nature of the good. Consider the first line of *Souls:* "Herein lie buried many things which if read with patience may show the strange meaning of being black here at the dawning of the Twentieth Century." Du Bois does not have to be irresponsible to induce wondrous contemplation. He does not pray by taking leave of social realities. Instead, he prays through the essays of *Souls* by immersing himself further in the social, political, and cultural conditions of black folk. In a sense, *Souls* is both a text that achieves Santayana-like ends and a spiritual practice of acknowledgement and blessing of the unappreciated and the vilified. Yet it does so by Deweyan means; Du Bois's readings are always conditioned by an awareness of power and politics, of race and racism. Here we come face-to-face with Du Bois's distinctive pragmatic religious naturalism. Its combination of politically inspired critical intelligence, contemplation, and recuperation of African American traditions represents the spiritual strivings of *Souls* itself.

Lest we forget, recall Du Bois's demand for a new religious ideal in *Souls*: "Back of this still broods silently the deep religious feeling of the real Negro heart, unguided might of the powerful human souls who have lost the guiding star of the past and are seeking in the great night a new religious ideal."[78] His search for a new religious ideal is a classic project in pragmatic religious naturalism. *Souls* itself is an embodiment, a true representation, of this hoped-for new religious ideal. It displaces the supernatural and ministers to *human souls* that gird themselves for battle against the politics of Jim Crow. "Religious feeling" is enlisted for critical and intelligent engagement with the history, rights, and ideals of the American republic. Finally, *Souls* makes clear that this new religious ideal is going to come only by reclaiming and reconstructing that guiding star; traditional religious practices such as song, prayer, and biblical exhortation are marshaled for providing meaning and goods for life as it is mortally lived.

In order to move forward, Du Bois makes his readers ever more dependent on the historical spiritual strivings of black folk. That is, he ties the forward-moving spiritual strivings of black folk present to those of black folk past. For pragmatic religious naturalists, these efforts can themselves become great acts of religious reverence. Indeed, they have a term for this: natural piety. In the next chapter I turn to Du Bois's "faith of his fathers," his African American natural piety.

3

"Love for These People"

Racial Piety as Religious Devotion

How we, too, are still pious...even we seekers after knowledge today, we godless anti-metaphysicians still take our fire, too, from the flame lit by a faith that is two thousand years old.

—Friedrich Nietzsche[1]

At the end of the preceding chapter I insisted that a crucial religious virtue of *Souls* is its particular type of critical intellection. Like Dewey, Du Bois's creative intelligence is geared toward action and change, and like Santayana, it is devoted to forms of historical (re)interpretation of both American and black American history. The combination represents Du Bois's distinctive African American pragmatic religious naturalism. Further, I insisted that this striving toward historical interpretation represents a religious virtue, which I named piety. In particular, Du Bois's piety is at its best when it is devoted to reclaiming and recovering the spiritual strivings of black America. *Souls,* in the way it critically honors and acknowledges the spiritual strivings of black folk, exhibits the virtue of piety.

I begin this chapter by acknowledging that it seems wrong to characterize Du Bois's selective and critically minded contemplation of things past as "piety." There are two traditional forms of piety. As conceived by Jonathan Edwards and Friedrich Schleiermacher in the nineteenth century, piety consists of a religious feeling of personal and prereflective closeness to God.[2] Conceived in Augustinian terms, piety is deferential in that it expresses the "human spirit's need for settled institutional and communal forms, including a structure of the church and authority to reign in spiritual excess."[3] On both counts, Du Bois appears little other than radically impious. On the one hand, he has little use for a personal relationship with God. On the other hand, he is wildly impious toward traditional forms of religious authority. His comments on the dogma and fairy tales of the church and on the mediocrity of preachers are legion. Together these criticisms seem to be utterly destructive of what might recognizably be called piety. Finally, we need to be clear that Du Bois is a thoroughgoing democrat who throughout his life pledges his allegiance to an individual's powers of self-determination and responsibility. Jeffrey Stout evocatively points out the apparent incompatibility of piety and democratic irreverence:

> Piety, if understood as deference to a hierarchy of powers on which social life depends, seems simply to be washed away in a tidal wave of democratic self-assertion. In deferential respect, common people once bowed down in gratitude and humility to everything higher than themselves in the chain of being. The value of such piety consisted partly in the contribution it made to education in the virtues. The reverence for authority implicit in it fostered docility, which in turn permitted an individual's character to be shaped by tradition and community toward virtue. Democracy, in contrast, trumpets self-reliance and holds docility in contempt. It encourages individuals to stand up, think for themselves, and demand recognition of their rights.[4]

Clearly, for Du Bois to be considered pious a different notion of piety is needed, one that is compatible with democracy and its impulses. Stout asks: "Can we succeed in giving [piety] a fresh, democratic air?"[5] Stout begins this process by questioning the assumption that democracy's spirit is necessarily corrosive of all aspects of piety. Is it not the case that particular aspects of classical forms of piety—community, tradition, and types of character—remain vital to democratic life? Indeed, a critical theme of Stout's recent work is the claim that democracy and its intellectuals, prophets, and social activists seek to develop character, shape virtues, and establish traditions of their own that help in both projects.[6] For example, his reading of Walt Whitman emphasizes Whitman's efforts to articulate a notion of the good for democratic life: "Whitman is not backing off from democratic commitment to the language of rights when he embarks on this program of culture and speculates on what the virtues of truly democratic individuals might be."[7] The point is that democracies are not without values, traditions, and patterns of behavior that complement forms of self-assertion and self-determination. Said slightly differently, the forms of self-assertion and self-determination that are conducive to democratic life are not intuitive; they have to be taught, and there is a remarkable collection of democratic voices devoted to explaining the types of values and ethical patterns that make democratic life worth living.

For these critics, one of the dangers of democracy is the way its powers of self-assertion and self-reliance can turn hubristic. Democrats become excessive when they operate under the illusion that they are entirely self-made—that they alone are responsible for their successes (or failures) and creative accomplishments. Under these conditions, democratically minded critics have taken pains to point out that self-reliance and self-assertion are far from sufficient for democratic vitality. One also has to work to acknowledge one's debts to and dependencies on others. Democratic life is a collective life, which is to say that nothing is accomplished politically or culturally without influence. These democratically minded critics call this virtue of critical acknowledgment and honoring of one's debts to others piety. One's fellow citizens, of course, are not supernatural but natural beings: one's neighbors and one's ancestors. Naturalistic piety is the art and virtue of acknowledging these natural sources of one's existence. This type of naturalistic piety does not consist of simply being historically minded, nor does it consist in uncritical devotion. Instead, democratic piety is represented by the activity of finding the right critical stance toward the natural sources of one's existence. Rituals and memorials can be effective tools here, as can an essay. Debts are celebrated while simultaneously being critically scrutinized. In its best forms, piety (democratically conceived) instills a sense of thankfulness and inspires right and loving action.

Santayana and Dewey have long been understood to be America's twentieth-century philosophers of piety. Piety, or what Dewey called "natural piety," is a central virtue in their pragmatic religious naturalism. In this chapter my claim is that Du Bois's religious voice—in his role as both a critic of religion and a critic who uses religion for his own pragmatic religious naturalism—is inhabited by a concept of "natural piety." Despite his frank willingness to flaunt traditional ways, Du Bois also expresses deep devotion to a critical appreciation of the natural sources of his being: "Cherish unwavering faith in the blood of your fathers, and make sure this last triumph of humanity."[8] This understanding of piety provides rejuvenated access to Du Bois's *Prayers for Dark People*. With its prayers for cleanliness, school study, temperance, and fiscal responsibility, the text can easily appear solely as a scolding, moralistic handbook. However, the richest and most philosophically significant prayers all collect around the spiritual importance of honoring the African American archive of effort and accomplishment. If we ever had any doubts that acknowledging the sources of his existence is a religious matter for Du Bois, this prayer of natural piety should dispel them:

> Remember with us tonight, O God, the homes that own us all. Make us true to the fathers and mothers of these children here—true to their hopes and ideals.... On the strength of the home hang many things—the training of children in a far deeper sense than we can train them here.... Give them grace to realize the vast significance of the family group in their lives and let us all know that here we but build on foundations laid there and we build best on homes where truth is taught and reverence and where Thy word is heard.[9]

Du Bois prayerfully exhorts black America to participate in this activity of natural piety: "Yonder lie ten million human beings writhing in sorrow and disappointment, bending beneath insult and hatred, choked with the blood and dust of battle. What do they need?... Only that work that is inspired by Love for these people—the work of hearts that sympathize and feel for them because they are flesh of their flesh and bone of their bone."[10] Black folk, he urges, need to be explicit and militant in their claim of their birthright, by which he means not only the rights due to them within American politics but also the treasuring and cultivation of the specific cultural, social, and aesthetic endeavors that black folk have accomplished in their collaborative efforts to survive and love. As we will see, this "Love for these people" is a complicated notion. It is not a fawning, uncritical, romantic love. Rather, it takes the struggles of African Americans seriously by honoring them with gratitude when it is due. However, it is a notion that also measures black life with unflinching standards. Du Bois's piety, in this way, is not simply a type of backward-looking historical consciousness. His piety is inseparable from the life of activity and social criticism it prepares its practitioners for. Here Du Bois differs slightly from Santayana, who separates piety from spirituality: "In honouring the sources of life, piety is retrospective...piety looks to the sources from which we draw our energies."

Spirituality, on the other hand, is forward looking, "the aspiring side of religion, the end toward which we move." A spiritual life is one led "in the presence of the ideal...for the sake of a true and ultimate good."[11] Du Bois, on the other hand, conjoins piety with spirituality, the retrospective with the prospective. For him, the two are practically identical.

Nowhere is this more evident than in *Souls*, which we return to as a powerful text of natural piety: *Souls* is an exhortation to black Americans to remain faithful—which is to say to commit the critical intelligence that is intense enough to be religious—to excavating and explicating their natural African

American sources of existence. Of course, *Souls* is not the only place where this type of natural piety flourishes. Natural piety vivifies Du Bois's midcareer essay titled "Of the Revelation of Saint Orgne the Damned." The piety of this essay is important for the way it very explicitly uses the retrospective powers of piety to develop the concept of the "democracy of race." It is a notion inspired by the idea of "Love for these people," but it is also capacious enough to be critical of narrow, race-based accounts of identity. The piety of this essay vividly engages in the democratic critique of self-assertion and individualism that Stout tells us is central to the natural piety of America's best democratic critics. Du Bois engages in this critique for the purpose of constructing black identity—first by honoring the sources of his existence and then by using the terms of this pragmatic construction to scrutinize the way in which that identity is used going forward. On both counts, Du Bois needs to be seen alongside other modern exemplars of democratic life whose accounts of natural piety teach us how to appropriately balance the honoring of traditions and communities with the creative energies of democratic ingenuity and self-making.

Pragmatic Natural Piety

Santayana describes piety as follows: "Piety, in its nobler and Roman sense, may be said to mean man's reverent attachment to the sources of his being and the steadying of his life by that attachment."[12] Santayana's distinguishing piety by its "Roman sense" is important, for he is marking his understanding of piety as classical and distancing it from the piety of Edwards and Schleiermacher. For Santayana, the sources of his being must be natural, which is to say that they are subject, as it were, to the elements—of time, contingency, luck, human desire, and the larger natural world in which the human drama plays itself out: "Natural beings have natural obligations, and the value of things for them is qualified by distance and by accidental material connections."[13] For Santayana, family both present and past, political associations both present and past, and "finally humanity at large and the whole natural cosmos" count as sources of his being, though in different ways depending on the times and context.[14] The point is that all of these natural sources are not self-derived, which leads to the Deweyan realization that "[t]he things in civilization we most prize are not of ourselves. They exist by grace of the doings and sufferings of the continuous human community in which we are a link."[15] Natural finitude carries with it a sense that one's existence is dependent on something larger than oneself.

Stout emphasizes that natural piety "is not to be understood primarily as a *feeling*, expressed in acts of devotion, but rather as a *virtue*, a morally excellent aspect of character."[16] The distinction is important and correct, but it needs further clarification. Stout is using virtue and character in an Aristotelian sense to mean a practice or an activity that needs to be cultivated and requires work. Natural piety is a self-consciously learned art that is exhibited in a great many contexts and settings. Dewey speaks of "the responsibility of conserving, transmitting, rectifying and expanding the heritage of values we have received."[17] Fulfilling these responsibilities requires long-term investments and explicit practices that engender a sense of obligation and indebtedness to historical trusts. At the same time, we should not forget that the virtue of natural piety is accompanied by a set of feelings and emotions. Though natural piety is not a feeling of closeness to God or church, it does deliver a feeling of wonder with the power to motivate action: "This consciousness that the human spirit is derived and responsible, that all its functions are heritages and trusts, involves a sentiment of gratitude and duty which we may call piety."[18] Explicating the natural loyalties of one's existence must be accompanied by a sense of gratitude, reverence, and blessedness. These are feelings. Dewey also recognizes the importance of the way natural piety generates such emotions: "A religious attitude, however, needs the sense of connection of man, in the way of both dependence and support with the enveloping world that the imagination feels is a universe."[19]

Santayana makes it clear that a critical aspect of the virtue of piety is learning not only to prioritize the sources of one's existence but also to hold these sources in appropriate and just balance. It is a demand that necessarily leads to deep conflict. On the one hand, piety begins with honoring local allegiances such as family and nation. Santayana writes, "It is right to prefer our own country to all others, because we are children and citizens before we can be travellers [sic] and philosophers....A specific inheritance strengthens the soul."[20] Yet, this very same process can produce the sort of malicious prejudices that come to violate other important natural pieties such as loyalties and sympathies toward people who are not from our own specific station. Local pieties, if they are just and appropriate, cannot utterly violate other natural dependencies with the larger world: "Indeed, piety is never so beautiful and touching, never so thoroughly humane and invincible, as when it is joined to an impartial intellect, *conscious of the relativity involved in existence* and able to elude, through imaginative sympathy, the limits set to personal life by circumstance and private duty."[21] Santayana's genius is his insistence that historical contingency, that very idea and insight on which local trusts and heritages depend, can also be a force for disciplining and, if need be, vitiating these same local loyalties. To realize that existence is shaped by adventitious contingencies is to comprehend that they can very justifiably be rendered less significant or even made to yield to other contingencies, which is to say, other natural pieties. On these terms, prioritizing and holding the sources of one's existence in a just balance requires constant attention. Natural pieties grow choked and deformed if they are not allowed to be constantly pressed and interrogated by competing loyalties. Indeed, part of the practice of piety is this art of holding multiple conflicts in tension.

The Natural Piety of *The Souls of Black Folk*

On what do loyalties to race, country, and community rest? Which loyalties should be honored and why? To what is reverence justified, and why is it due? *Souls*, in its use of historical criticism to answer these questions, is a text of African American natural piety. Its essays critically review the natural sources of African American existence in an effort to inspire a sense of gratitude, grace, and duty. This disposition can be seen in details small and large. Consider the small: Du Bois, as I note in chapter 2, changed the title of earlier written essays, "Strivings of the Negro People" and "The Religion of the American Negro," to "Of Our Spiritual Strivings" and "Of the Faith of the Fathers" for the publication of *Souls*. As I read them, these changes are acts of natural piety that insist that the radical interpretations that follow (i.e., the complexities of double consciousness and the uncertain modern place of religion, both of which threaten to unsettle pat accounts of identity) find their feet in the black community. In *Souls*, we need to acknowledge that, for all of the text's insistence on change and for the way that its radical interpretations anticipate something new, it roots these radical aspirations in the natural sources of black existence, particularly African American religion, and feeds them there as well.

Consider the large: There are two centerpieces to *Souls* as a text of natural piety. The first is the way Du Bois honors black American heritages and trusts as a way of demanding right of place in the United States. This cannot be emphasized enough. His piety honors black ancestors as a way of making claims on the firmament of the nation. Black people do not just belong in America; black people founded it. The chapter titled "The Sorrow Songs" epitomizes this form of Du Boisian piety. Du Bois's readings of the songs themselves embody a critical obedience to what he calls "the spiritual heritage of the nation."[22] His symbolic use of the songs as a window of access to his grandmother and those before her, his family's African ancestors, represents a fulfillment of Deweyan responsibilities of interpreting and transmitting a heritage of values. Moreover, it should not escape notice that Du Bois concludes this chapter with a jeremiadic entreaty that enjoins black Americans to embrace their contributions to the construction of the American nation as a whole: "Around us the history of the land has centred for thrice a hundred years; out of the nation's heart we have called all that was best to throttle and subdue all that was worst; fire and blood, prayer and sacrifice, have billowed over these people....Actively we have woven ourselves with the very warp and woof of this nation."[23]

These urgings are prominently echoed in his "Credo" and the essay "Jacob and Esau," where Du Bois insists that black America claims its heritage as a birthright.[24] In addition, his "Credo" calls for the "training of children" "lit by some large vision of beauty and goodness and truth" as a way of honoring "the sons of the fathers," who, "like Esau, for mere meat barter their birthright in a mighty nation."[25] The point is that, for Du Bois, the stakes of acknowledging and honoring heritages and trusts like the "sorrow songs" and the sons of the fathers involve claiming ownership of America. Consider in the same breath of the jeremiadic ending to "The Sorrow Songs" that Du Bois also demands that white America take pious responsibility for itself by acknowledging African Americans' contributions to institutions and ideas it calls its own: "Your country? How came it yours?"[26] Again, the idea is that piety—just acknowledgment of the sources of America's existence—lead to black America's rightful claim of ownership of the nation itself.

The second pivotal point of piety in *Souls* is Du Bois's chapter on Alexander Crummell. It is an essay that has long perplexed critics. On the surface, it reads like an encomium to Du Bois's mentor, father figure, and religious forebear. Du Bois portrays Crummell as a compassionate saint and a solitary, Christian, suffering servant willing to sacrifice himself for the sake of his people. However, this surface appearance has never satisfied critics. Historian Wilson Moses tells us that Du Bois's depiction of Crummell is wildly inaccurate: "Crummell was an entirely different breed of cat."[27] Crummell was imperious, authoritative, and withering in his Victorian commitment to all things mannered and Christian. He was no friend of the common person. Further, Crummell, the stalwart Christian missionary, saw all things un-Christian related either to Africa or African American slave culture as uncivilized and atavistic. For all of Du Bois's own Victorian and authoritarian tendencies, he always found cultural and spiritual richness in slave culture and religion.[28] Indeed, this acknowledgment is central to Du Bois's piety, and thus Crummell's inability to exhibit appropriate natural piety represents a very significant difference between Crummell and Du Bois. And yet, Du Bois's chapter on Crummell mutes this conflict by never explicitly addressing this crucial difference. Robert Gooding-Williams artfully and suggestively argues that Du Bois's essay actually contains an indirect and a "sublime" yet "substantive critique of "Crummell's...repudiation of slave culture."[29] This is undoubtedly right. In the essay, Du Bois effects this by depicting Crummell as sympathetic to common folk and their ancestry. In other words, Du Bois's "inaccurate" depiction of Crummell represents Du Bois's own correction of Crummell's unsympathetic views of the souls of black folk.

However, there is more to the story than this. What Gooding-Williams's account lacks is a close reading of how Du Bois effects these qualities in his Crummell. The tale that Du Bois writes of Crummell is not one that begins with Crummell triumphantly embracing the culture of black folk. Instead, the story he tells is of Crummell's struggles to find the appropriate way to attach himself to the sources of his existence, his own people. In other words, Du Bois creates for Crummell a narrative depicting the emergence of Crummell's natural piety. Whether Crummell actually exhibited anything like this is beside the point. Du Bois's narrative about Crummell is ultimately revealing of Du Bois's own religious values.

Du Bois begins his narrative of the young clergyman Crummell as he is founding a chapel dedicated to the education of black folk. He quickly becomes disappointed with and judgmental of the perceived lack of moral virtue in black folk: "The dearth of strong moral character, of unbending righteousness, he felt, was their greatest shortcoming, and here he would begin."[30] His intentions founder; he is unable to raise a congregation; and he is, in effect, rejected by his people. Frustrated, he is plagued by "the temptation of Doubt...to doubt the destiny and capability of the race his soul loved because it was his...he closed the door, and sank upon the steps of the chancel, and cast his robe upon the floor and writhed."[31] Crummell appeals to his church's white Methodist authorities; he insists that he has failed with this small congregation and wants to minister to a larger black constituency: "There are few Negroes here, and perhaps they are not of the best. I must go to where the field is wider, and try again."[32]

Yet, when he goes to face the bishop of Philadelphia, he encounters the prelate's harsh racism: "No Negro priest can sit in my church convention, and no Negro church must ask for representation there."[33] This is the key moment of the essay, and Crummell responds with a statement of love for his people:

But this I know: in yonder Vale of the Humble stand to-day a million swarthy men, who willingly would

"...bear the whips and scorns of time,
The oppressor's wrong, the proud man's contumely,
The pangs of despised love, the law's delay,

> The insolence of office, and the spurns
> That patient merit of the unworthy takes."[34]

Crummell's turn to the sufferings of his people—and not their "moral character"—represents a crucial moment of piety. It speaks to a sense of grace and reverence at their accomplishments and to their abilities to live through sufferings and hardships. It is the beginning of his appreciation of the sources of his existence. At the same time, it is important not to overstate matters. Du Bois's Crummell, even after this détente with the folkways of his people, is never fully comfortable with the folk. When Crummell goes to Africa to search for sources of his existence there, he finds himself bereft: "In the wild and fever-cursed swamps of West Africa he stood helpless and alone."[35] Thus, of Crummell at the end of his life, Du Bois describes a continuingly tendentious relationship between the man and his people: "He fought among his own, the low, the grasping, and the wicked, with that unbending righteousness which is the sword of the just."[36] Finally, Du Bois concludes with a sad vision of Crummell, who is never fully embraced by his people: "He did his work,—he did it nobly and well; and yet I sorrow that here he worked alone, with so little human sympathy. His name to-day, in this broad land, means little, and comes to fifty million ears laden with no incense of memory or emulation."[37]

Du Bois's narrative on Crummell is thus a two-sided story of natural piety. On the one hand, Du Bois has Crummell make a crucial realization about the dignity of common black people and the need to recognize a debt to them. At the same time, Crummell's relationship with common folk is never fully without conflict. The folk are described in harsh ways: the low, the grasping, and the wicked. What is more, Crummell never feels their warm embrace. This tension between love and reverence and continued criticism is a dramatization of a dynamic Santayana describes so well: "As a man dies nobly when, awaiting his own extinction, he is interested to the last in what will continue to be the interests and joys of others, so he is most profoundly pious who loves unreservedly a country, friends, and associations *which he knows very well to be not the most beautiful on earth*."[38] Indeed, Santayana's standard of piety does not preempt but thrives on and demands constant criticism of the imperfections of one's own roots.

I believe this is what Du Bois is after in this depiction of Crummell. Crummell comes to love his people in full recognition of those shortcomings. Moreover, I believe that the essay also represents Du Bois's own critically pious relationship to Crummell on the same terms. Du Bois loves Crummell and is indebted to him while, as Gooding-Williams suggests, critical of Crummell's real-life dismissal of slave culture. For Du Bois, Crummell is a flawed figure; for Du Bois, he is not the most beautiful person on earth. Precisely because of this, the essay on Crummell, at the end, exemplifies the spirit of Du Bois's own natural piety: critical and backlit by love. Stout reminds us that "from a democratic point of view, the only piety worth praising as a virtue is that which concerns itself with *just* or *fitting* acknowledgment of our existence and progress through life."[39] Within democratic life, just and fitting acknowledgment must include critical notes mixed in with purer sounds of reverence. There is no better description of *Souls* as a text of natural piety.

The Pious Revelations of Saint Orgne

"Orgne" is an anagram for "Negro," and Du Bois first delivered what would become the essay he titled "Of the Revelation of Saint Orgne the Damned" in his 1938 Fisk University commencement address. In the essay, Orgne wakes up on "his Commencement morning" and asks himself the question, am I damned because of the color of my skin? Du Bois's answer is representative of his pragmatic meliorism of a hope not hopeless but unhopeful: "In the very truth, thou art damned, and may not escape by vain imagining nor fruitless repining. When a man faces evil, he does not call it good, nor evade it; he meets it breast-forward, with no whimper of regret nor fear of foe."[40] And yet, from this dejecting beginning comes Du Bois's notion, with his typical idealism, of the Democracy of Race: "Through cooperation, education, and understanding the cultural race unit may be the pipe line through which human civilization may extend to wider and wider areas to the fertilization of mankind."[41]

Before I explicate more fully the Democracy of Race, in many ways the real revelation of Orgne is in the development of this type of creative energy and vision from such a clear-eyed recognition of racial realities. By "clear-eyed recognition" I mean not simply the sober way in which Du Bois evaluates American life and concludes that distinctions and discriminations based on race are relentless ("the Jim Crow seats on the street cars every day, the Jim Crow coaches on the railroad, the separate sections of the city where the races dwell") and practically persistent ("Absorption into the nation, save as a long, slow intellectual process, is unthinkable."[42]). I also mean the way Du Bois develops his surging and inspiring notion of race and democracy while emphatically insisting throughout the essay that race is nothing more and nothing less than a socially constructed reality: "There are certainly no biological races in the sense of people with large groups of unvarying inherited gifts and instincts thus set apart by nature as eternally separate."[43] Of course, this does not demote race's social relevance, which is as real as marriage, money, or nationhood and ignored only willfully and at one's peril. Du Bois imagines black America, to reinvoke his phrase, as a "cultural race unit" that he understands as a "perfectly definite group, not entirely segregated and isolated from our surroundings, but differentiated to such a degree that we have very largely a life and thought of our own...we form in America an integral group, call it by any name you will, and this fact in itself has its meaning, its worth and its values."[44] Indeed, the very concept of race that Du Bois proffers is itself a form of natural piety. For race (pragmatically conceived) can be built only by acknowledging collective efforts from yesterday and today.

In no small way, the essay of Saint Orgne is devoted to enhancing the meaning, worth, and value of race groups for democratic life. To our ears, this may not seem so controversial or objectionable. Perhaps we live too comfortably in an age of mutlicultural pluralism, where distinct cultural groups do not seem an anathema to democratic life. Yet, Du Bois does not make this assumption. For him, the idea that race matters—but only when conceived of as a necessary social construct—runs against the regnant liberal assumptions about the nature of democracy: "In theory we know it by heart: all men are equal and should have equal voice in their own government."[45] This simple construal depicts humans as isolated individuals who all bear a packet of rights for their own use. Additionally, Du Bois knows too well that both in the United States and abroad, this is not how power works. It is this discrepancy that "compels us today as never before to examine and re-examine the problem of democracy." That is, Du Bois wants to use his pragmatically conceived notion of race to help us think critically about what it means to strive and live for the good within a democracy where power is exerted unequally against racial groups. What he is saying here about race and its uses is profound. He is not simply saying that race is not a biological fact but a social construct. He is also claiming that thinking about race as a social construct can be a crucial means for helping us rethink the meaning, worth, and values of democratic life:

> For this task we have to create a new family group; and a cultural group rather than a group merely biological. The biology and blood relationship of families is entirely subordinate and unimportant as compared with its cultural entity; voluntarily the sacrificial priesthood of parents to children...who can and will train in the elements of being civilized human beings; how to eat, how to sleep, how to wash, how to stand, how to walk, how to laugh, how to be reverent and how to obey.[46]

Of course, the closing of this passage is marked by Du Bois's imperious moralistic side. However, if we put this aside, we can hear something else: an account of democracy that is deeply concerned with virtues, values, their source, and their dissemination. These are the concerns of democratic piety. They sit in contrast to the hubristic tendency of democracies to value raw self-expression and individuality as their highest achievement. Instead, Du Bois is saying that the experience of black people in the United States needs to be pressed into service as an alternative form of democratic selfhood. It is one that, to be sure, values each individual. Du Bois waxes poetically liberal about the necessities of "emotion and dream...of creative power; in building, painting and literature there is a chance for the free exercise of the human spirit, broad enough and lofty enough to satisfy every ambition of the free human soul."[47]

Nonetheless, he understands that all of these are opportunities that are controlled by political and social occasion. His reflections on the human spirit show how it is tied to thick social structures,[48] and this is the value of the concept of race for Du Bois: It reveals that individuality is deeply social. For Du Bois, the black experience teaches that democratic forms of individuality derive from recognition by the state: "Every individual who is part of the state must have his experience and his necessities regarded by that state if the state survives." Moreover, democratic individuality is also rooted in a set of experiences that, "as any man has lived it, is part of that great national reservoir of knowledge without use of which no government can do justice."[49] This idea of a "reservoir of knowledge" is a version of Dewey's and Santayana's natural dependencies. What Du Bois is centrally saying through Saint Orgne is that democratic citizens have natural dependencies that are responsible for and fuel their contemporary projects and aspirations. Thus, Saint Orgne preached "the word from Jeremiah, Shakespeare, and Jesus, Confucius, Buddha and John Brown" as he "organized a cooperative story in the Sunday school room." And as he worked with sharecroppers who were demanding their freedom, "[a]lways the swinging thunder of song surged above—Jordan rolled; the rocks and the mountains fled away, the Way was crowded; and Moses went down." Finally, "across the swamp and across the world and up from the cotton fields of Georgia rolled a Negro folk song. Orgne saw in music Jehovah and his angels, the Wheel in a Wheel."[50]

These are, one could contend, overly romantic or nostalgic images of piety, homages to the religious ways of common black folk. Yet, each time Du Bois invokes them, he does so for the purposes of a modern project of social or political agitation. That is, he crafts what Dewey and Santayana refer to as "connections" not for the sake of prizing them in and of themselves. Instead, the lineaments of racial piety have contemporary, active uses for Du Bois: "The way to democracy lies through race loyalty if only that is its real and consciously comprehended end. Selah and Amen."[51] In what is clearly a prayer, he qualifies the uses and purposes of "race loyalty." Racial solidarity is something to be nurtured and prized in that it reflects the immanent conditions of living under the damning pressures of race in the United States. Here Du Bois marries natural piety with a pragmatic case for the conservation of race. On these terms, "race loyalty," "Love for these people," or the "swinging thunder of song" are not essentialized claims of racial solidarity or superiority. In this we hear the piety of someone conscious of the condition that Santayana called "the relativity involved in existence." Instead, "race loyalty" is both a strategy for living and a tool for mounting a sharp critique of dangerous liberal bromides that Americans like to tell themselves about this as a land of opportunity.

Race, when it is pragmatically conceived as a social reality, becomes a critical concept for uncovering the pernicious assumptions and democratic blind spots that can flourish under democratic guise. Race itself is what gives Du Bois access to the virtues and forms of excellence that are not often prized within democratic life—reverence, proper training, devotion of parent to child and child to parent, and finally the just sacrifices we all need to make for each other. Not all of these are confined to the privacy of home, and they all have socially ramifying effects: "It is to this use of our racial unity and loyalty that the United States impels us. We cannot escape it. Only through racial effort today can we achieve economic stability, cultural growth, and human understanding."[52] Du Bois's insistence on remaining grounded in the United States despite its all too pernicious flaws is characteristic of the heightened awareness of the finitude of one's conditions that one finds in natural piety; this is a form of immanent critique and should not be mistaken for liberal complacency.

Up to this point I have not spoken of the importance of sacrifice to Du Bois. In chapter 5 I turn more fully to his discourse of sacrifice, and there we will see that Du Bois was steadfastly committed to honoring the memory of those who sacrificed for the sake of others. I want to close this chapter on piety by insisting that piety and sacrifice are intimates, for in Du Bois's hands, sacrifice becomes a way of honoring and recognizing the natural sources of black existence. As we can see in this prayer of pragmatic religious naturalism, pious groundings in sacrifice shape Du Bois's natural religious hopes for the future:

We thank Thee, O Lord, for the gift of Death—for the great silence
that follows the jarring noises of the world—the rest is Peace. We
who live to see the passing of that fine and simple Old Man, who has

so often sat beside us here in this room, must not forget the legacy he leaves us or the Hope he still holds to us: we are richer for his sacrifice, truer for his honesty and better for his goodness. And his living leaves us firm in the faith that the Kingdom of Heaven will yet reign among men."[53]

4

Rewriting the American Jeremiad

On Pluralism, Black Nationalism, and a New America

The final words in W. E. B. Du Bois's *The Souls of Black Folk* are a prayer of remonstration and hope: "*Let the ears of a guilty people tingle with truth, and seventy millions sigh for a righteousness which exalteth nations, in this drear day when human brotherhood is mockery and a snare.*"[1]

This concluding prayer bears the markings of the classic form of American religious rhetoric, the American jeremiad. It is just this juxtaposition of remonstration and hope—on the one hand rebuking white America for its sins of racial oppression and its failure to live up to an exalted ideal and on the other hand yearning for reconciliation and envisioning an ideal community—that makes it most jeremiad-like. Archetypically, this is what jeremiads do: They move from denunciation to restoration. They hold up a standard of lawfulness and godliness; they use the rhetoric of indignation and discontent to make it clear that the present state of affairs is unlawful and ungodly. And in the end they conditionally hold out visions and paths of redemption.[2] Jeremiads were the crucial rhetorical mechanism by which the early Puritans gave shape to their "errand in the wilderness": Sharp castigation and rebuke were necessary to create a redeemed community. Du Bois saw his relationships to the American nation in similar terms. In *Souls* he calls out for "hearing my errand."[3] This chapter gives Du Bois's errands—his jeremiads—just that.

It is impossible to give any American jeremiad a hearing without engaging with the work of Sacvan Bercovitch. He is best known for his claim that the American jeremiad was a politically homogenizing rhetoric: Jeremiads produced an "ideological consensus" that proclaimed Americans as a chosen people whose political life was impelled by divine inspiration. At the heart of this reading is a remarkable rhetorical insight. Bercovitch argues that it was only through denunciation that jeremiads came to normalize and insist upon the terms by which American democracy became divine. In other words, by decrying Americans' *not* living up to the laws of the "new Jerusalem," "the new Eden," and the exceptional "city on the hill," jeremiads introduced the very terms that came to mark the rhetoric of American political life: a single ideological vision of American exceptionalism, "unshakeable optimism," and "unswerving faith in the errand."[4]

The problem with Bercovitch's account of the American jeremiad is that it swallows the African American jeremiad whole. For Bercovitch, African American jeremiads affirm this American ideology as much as John Winthrop's original 1630 sanctification of America. As Bercovitch has it, though the surface nature of African American complaints is different—against slavery and racial discrimination—these are not complaints against the content of the American divine covenant, which remains good and true. For Bercovitch, black American jeremiads maintain the American consensus and extend it to include African Americans. American exceptionalism and triumphalism remain intact.[5] An example of the way this normative understanding of the American jeremiad influences accounts of the African American jeremiad can be vividly seen in the account by Wilson Moses: "The purpose of the black jeremiad was ... a means of loyalty—both to the principles of egalitarian liberalism and to the Anglo-Christian code of values."[6]

Others, most prominently David Howard-Pitney and Moses, have suggested seeing Du Bois as part of a tradition of African American jeremiads, yet their accounts do little to distinguish the dynamics of Du Bois's forms of race-conscious jeremiads from the larger American tradition of jeremiads.

We need a new model for understanding African American jeremiads. Bercovitch resolutely insists that racist American ways represent betrayals and not expressions of American ideals. He sees the American consensus as an ever-flexible canopy that extends without rupture to include African Americans, he never considers the notion that the very idea of African Americans challenges the meaning of the American consensus. Here I build on Eddie Glaude's work: "Bercovitch grossly underestimates the entrenched nature of America's racial beliefs, particularly the fact that the idea of chosenness was racialized such that members of the chosen people were all white men delineated from those who were not chosen on the basis of race."[7] For Glaude, seeing the African American jeremiad through this lens changes the very terms by which the black jeremiad remonstrates and hopes for America: "The black jeremiad as a rhetorical form ought to be understood as a paradigm of the structure of ambivalence that constitutes African Americans' relation to American culture."[8] The ambivalence that Glaude refers to here "helps account for the tortuous relation of African Americans to American culture: their lingering sense of being in but not of a nation ambivalent about its own identity."[9] Glaude does not understand ambivalence as a form of weakness. African American expression of ambivalence represents the airing of real doubts about the American project as it has been conceived. When Glaude says that the African American jeremiad takes part in this ambivalence, I take him to mean the following. The African American jeremiad remonstrates the nation not to call it back to the consensus ideal of American triumphalism but to rebuke it in order to offer a version of America that emphasizes the democratic conditions of pluralistic dissent and difference. In other words, the race consciousness of the African American jeremiad distinguishes it from the larger American tradition of the jeremiad.

In this chapter I argue that Du Bois's jeremiadic writings—in particular *Souls* and *Darkwater*—represent just such a pluralistic alternative. Like his prophetic predecessors, Du Bois sought redemption through the jeremiad by using the language of denunciation to introduce the terms for a language of affirmation. In 1914 Du Bois declares:

> When the Hebrew prophets cried aloud there were respectable persons by the score who said:
> "Unfortunate exaggeration!"
> "Unnecessary feeling!"
> "Ungodly bitterness!"
> Yet the jeremiads were needed to redeem a people.[10]

If jeremiads are needed to redeem a people, Du Bois differs decisively from his Puritan predecessors and Bercovitch's model in the conception of what it means to be a people and what it means to be redeemed. The notion of redemption he introduces is not one that harkens back to America as a triumphal consensus or produces a discourse of "ritual leveling"[11] "to blur discrepancies"[12] in the service of a "whole people."[13] Instead, they actively dissent from the very idea of an American consensus as it has been classically conceived. Du Bois's jeremiads try to imagine a new type of America, a pluralistic nation that does

not suppress its fraught history. Du Bois does this in two ways. First, his jeremiadic criticisms resist either exalting America as a supernaturally blessed
mission or succumbing to the nihilism of "reading into America the futility
and fraud of hope itself."[14] For Du Bois, the nation is not an object of worship;
his jeremiads reject the idea of America's divine guarantee, just as they reject
a steadfast optimism and unshakeable faith in the American experience.
Nonetheless, the nation provides the democratic conditions for achieving
ideals that come only from humans working together. Du Bois's jeremiads
imagine community between black and white America, but only when conceived of as a project of *e pluribus unum:* "The meaning of America is the
beginning of the discovery of the Crowd.... What a world this will be when
human possibilities are freed, when we discover each other."[15] Du Bois's interest in the "crowd" represents a democratic populism that speaks to values that
are starkly different from the self-congratulatory grandiosity of Bercovitch's
American jeremiad. A "people" for Du Bois is a motley mix of individuals
who have different interests and traditions but share a concern for the earthly
conditions of the dispossessed. His jeremiads envision redemption on the
basis of "mutual respect and growing intelligence."[16] Implicit is a notion of
disagreement and dissent.

The second critical way in which Du Bois's jeremiads disrupt Bercovitch's
norm is his use of them to establish and consolidate what Du Bois calls "A
Negro Nation within the Nation."[17] What does Du Bois mean here by "nation"?
He does not mean a separate political entity of African Americans but a type
of cultural, political, and social solidarity within the United States. I argue that
this emphasis on the integrity of black American culture represents a viable
form of black nationalism. A people also include a nation of black people with
interests of their own. Finally, this notion of a nation within a nation represents an extension of Du Boisian double consciousness, and on these terms
Du Bois's jeremiads are part of his identity project.

Du Bois's jeremiads introduce a pluralistic concept of peoplehood that
survives—even thrives—on the differences. This complex rendering of pluralism leaves his readers neither entertaining the spiritual exceptionalism
of their own existence nor believing that divine grace is ensured. Instead,
Du Bois suggests a temporal politics wherein his readers are left to understand that communal consensus is a precarious proposition that must be
tended to daily in light of human encounters and limitations. Here, of course,
we reencounter the language of pragmatic religious naturalism. These are the
ultimate ends of America that are, as Du Bois says, discovering each other.
The terrain of this goal is a far cry from hoping to establish a new Jerusalem
for God.

Writing the American Consensus Anew

The making of the Du Boisian consensus—a political vision fundamentally grounded in democracy, equality between the races, and legal protection of natural rights—is not for the faint of heart. It begins not with conciliatory appeals to American ideals. Make no mistake, Du Bois's consensus vision of a just and righteous society begins with a diagnosis of the American sickness. In *Souls*, Du Bois describes racism in the United States as "the enormous race complications with which God seems about to punish this nation."[18] More powerful is the essay "The Souls of White Folk" in *Darkwater*, which, in its unvarnished and raging denunciations of America's sins, casts an enormous jeremiadic shadow over the text as a whole:

> Merciful God! in these wild days and in the name of Civilization, Justice, and Motherhood,—what have we not seen, right here in America, of orgy, cruelty, barbarism, and murder done to men and women of Negro descent.... But say to a people, "The one virtue is to be white," and the people rush to the inevitable conclusion, "Kill the 'nigger'!" Is this not the record of present America?... Are we not coming more and more, day by day, to making the statement "I am white," the one fundamental tenet of our practical morality?... We, as a folk of simpler souls and more primitive type, have been most struck... by the utter failure of white religion. We have curled our lips in something like contempt as we have witnessed glib apology and weary explanation.... A nation's religion is its life, and as such white Christianity is a miserable failure.[19]

What is critical to see in Du Bois's words is the depth of his denunciation of white America. Du Bois does not simply rail against an America that has betrayed its finer political and religious commitments with a rancid racism. In fact, he suggests that its political and religious commitments are devoted to these rancid ideals. He lambastes America not for the way its politics belie its purported moral and religious convictions; rather, he suggests that its moral and religious convictions have given rise to its politics. In other words, *this* is the American consensus, and it fundamentally involves a white supremacist mission: "Stripped of its verbiage and subterfuge and in its naked nastiness the new American creed says: Fear to let black men even try to rise lest they become the equals of the white. And this is the land that professes to follow Jesus Christ. The blasphemy of such a course is only matched by its cowardice."[20] Du Bois's protest is less against America's betrayal of its consensus ideology and more against just this American consensus ideology—of religious and political deformities designed to subjugate and oppress African Americans.

Du Bois raises the question of the importance or centrality of race in conceiving of America. More directly, he insists that, indeed, racist ideology and racist social practices—slavery and its legacy of continued discrimination—contribute as strongly to the American ideology as abstract Christian ideals and natural rights. He insists—or demands acknowledgment—that race was one of the terms by which the American consensus was conceived. Being white is not an incidental component of the American ideology but an essential, subjective position with practical moral effects. One need only turn to the jeremiadic sections of Jefferson's *Notes on the State of Virginia* and his famous gnashing of teeth about how God is going to deal with the American legacy of slavery to bear this out: "Indeed, I tremble for my country when I reflect that God is just; that his justice cannot sleep forever.... The Almighty has no attribute which can take side with us in such a contest."[21] What is obvious is that extending citizen status to black folks makes the idea of a coherent political life impossible for Jefferson.[22] Du Bois's jeremiads emphasize the way that religious and racist doctrine are made compatible in creating the American ideology.

Implicit in this is a deeper point about the very nature of ideology. For Du Bois, American ideology is inseparable from American social practices and experiences. He is unwilling to separate the social manifestations of discrimination and prejudice from America's high-minded egalitarian proclamations. A proper understanding of American ideology needs to be read out of those discriminatory social practices. Ideology does not reside simply in articulated sets of beliefs and commitments but also in social practices that reflect deeply held sets of beliefs and commitments that are not otherwise officially expressed.[23]

Du Bois's complication of the American ideology with the terms of race reveals a crucial difference between the American and the African American jeremiads. The American jeremiah can make an assumption about the consensus that the African American jeremiah cannot. The former can be certain that the consensus vision—the moral and social standard according to which the jeremiah upbraids and imagines the community—is already understood by the community as righteous and correct. The American jeremiah thus does not have to convince the community that these standards are the right ones. The community may not want to abide by this vision, however: Because it is not easy to live righteously, the jeremiah has to persuade by threats. Nonetheless, the community certainly acknowledges and recognizes the rectitude of the Jeremiah and the righteousness of the message. It is *not the very terms of the consensus itself* that need fashioning but the community that lives by them.

By insisting on seeing African Americans as part of American democracy, the African American jeremiah cannot make the same assumption for it is not at all certain that the larger American community already accepts that consensus vision. In fact, the African American jeremiah knows that a vision of pluralistic democracy is in fact not a sanctioned consensus in white America's eyes. The challenge that Du Bois faces is not simply claiming that discrimination is immoral but also convincing white America of the legitimacy of the very notion of a consensus that fully includes African Americans. He repeatedly demands that African Americans be recognized for all of their contributions to American life and in doing so calls not only for justice but also for changes in the very vocabulary of justice. Consider "Awake, America!" Here Du Bois wields a divine standard to renounce the nation: "We Americans, black and white, are the servants of all mankind and ministering to a greater, fairer Heaven. Let us be true to our mission. No land that loves to lynch 'niggers' can lead the hosts of Almighty God."[24] By unequivocally calling for the inclusion of African Americans, Du Bois is not so much calling the nation back to its principles and promises or restating a consensus already acknowledged by the larger community as pious and righteous as he is crafting, creating, and articulating to the nation principles and promises *for the first time.*

On these terms, the African American jeremiad's move from rebuke to reform is not only a complaint about America as it is (or about what America hopes itself to be); it demands that America become a type of nation not yet imagined by the American consensus. Walker's *Appeal* is a perfect example of this: "The whites may say it is impossible, but remember that nothing is impossible with God."[25] To me this is the crucial premise on which the *Appeal* rests: White America officially sanctions the nation's brutal practices. In light of those practices, Walker surmises that *white Americans believe the appeal is impossible to fulfill.* Throughout the entreaty, Walker fears not simply that his complaints are not being heard but that they are not even intelligible: "It is surprising to think that the Americans, having the Bible in their hands, do not believe it... while you keep us and our children in bondage... we cannot be your friends. You do not look for it, do you?"[26] This is the complaint of a jeremiah who does not simply feel that whites have transgressed God's standard. It is also the complaint of a jeremiah who senses that whites simply do not register his standard as godly.

This is the important context in which Du Bois's eventual embrace of the United States must be placed. His embraces—his visions of interracial cooperation—stand as radical rewritings of the American consensus. Du Bois's consecrations of America represent new imaginings: "We raise our hands to Heaven and pledge our sacred honor to make our own America a real land of the free....Awake! Put on thy strength, America—put on thy beautiful robes."[27] These robes, as I say, are his original weavings.

In *Souls*, Du Bois begins to imagine a clear (if at times overwrought) humanist universalism: "Hence arises a new human unity, pulling the ends of the earth nearer, and all men, black, yellow, and white."[28] He develops this internationalist outlook in one of his (and for that matter, one of the nation's) greatest jeremiads, his 1905 "Address to the Country," given at the first meeting of the Niagara Movement. Promising to "never cease to protest and assail the ears of America" and after inveighing against the contradiction between the racism of American politics and its professed religious commitments, Du Bois imagines a swelling of great international concord: "All across the skies sit signs of promise. The Slav is rising in his might, the yellow millions are tasking liberty, the black Africans are writhing toward the light, and everywhere the laborer, with ballot in his hand, is voting open the gates of Opportunity and Peace. The morning breaks over the blood-stained hills. We must not falter, we may not shrink. Above are the everlasting stars."[29]

In *Darkwater* Du Bois more fully develops and commits himself to a pluralistic and multiracial vision of democracy. Du Bois's new American consensus looks to America's deep troubles and trials in order to chart an internationalist plan of cooperation between the races: "The unity beneath all life clutched me. I was not less fanatically a Negro, but 'Negro' meant a greater, broader sense of humanity and world-fellowship."[30] Indeed, he disavows the sort of divine chauvinism that is characteristic of the American jeremiad: "We are not better than our fellows, Lord."[31] Du Bois has clearly learned from the failures of American democracy. Democracy can succeed only if it values and nurtures *differences* among men and women. Here is *Darkwater*'s new American consensus, the vision of reform at the end of Du Bois's jeremiads. It is a vision that values cooperation between races and people and not the eliding of differences. It embraces history and experience as key ingredients for a democratic ideal. By embracing a vast variety of experiments in living as a route to greater knowledge, it also has a liberal Millian cast to it. However, unlike John Stuart Mill, whose utilitarian telos seeks to solve practical problems and conflicts with right answers, Du Bois's telos centers on a utopian, essentially divine coexistence of different cultures:

> The real argument for democracy is, then, that in the people we have
> the source of that endless life and unbounded wisdom which the
> rules of men must have. A given people today may not be intelligent,

but through a democratic government that recognizes, not only the
worth of the individual to himself, but the worth of his feelings and
experiences to all, they can educate, not only the individual unity,
but generation after generation, until they accumulate vast stores of
wisdom. Democracy alone is the method of showing the whole experience of the race.[32]

The Black Nationalism of Du Bois's Jeremiads

To speak of the black nationalism in Du Bois's jeremiads is to introduce an
unusual combination of categories. As we have already heard, the African
American jeremiad is thought to be a tool for the reconciliation and affirmation of a readily identifiable American project. Black American jeremiads are not supposed to affirm notions of the national distinctness of black
American identity. Moreover, black nationalism, however we define it (and
I will define it shortly), is at heart about constructions of black specificity.
Thus, what is uncommon is thinking of the jeremiad and black nationalism
as complementary; that it is possible to ply a form of black American nationalism *within* an American jeremiad. For example, Wilson Moses describes
Frederick Douglass's classic jeremiad, "The Nation's Problem," as the great
example of black American opposition to a black nationalist impulse: "The
trouble is... when we assemble in great numbers anywhere we are apt to form
communities by ourselves.... When we isolate ourselves we lose, in a large
measure, the common benefit of association.... A nation within a nation is an
anomaly."[33]

    With all due respect to Douglass, the idea of a black nation within the
nation is not an anomaly. Philip Foner writes: "As early as 1852, Martin R.
Delany in the appendix to his book, *The Condition, Elevation, Emigration and
Destiny of the Colored People of the United States*, wrote 'We are a nation within
a nation;—as the Poles in Russia, the Hungarians in Austria, the Welsh,
Irish, and Scotch in the British dominions.' "[34] To be sure, what Delany means
here by "nation" is open to debate. What first needs to be acknowledged is
that "black nationalism" is an extremely capacious category—we use it to
describe the political philosophies of Edward Blyden, Alexander Crummell,
and Malcolm X.[35] For my purposes in reading Du Bois, however, I single out
a particular form of black nationalism. Here my thinking follows Glaude's
work on black nationalism. Glaude argues that the language of "nation" is both
historically and epistemologically appropriate for describing notions of racial
solidarity that do not aspire to a separate, black nation-state.[36] On Glaude's

reading, black American political and religious thinkers have long imagined black national constructions and used nation-talk to build political, social, and cultural solidarity: "A concept of nation or peoplehood or 'we-ness'—what can be generally called racial solidarity—informed all forms of black politics in the early nineteenth century."[37]

Moses, for all of the problems that Glaude encounters with his emphasis on racial essentialism in black nationalism, nicely articulates the central importance of solidarity to black nationalism: "If there is one *essential* quality of black nationalism, however, it is the feeling on the part of black individuals that they are responsible for the welfare of other black individuals, or of black people as a collective entity, simply because of a shared racial heritage and destiny."[38] This produces a sense of peoplehood that is rooted in the black community's common sufferings and survivals, and this sense is easily translated into a metaphorical language of nationhood.[39] We may be tempted to think of this as a minimalist definition of black nationalism because it does not make any specific political claims. However, we should not mistake its flexible potential for a lack of power. This, I think, is a great lesson of Benedict Anderson's *Imagined Communities,* which roots nationalism "not with self-consciously held political ideologies, but with the large cultural systems that preceded it."[40] It is helpful in this context to think of this form of black nationalism as a cultural system of solidarity.[41]

In this way, Du Bois's black jeremiads defy simple assimilation into the "Anglo-Christian code of values." Furthermore, when Du Bois does express admiration for an American liberalism and democracy, the loyalties he is often interested in adumbrating and extolling are examples of the embodiment of those ideals by his black American predecessors and African ancestors.[42] In short, Du Bois's jeremiads are marked by their efforts to imagine black America as a distinct people within the American nation. Where Moses suggests that one cannot be both a black nationalist and a black jeremiah, I insist that Du Bois shows it possible.[43] In Du Bois's jeremiads, a vibrant form of black nationalism—the sense of separate and distinct peoplehood that black people feel—coexists with Du Bois's hopes to redeem the United States as a whole. In fact, the two projects are related. Du Bois's opening statement in *Souls* on double consciousness and his hopes neither to "Africanize America" nor to "bleach his Negro soul in a flood of white Americanism" stand as the monumental example of his searching for black integrity within the American nation. *Souls* also includes another stunning articulation of the ambiguities of black nationalism (one that is not heard often enough): "In the soul-life of the land he is to-day, and naturally will long remain, unthought of, half forgotten...To-day the ferment of his striving toward self-realization is to the strife of the white world *like a wheel within a wheel*...Few know of these problems, few who know notice them; and yet they are there, awaiting student, artist, and seer,—a field for someone to discover."[44]

Du Bois's use of Ezekiel 1:16—"a wheel within a wheel"—is an alternate Du Boisian articulation of "a nation within a nation."[45] It is jeremiadic in that it emerges from a rhetoric of denunciation. Pointedly, Du Bois's black national imaginings are about neither black separatism nor essential racial differences. In this jeremiad, Du Bois seeks to create a notion of a black nation strong enough to provide coherence and integrity to the black community while remaining flexible enough to acknowledge the way in which the black nation is necessarily enmeshed in America at large. What is arresting here is the swiftness and starkness of the opposition he sets up between the felt integrity and the felt marginality of black America with regard to American life. Black nationhood is truly marked by the coexistence of oppositions; the "wheel within" is critical to the operation of the larger wheel but all too often overlooked. What is radical about Du Bois's jeremiad is that his framing, shaping, and arguing for a politically and culturally distinct African America are not terms that *sui generis* obstruct a conception of national consensus. Instead, this jeremiad mirrors the necessarily fraught doubleness of his famous notion of self-consciousness. In addition, we should again hear Glaude's insistence that African American jeremiads reflect deep ambivalence about the very terms of the American project.

Du Bois's efforts to symbolically construct black peoplehood rest on a skein of natural, contingent, and immanent experiences and conditioned interactions with lived life: "Herein the longing of black men must have respect; the rich and bitter depth of their experience, the unknown treasures of their inner life, the strange rendings of nature they have seen, may give the world new points of view and make their loving, living, and doing precious to all human hearts."[46] To be sure, Du Bois repeatedly claims—not only in *Souls* but throughout his career as well—that black Americans have given certain gifts to America—"the gift of story and song...of sweat and brawn...and a gift of the Spirit."[47] However, he equally makes it clear that each of these gifts has developed over time—survival techniques in response to clear political and social conditions.[48] It is easy to mistake the romantic intonations of Du Bois's language for a commitment to "theological racialism in which...each race was the manifestation of a spiritual ideal, a sacred mystery that existed in the mind of God."[49] I find little evidence for this. Instead, the "wheel within a wheel" is a conceptual category designed to do the specific work of creating the moral, imaginative, and social space for surviving and struggling against racist America. For Du Bois, this includes not only joining but also remaining distinct from America writ large. From it emerges a form of black nationalism that thrives on the structures of American ambivalence.

Glaude convincingly locates this form of black nationalism in Walker's great jeremiad. Where Moses sees the Walker's *Appeal* as addressed mostly to whites, affirming its national myths—"It can be conceived with American interests at heart"[50]—Glaude's focus is more on the internal conversation Walker is conducting with black America. As Glaude has it, Walker directs his jeremiad to black America as much as white America. This crucial point changes the basic model of the African American jeremiad, which not only remonstrates the larger white nation but also issues warnings and demands to black America. In fact, it is precisely these sorts of issuances that make for a notion of a nation within a nation. Black jeremiahs need to be able to conceive of black peoplehood in order to make demands on and for black solidarity.

Thus throughout his *Appeal,* Walker can be heard pleading for black solidarity: "Men of colour, who are also of sense, for you particularly is my Appeal designed.... I call upon you therefore to cast your eyes upon the wretchedness of your brethren...*go to work and enlighten your brethren!*—Let the Lord see you doing what you can to rescue them and yourselves from degradation."[51] And here are Walker's stated goals in the preamble to the *Appeal:* "My object is, if possible, to awaken in the hearts of my afflicted, degraded and slumbering brethren, a spirit of inquiry and investigation respecting our miseries and wretchedness in this Republican Land of Liberty!!!"[52] For Glaude, Walker's jeremiad is distinctive in its appeal to black people for "inquiry" and "investigation": "Walker's use of the jeremiad not only urged the nation to turn from sin; he also exhorted African Americans to act intelligently for themselves."[53] This sort of self-conscious effort to figure out what is best for black America presupposes a thick notion of black solidarity, thick enough, in Glaude's view, to elicit a conception of black nationhood that is tailored to contribute to American democracy by reforming it through practices of black self-help.

This spirit of Walker's lives in Du Bois. The need to develop free, imaginative, and creative thinking skills is a thread that runs throughout the jeremiadic *Souls.* Following Walker, Du Bois is intently focused on urging or promoting independent critical intelligence for black America: "a responsibility to themselves, a responsibility to the struggling masses, a responsibility to the darker races of men whose future depends so largely on this American experiment, but especially a responsibility to this nation."[54] Thus, Du Bois warns against "the Mammonism of America" and frames his horror at the "budding Mammonism" in black America with a demand for critical thinking: "What if the Negro people be wooed from a strife for righteousness, from a love of knowing, to regard dollars as the be-all and end-all of life?"[55] By couching the sort of self-criticism and review that is required for critical intelligence in the form of a jeremiad, Du Bois designates self-determination as a spiritual practice and exercise. In turn, the chapter titled "Of the Training of Black Men" becomes, in essence, a sermon about the necessity for black self-determination: "Internal problems of social advance inevitably come,—problems of work and wages, of families and homes, of morals and the true valuing of the things of life; and all these and other inevitable problems of civilization the Negro must meet and solve largely by himself...and can there be any possible solution other than by study and thought and appeal to the rich experience of the past?"[56] In this light, Du Bois's chapter on Booker T. Washington, with its impassioned calls for the salvation of criticism, becomes a jeremiad. Without criticism and debate, there is an "irreparable loss,—a loss of that peculiarly valuable education which a group receives when by search and criticism it finds and commissions its own leaders."[57] Often Du Bois's calls for self-determination based on education, contemplation, and critical self-review are seen as part of his Victorian elitism and moral priggishness. Yet it is in coming to understand the African American jeremiad as a rhetorical vehicle for just this sort of criticism and review that we can properly locate this language in Du Bois.

Here, then, is a crucial point at which Du Bois's jeremiads, as well as the African American jeremiad more generally, swerve from the Puritan model. His jeremiads express the "structural ambivalences" of black life by calling for self-critical discussions among African Americans. Black jeremiads turn into a way of strategizing as black Americans in order to best survive and thrive within the United States. In doing so, Du Bois transforms the classic idea of chosenness in the American jeremiad. His emphasis on African American chosenness is not based on the divine superiority of African Americans as such. Rather, his focus on an internal conversation among black Americans bespeaks, in essence, a type of chosenness that is a *response* to sufferings. This is the best context in which to understand Du Bois's repeated claims for "The Gift of Black Folk." These gifts—"The Emancipation of Democracy" and "The Gift of the Spirit"[58]—are not gifts given to African Americans but are *achieved* by them by struggle, acumen, and collective effort. Du Bois's jeremiads represent calls for black Americans to *realize* their chosen status—in the eyes of each other, the nation, and the Lord—by virtue of their creative and active response to racism.

In using the jeremiad to focus on the specificity of the black experience, Du Bois turns Bercovitch's model on its head. In their call for critical analysis of the African American life, Du Bois's jeremiads do not blur differences; they do not compress America into an undifferentiated unity. Instead, they help bring distinction to black life. Moreover, they create a ready sense of black nationhood that is designed to *express* and not to denigrate the ambivalences of black life. It is by virtue of those ambivalences—by confronting the paradoxical way that American democracy becomes vibrant as black America develops and contributes its own identity markers—that African Americans build nationhood: black nationhood and American nationhood. That is, with Du Bois, only by giving voice to themselves as a black nation do black Americans give voice to the nature of their lives as Americans.

The Idealism of Du Bois's Jeremiads

I do not want to misstate the tenor of Du Bois's redemption. Yes, his jeremiads finish in a vision of democracy and experience, but they also finish in a utopian fervor that seems to belie their pragmatism. Here are examples from three different pieces in *Darkwater*: "Beyond all this must come the Spirit—the Will to Human Brotherhood of all Colors, Races, and Creeds; the Wanting of the Wants of All"; "O Truce of God! / And primal meeting of the Sons of Man, / Foreshadowing the union of the World!"; "Bid the black Christ be born! / Then shall our burden be manhood, / Be it yellow or black or white."[59]

It is passages like these that lead Wilson Moses to see an other-worldly messianism, "conjuring up visions of black gods and goddesses,"[60] in the "quasi-religious vignettes of *Darkwater*."[61] To be sure, there is an undeniable romanticism in moments like these, heavy in their portent of a perfect End of Days. As political philosopher Michael Walzer points out, biblical jeremiah was a "leading romantic" who foretold a return to the promised land after exile.[62] His prophesies were messianic; time and politics as we know them vanish to be replaced by perfect righteousness: "What Jeremiah promises, in effect, is a transformation of human nature, or better, the reappearance of the original Adam."[63] So goes the classic view of jeremiadic messianism; Bercovitch's account of American exceptionalism emphasizes the ways in which Americans came to think of themselves as symbols of these sorts of radical transformations. And so goes the account of Du Bois's jeremiads by Wilson Moses. At the end of the day, they too disparage mortal existence and abandon its all-too-human contingencies for the rarified divine event at the End.

It is true that in the fashion of the jeremiah, Du Bois criticizes the real in light of the ideal. What is more, if Du Bois's articulations of that ideal are taken out of context—read alone in bare light—Du Bois can begin to sound chiliastic. However, when his accounts of the ideal are counterbalanced and contextualized by his concern with the historical and real conditions of life, it becomes clear that he reverses the classic jeremiad's relationship between the real and the ideal. In Du Bois's hands, the idea of an End of Days and ideal existence is made to serve both the real and the deeper purpose of his jeremiads: unveiling through critical self-review the historical, social, and political forces that shape black existence. My idea here builds on Glaude's suggestion that messianism, particularly as it was expressed in African American life, can be understood as a more variegated phenomenon than the single desire "to force the End": "This drive is not so much the result of longing for the apocalypse or an unconditional victory as it is the outcome of psychical and physical scars and bruises resulting from repeated indifference—people simply refusing to suffer any longer (and this need not be imagined in terms of ultimate purposes, but may be the source of messianic attraction)."[64] In other words, what Glaude suggests here is that messianism can be used in a pragmatic fashion to motivate and galvanize intelligent analysis of immediate and contingent crises. This is not to offer an apologetics for Du Bois's messianism. It is to say, however, that, in Du Bois's jeremiads, the ideal functions as a rhetorical tool for prompting analysis of the contingencies of existence. Visions of restoration in Du Bois's jeremiad help shape the real.

For example, in *Souls,* Du Bois presents what seems to be a classically sterile idealist quest for "founding Right on righteousness and Truth on the unhampered search for Truth." It is the sort of idealism that seems at home with his visions of a "new human unity" between all men and women. Yet, in the same breath, Du Bois insists that "All this is gained only by human strife and longing; by ceaseless training and education."[65] His priorities are, in fact, rather low flying and grassroots: "Nothing new, no time-saving devices,— simply old-time glorified methods of delving for the Truth and searching out the hidden beauties of life, and learning the good of living."[66] It is politics whose idealism is in the daily and the common.

Further, the human unity of which he speaks is ultimately found in time-bound interactions: "The larger humanity strives to feel in this contact of living Nations and sleeping hordes a thrill of new life in the world, crying, 'If the contact of Life and Sleep be Death, shame on such Life.'"[67] Du Bois's particular emphasis on "Life" signals the prevailing drive in his messianism: In privileging life over death, Du Bois is intent on struggling with conditions as they are. In fact, he sees little more than cowardice and expediency in creating a messianic vision that obviates a responsibility to engage in current conditions: "It is not difficult now to say to the young freedman, cheated and cuffed about, who has seen his father's head beaten to a jelly and his own mother namelessly assaulted, that the meek shall inherit the earth."[68] Instead, the pursuit of "Right" and "Truth" requires a commitment to what Du Bois calls "mutual respect and growing intelligence" for the life experiences of black people.[69] To cite an earlier passage: "Herein the longing of black men must have respect: the rich and bitter depth of their experience...may give the world new points of view and make their loving, living and doing precious to all human hearts."[70] With messianic fervor, Du Bois creates an ideal whose boundaries do not exceed the limits of finitude.

More than any other notion, sympathy for the other—a fair and just appraisal of the experiences of someone not oneself—is the foundation of Du Bois's jeremiadic reconciliation in *Souls:* "The nineteenth was the first century of human sympathy,—the age when half wonderingly we began to descry in others that transfigured spark of divinity which we call Myself; when clod-hoppers and peasants, and tramps and thieves, and millionaires and—sometimes—Negroes, became throbbing souls whose warm pulsing life touched us so nearly that we half gasped with surprise, crying, 'Thou too! Hast Thou seen Sorrow and the dull waters of Hopelessness? Hast Thou known Life?' "[71] For Du Bois, sympathy leads to human unity not through an undifferentiated monism but through mutual cooperation, so that "acute race-sensitiveness must eventually yield to the influences of culture." Sympathy is nothing if not the development of the virtue of finding points in common in a irrevocably pluralistic world. To be sure, Du Bois's version of the "points of transference where the thoughts and feelings of one race can come into direct contact and sympathy with the thoughts and feelings of the other" can be remarkably elitist:[72] He holds deep hopes that the cultured classes, black and white, will interact. Yet, to emphasize his elitism exclusively is to ignore his use of sympathy to craft simple but profound democratic sentiments: "We often forget that each unit in the mass is a throbbing human soul. Ignorant it may be, and poverty stricken, black and curious in limb and ways of thought; and yet it loves and hates, it toils and tires, it laughs and weeps its bitter tears, and looks in vague and awful longing at the grim horizon of its life,—all this, even as you and I."[73]

Twenty years later, Du Bois develops the same themes in *Darkwater,* in which he still mourns the lack of sympathy born of mutual interaction: "All this goes to prove that human beings are, and must be, woefully ignorant of each other. It always startled us to find folks thinking like ourselves. We do not really associate with each other, we associate with our ideas of each other, and few people have either the ability or courage to question their own ideas."[74] To demand "associating" is to insist that meaning, even ideal meaning, comes from the meaning of time-bound actions with and on others—not oneself. Du Bois's frightening poem, "The Prayers of God," in its rank morbidity— "Death is here! / Dead are the living; deep-dead the dead. / Dying are earth's unborn"[75]—is a narrative of the dawning realization of the real effects actions have on others. Death here is not the goal; it serves as a frame by which to focus attention on the brutalities of life. In turn, Du Bois defines godliness as coming to realize the sacredness of the here and now: "Is this Thy kingdom *here*, not *there*, / This stone and stucco drift of dreams?"[76] This realization culminates in a theology of social action and what can be considered a messianism of worldly struggle: "Thou needest *me*? / Poor, wounded soul! / Of this I never dreamed. I thought—" The only thing that is other-worldly about this poem, perhaps, is Du Bois's fantasy that a white America would become sympathetic to this degree. However, the terms of the fantasy itself fight against what Du Bois sees as the clear irresponsibility and ungodliness of otherworldliness. It is a fantasy not of the end of days but of redoubled effort fueled by the dawning of sympathetic feelings to find purchase in the world. In essence, the poem is an account of not only the emergence of human sympathy but also the sacredness of this emergence.

Darkwater, for all its mystic overtones and calls for human brotherhood, does not try to force the End of Days. Amid the text's rhetorical flourish is a steadying and sober gradualist politics of reform and struggle. Du Bois invokes the myth of Ethiopianism in "The Hands of Ethiopia" not to usher in a black-ruled apocalypse but to insist that black hands "rather are they hands of pain and promise; hard, gnarled, and muscled for the world's real work...they are the hands of helpfulness for an agonized God!"[77] In "Of Wealth and Work" he locates sympathy, intelligence, and even human kinship in the daily contingencies of education: "—it comes daily, bit by bit and step by step, as men and women learn and grow and as children are trained in Truth."[78] The essay titled "The Immortal Child" ironically plays on the idea of an everlasting Christ by laying out an immortal plan of doing the daily hard work of educating children from generation to generation. Indeed, generational immortality is based on a pragmatic realism: "We may teach frankly that this world is not perfection, but development; that the object of education is manhood and womanhood, clear reason, individual talent and genius and the spirit of service and sacrifice."[79] Instead of messianism, Du Bois envisions an ideal world of critical thought and intelligence that contests and serves: "With this Power comes, in the transfiguring soul of childhood, the Glory: the vision of accomplishment, the lofty ideal."[80] One does not rest complacently in this ideal world. Its loft comes from the insistence that great good can be achieved as we naturally are.

Ultimately, this naturalistic idealism of Du Bois's jeremiads transforms the place of the nation in American jeremiadic discourse. The classic American jeremiad conceives of the American nation as an object of national worship, a nation to which God made exclusive promises unknown and unavailable to other nations and peoples. Du Bois's jeremiads conceive of the American nation as a place to enact the promise of the United States as one landscape among many in which humans can work to create political conditions to reflect godly virtues.[81] He invokes "the highest ideals of American democracy," but, as I have shown, his conception of those ideals represents a wholesale rewriting of the American political imagination.[82] In America Du Bois seeks "not perfect happiness, but plenty of good hard work, the inevitable suffering that always comes with life; sacrifice and waiting, all that—but, nevertheless, lived in a world where men know, where men create, where they realize themselves and where they enjoy life. It is that sort of world we want to create for ourselves and for all America."[83] His version of salvation is a variety of critical intelligence that joins thought to deed. American democracy is valued as a set of conditions that allows citizens to jointly accomplish something greater than themselves. The redemptive zeal of this passage is reserved for closer and better understandings of the details of human desires and politics. Those worthy of being called Jeremiahs face *those* details unflinchingly:

> Humanity is progressing toward an ideal; but not please God, solely
> by help of men who sin in cloistered ease, hesitate from action and
> seek sweetness and light; rather we progress today, as in the past,
> by the soul-torn strength of those who can never sit still and silent
> while the disinherited and the damned clog our gutters and gasp
> their lives out on our front porches. These are the men who go down
> in the blood and dust of battle. They say ugly things to an ugly world.
> They spew the lukewarm fence straddlers out of their mouths, like
> the God of old; they cry aloud and spare not; they shout from the
> housetops, and they make this world so damned uncomfortable with
> its nasty burden of evil that it tries to get good and does get better.[84]

Here again, in the move that distinguishes his jeremiads and undermines American exceptionalism, we see Du Bois putting the ideal in the service of the real. Salvation is clearly not an act of theonomy, beholden and subject to the external rule of God. The ideal for Du Bois is never without—in fact, it is entirely dependent on—a type of critical intelligence that finds salvation in the day-to-day. If we return to the "Afterthought" with which the chapter opens, we find a distinctly Du Boisian version of this utopia: "*Let there spring, Gentle One, from out its leaves vigor of thought and thoughtful deed to reap the harvest wonderful.... Thus in Thy good time may infinite reason turn the tangle straight, and these crooked marks on a fragile leaf be not indeed.*"[85]

The overtones of Kant are significant: Du Bois the rationalist, the so-called idealist, calls for straight, not crooked, marks. However, let us read more closely. Du Bois joins infinite reason to practical reason, and he looks not to God to fix the nation's racial myopia but to principles and values that are ultimately rooted in each and every soul. Du Bois the pragmatist recognizes that the leaf—the territory in which the marks have meaning—remains fragile, inconstant, and trembling. Moreover, though the principles that would fix racial ills sit autonomously in every human, they necessarily emerge and play themselves out on a thatched field of mutual interdependence. Here we are not autonomous but heteronomous all the way down. In order for thought and deed to be vigorous, we must ascertain as best as we can the coordinates of others' experiences: on the porch, in the gutter, mixed with blood and dust. This is the legacy of Du Bois, the African American Jeremiah, who finds the hope of salvation in the politics of mortal struggle.

5

"Behold the Sign of Salvation— A Noosed Rope"

The Promise and Perils of Du Bois's Economies of Sacrifice

Bewildered we are and passion-tossed, mad with the madness of a mobbed and mocked and murdered people; straining at the arm-posts of Thy throne, we raise our shackled hands and charge Thee, God, by the bones of our stolen fathers, by the tears of our dead mothers, by the very blood of Thy crucified Christ: What meaneth this? Tell us the plan; give us the sign!

—Du Bois, "A Litany at Atlanta"[1]

In W. E. B. Du Bois's 1933 short story, "The Son of God," a black American Christ figure named Joshua preaches a gospel of nonvio-lence, the godliness of the poor and the wretched, and the equality of the races. It is a message that deeply threatens the whites in the story's fictitious Southern town. A white mob gathers, demands Joshua's life, and finally lynches him: "They had hanged him at sunset."[2] Joshua's mother, Mary, mourns her son's death and pro-claims him the Christ: "He is the Son of God!" Just as the cross sig-nifies Jesus's victory over death, so the apparatus of Joshua's hanging comes to symbolize his sanctification. Du Bois writes: "Behold the Sign of Salvation—a noosed rope."[3]

That the noose, the execrable symbol of the terror of lynch-ing, would possess salvific qualities for Du Bois is, to the say the least, unexpected for the twentieth century's most relentless critic of American lynching. Yet the religious archetype of which it is a part—a black Christ, in the American South, lynched because his preachings or actions threaten the racist mores of white America—occurs repeatedly in Du Bois's early writings.[4] Between 1900 and 1935 Du Bois consistently revisits this religious narrative, writing close to a dozen stories and poems that model Christ's original sacrifice. Literary critic Trudier Harris describes African American writers who write about lynching as "ritual priests ever keeping in sight of their people those mysteries which affect their lives."[5] Du Bois is clearly such a priest. His stories, which I call Du Bois's lynching parables, have gone almost entirely unexplored and, when taken together, constitute a distinct discourse in Du Bois's writings—a discourse of sacrifice.

These lynching parables, however, represent only one half of Du Bois's sacrificial discourse. The other half consists of his normative *prescription* of acts of sacrifice. That is, Du Bois consistently makes a plea for a sacrificial ethic, one that he makes explicit in *The Souls of Black Folk* as a "Gospel of Sacrifice": "the determination to realize for men, both black and white, the broadest possibilities of life, to seek the better and the best, to spread with their own hands the Gospel of Sacrifice."[6] By and large, the sacrificial acts he envisions center on the willingness to put aside personal interests and subsume one's own ego for the sake of a larger communal cause. For example, Du Bois's idealization of John Brown presents an activist version of Christianity based on "broad, generous, self-sacrificing principles" committed to fighting racial inequality.[7] In Du Bois's vision, activist acts of sacrifice—a willingness to self-abnegate in order to contribute to a cause bigger than oneself—are needed for the sake of African American advancement, not to mention for America and the larger international community as well: "Work and Sacrifice is [sic] the true destiny of humanity,"[8] and he grandly imagines "a wide vision of world-sacrifice."[9] On these terms, Du Bois's Gospel of Sacrifice amounts to a civic ethic of sacrifices for the greater good.

Thus, it is clear that Du Bois has two ways of speaking of sacrifice. He writes literary representations of black Christ lynchings, as well as more normative, much more moralistic works that urge African Americans to adopt a civic ethics of sacrifice, the Gospel of Sacrifice. The questions at the heart of this chapter revolve around an understanding of these two halves of Du Bois's sacrificial discourse. What sort of work do they do? Are they related? Is there a way in which his typological depictions of black Christ lynchings contribute to his Gospel of Sacrifice? Or are we better off thinking of his lynching parables and his Gospel of Sacrifice as separate discursive streams?

These are complex and (given the utterly monstrous history of lynching in the United States) potentially dangerous questions. Indeed, perhaps the most poignant question of all is why Du Bois would want to persist with and create a sacrificial discourse in the first place. During the time that Du Bois was writing his multivalent sacrificial discourse—during the horror of the late nineteenth and early twentieth century, which came to be known as the Nadir—African Americans were being lynched at a staggering rate.[10] Ralph Ellison recounts lynching as "ritual sacrifice...dedicated to the ideal of white supremacy."[11] This is a startling insight: The implication is that lynchings are embedded in an economy of religious practice. René Girard's theoretical work on ritual sacrifice and the scapegoat uncannily describes American lynching and confirm what Ellison and black America writ large intuitively knew long ago: African Americans were being subjected to a system of human sacrifice by a white Christian America.[12] In the past decade, scholars such as Orlando Patterson, Donald Mathews, and Anthony Pinn began doing the historical and cultural critical work to show the ways that Christianity was enmeshed and implicated in the practice of lynching.[13]

It is precisely this horror that makes us ask why Du Bois did not conclude that sacrifice was an American category thoroughly rooted in blood, abuse, and suffering and thus forever tainted and one that society is better off working to live without. Certainly, this has been a common conclusion of post–civil rights African American thinkers. James Cone, Delores Williams, Joanne Marie Terrell, and Pinn all consistently reject sacrifice and suffering as viable categories for theological, political, or social work.[14] For each of these thinkers, to find value in discourses of sacrifice is to capitulate to white power structures. For example, Terrell sees political, psychological, and spiritual peril in the ethics of sacrifice because sacrificial hermeneutics emphasizes "pacifism" and "nonacquisitive love," which in turn "cause many people within the black Christian community to 'tremble, tremble,' their trepidation perhaps also a mirror of their sometimes hesitation to engage opposing powers more proactively."[15]

Again, care is needed here. The easy temptation is to judge Du Bois's discourse of sacrifice as a form of political quiescence. And it certainly has. Wilson Moses holds that Du Bois's depictions of "the redemptive suffering of Jesus Christ" reinforces a politically conservative thrust of the "widely held notion of black people as innately predisposed to...such Christian virtues as patience, forgiveness, and the ability to endure pain with dignity and silence."[16]

Conclusions like these are too easy and too peremptory. *Pace* Moses, Du Bois never portrays black people as *inherently* better sufferers; for Du Bois, only the contingencies of slavery and Jim Crow, not a metaphysical disposition, explain black people's sufferings and their responses. Moreover, the assumption that Du Bois's discourse of sacrifice is designed to engender nonconfrontational acceptance of white power structures should give us pause. There is scant evidence that Du Bois ever "trembled, trembled" at the prospect of confronting white political power. By and large, his denunciations of injustice come unvarnished.[17] Furthermore, throughout his career Du Bois consistently derides the penchant of African American religion for "doctrines of passive submission" through which "courtesy became humility, moral strength degenerated into submission, and the exquisite native appreciation of the beautiful became an infinite capacity for dumb suffering."[18] It would be awfully curious and even self-contradictory were Du Bois to develop a discourse of sacrifice that engendered the very values he fundamentally set out to combat. Yet, this is what criticisms like those of Moses force us to conclude: that Du Bois's discourse of sacrifice represents an enormous self-contradiction and egregious blind spot in his work. In addition, criticisms like Terrell's, which reject discourses of sacrifice out of hand, leave us with only the ability either to denounce the politics of Du Bois's discourse or look on it as a sad anachronism of a politically unenlightened age.

These seem like a set of particularly ungenerous and themselves historically anachronistic assumptions. Du Bois's discourse of sacrifice may be from another age, but it does not mean that the category of sacrifice means to him what it means to contemporary critics. Instead, this chapter follows a set of more generous assumptions. Let us assume that Du Bois is not caught in an enormous self-contradiction, which is to say that he does not develop his discourse of sacrifice in order to capitulate to white power. Instead, let us assume that he constructs it, in keeping with the larger force of his career efforts, to challenge white power. On these terms we can conclude only that Du Bois sees his discourse of sacrifice as empowering and understands that it challenges and combats America's baneful tradition of blood sacrifice. In other words, might it be the case that Du Bois battles America's sacrificial perversions with an empowering discourse of sacrifice of his own? Sacrifice on these terms would signify a way of emboldening black America. Of course, crucial questions follow. How can this be? Is there a discernable logic to sacrifice that makes this possible? What does Du Bois see in sacrificial discourse that allows for these sorts of galvanizing ends? How can he use the language of sacrifice without capitulating to its destructive history?

This chapter is devoted to explaining Du Bois's potentially dangerous turn toward sacrifice. I argue that, by engaging the language of sacrifice, Du Bois works, following Theophus Smith's account, as a classic African American conjuror. He co-opts a body-breaking discourse of sacrifice, dislodges it as a domain of white supremacy, and turns it into a resource for repair and renewal for black America. Susan Mizruchi's observations here are apposite, as she recognizes that Du Bois uses his sacrificial discourse in an antidotal fashion to combat what amounted to white America's commitments to actual human sacrifice: "American Blacks have been much sacrificed, [Du Bois] suggests, but they are not without their own form of sacrificial agency. Du Bois's preoccupation with death and sacrifice form a central part of his legacy, to confront them is to recognize how the identification of a negative cultural typology can be a source of creative inspiration, critique, and even renewal."[19] This is an invaluable insight. However, Mizruchi does not fully explicate it. She does not identify a specific body of literature by Du Bois devoted to sacrifice, nor does she explain how the dynamics of sacrifice are particularly well suited for combating and reversing sacrificial evils. Additionally, we do not hear what sorts of goods Du Bois is trying to acquire through his discourse of sacrifice. This chapter attempts to fill in these holes.

Du Bois's choice to conjure with the language of sacrifice reflects a turn-of-the-century sociologist's wisdom. Contemporaneous to Du Bois, Durkheimian theorists of sacrifice Henri Hubert and Marcel Mauss argue that systems of sacrifice are not, despite their surface logic, about giving things up. They argue that, for those who participate in them—that is, for those who do the sacrificing (not, of course, for those who are sacrificed)—sacrificial systems are deeply *acquisitive*. In other words, sacrificial systems are marked by a buried and inchoate logic that assumes that *participants* in sacrificial systems—those who conduct the sacrifices—expect to receive certain communal and social goods in return for acts of self-denial. On these terms, sacrificial systems are about consolidating and managing the terms by which people form and interact within communities.

I maintain that, through the Gospel of Sacrifice and his lynching parables, Du Bois presides as a Durkheimian sacrificial priest who attempts to practice the acquisitive and consolidating dynamics of sacrificial discourse. Translating the extant sociological theory of sacrifice for his own purposes, Du Bois attempts to transform black Americans from the victims into the agents of a sacrificial system, who can then make claims on its political, social, and even material goods. In "The Joy of Living he writes: "Hard and thoughtful toil inspired by large sympathy with your fellow men and infinite patience with their sorrows and difficulties will soon bring you face to face with the greatest thing in life—Sacrifice. I do not mean by sacrifice, aimless renunciation—I do not mean giving up the Joys of Life simply for the sake of the discipline."[20] In pragmatic religious naturalistic fashion, Du Bois does not use sacrifice as a way of retaining God's favor or expiate sins but as a political tool for gaining ownership of the rights and goods that make this life worth living.

Du Bois writes his discourse of sacrifice to affect both white and black America. In this, he exemplifies what James Weldon Johnson called "The Dilemma of the Negro Author": "But the Aframerican author faces a special problem which the plain American author knows nothing about—the problem of the double audience. It is more than a double audience; it is a divided audience, an audience made up of two elements with differing and often opposite and antagonistic points of view. His audience is always both white America and black America."[21] Part of Du Bois's conjuring wisdom is the realization that, for better or worse, the language of sacrifice is the language of both of his Americas, black and white.

On white America, Du Bois plies his sacrificial discourse to acquire the host of political rights and opportunities due American citizens as a whole. He also calls for recognition by white Americans of the irreplaceable contribution of black Americans to the development of this nation. On black America, Du Bois develops his sacrificial discourse to impress upon black Americans that they themselves must self-consciously recognize their contributions to America. This contributes to two dynamics. First, the consolidating forces of sacrifice nurture the form of black nationalism I emphasize in the previous chapter on jeremiads. Second, Du Bois's discourse of sacrifice represents a way of honoring and recognizing the natural sources of black American existence. As such, his sacrificial discourse stands as a form of natural piety. As we will see, sacrifice and piety are intimates.

In the end, Du Bois's sacrificial discourse is an extension of his pragmatic religious naturalism. Neither the Gospel of Sacrifice nor the lynching parables function to confirm belief in a transcendent, other-worldly God. Du Bois's sacrificial conjurings are utterly unconcerned with supernatural redemption and are instead intent on explicitly bringing to the fore the earthly social and political goods and values for which life is worth living. This is particularly true of his depictions of the death and suffering of the black Christ, which bespeak a naturalistic worldview limited by human finitude. They confirm the importance of continued commitment to a mortal version of justice. Additionally, in a crucial act of natural piety, the lynching parables resurrect rich memories of the lynched dead. It is only when these sources of black existence are properly honored that the Gospel of Sacrifice finds its truest traction moving forward.

To be sure, these dynamics present certain dangers; the nationalistic and xenophobic tendencies of discourses of sacrifice should make us cautious. Du Bois, I believe, is conscious of these tendencies in his own discourse, and he attempts to modulate them as he capitalizes on their strengths. I am far from certain, however, that he is able to save sacrifice from its barbaric and atavistic tendencies. Still, Du Bois's response to black America's having been a sacrificial victim by creating a discourse of sacrifice in which black Americans become sacrificial agents deserves a full reckoning.

Why Du Bois Persists with a Sacrificial Discourse:
What Sacrifice Is Good For

René Girard, the great contemporary French theorist, provides a theoretical undergirding to contemporary misgivings about the act of sacrifice. Girard's work is famous for exposing the dynamics of scapegoating as a sacrificial system that displaces the violence that members of the community feel for each other onto a "'sacrificeable' victim,'" a "'monstrous double,'" whose death, in effect, absorbs the violence that members of the community would otherwise exact on each other.[22] As I read him, Girard sees sacrificial dynamics underlying not only explicit ritual slaughterings but also all religions and politics that rely on us/them, insider/outsider, and friend/enemy distinctions.[23] For Girard, the only solution to the basic injustice of the very category of sacrifice is to step out of it entirely. His hopes are that by explicitly exposing the inchoate logic of sacrifice—by saying out loud that sacrifice functions not to appease God but to allay the anxieties of social disorder—society will willingly renounce sacrifice because of its clear and brutal oppression. To this end, Girard unapologetically turns to Christianity and insists upon a "non-sacrificial reading of the gospel text," arguing that "Jesus dies, not as a sacrifice, but in order that there may be no more sacrifices."[24]

That Du Bois *does* develop a sacrificial discourse (in particular, one that depicts the death of a black Christ) should make us pause for a moment and consider the adequacy of Girard's prescriptions. Indeed, Du Bois's effective defiance of Girard reveals an easy-to-overlook but crucial attribute of Girard's account of scapegoating—nowhere does Girard speak of how *the scapegoat might assert its agency and rightful place within the society that sacrifices it.* That is to say, he theorizes exclusively from the standpoint of those who are *participants*, however reluctant, in the system of scapegoating and who understand themselves as possessing the agency to confound the system if they protest hard enough. Girard's strategy of disrupting systems of sacrifice by exposing their inchoate and undesirable logic—"for the first time...to expose to the light of reason the role played by violence in human society"[25]—assumes that those who make this critique speak from a social position where their voices are recognized as cogent and legitimate.

This, of course, is decidedly not the position of the scapegoats, who must assume that their direct criticisms will not be readily heard. I am reminded of Burton Mack's criticism of Girard, a wisdom that scapegoats are surely all too familiar with: "We might also want to ask whence the confidence that...such criticism could really make a difference in our world."[26] My point is that Girard does not theorize or adequately consider how the scapegoats might combat the larger sacrificial system in which they function as the "monstrous double." Talal Asad addresses the same concern in considering the limitations of free speech:

> The enjoyment of free speech presupposes not merely the physical ability to speak but *to be heard,* a condition without which speaking to some effect is not possible. If one's speech has no effect what-ever, it can hardly be said to be in the public sphere, no matter how loudly one shouts. *To make others listen* even if they would prefer not to hear, to speak to some consequence so that something in the political world is affected...—these are all presupposed in the idea of free public debate as a liberal virtue. But these performatives are not open equally to everyone because the domain of free speech is always shaped by preestablished limits.[27]

Du Bois knew that white America—from its political representatives to its clergy to the citizenry at large—was in the first half of the twentieth century deaf and unreceptive to antilynching discourse. In 1927 he writes in outrage at white recalcitrance: "The recent horrible lynchings in the United States, even the most incredible burning of human beings alive, have raised not a ripple of interest, not a single protest from the United States Government, scarcely a word from the pulpit and not a syllable of horror of suggestion from the Defenders of the Republic, the 100% Americans, or the propagandists of the army and navy."[28] So great was white recalcitrance that Du Bois surely believed that nothing short of military intervention was going to stop lynching and that that force was not forthcoming.[29] In short, if the scapegoats want to criticize the society that sacrifices them *while having to survive and remain within that very same society,* they must come up with another strategy.

Josiah Royce, one of Du Bois's mentors at Harvard, described in his 1913 text *The Problem of Christianity* an ideal Christian spirit. This "greatest of mys-tics" has suffered greatly, knowing "what it is to be despised and rejected of men, and to be brought to the very depths of lonely desolation."[30] What is dis-tinctive about the suffering of this spirit is that it has come at the hands of his own society, which has treated him with treachery and deceit. This spirit has "suffered thus through a treason which also deeply affected, not one individ-ual only, but a whole community." What is exceptional to Royce and funda-mentally distinguishes this mystic is the sufferer's response to and strategy for overcoming the treasonous violation: "Such a soul...triumph[s]...over the grief that treason has caused" by "us[ing] *the very lore which just this treason has taught, in order to begin a new life work."*[31] In other words, this spirit takes the very substance of the treason and turns it into an antitoxin not by hiding in "all his illuminations...all his mere experiences of fulfillment, or of the immediate presence of the Divine" but by engaging with the real-life contingencies that stem from where the treason took place: "I must insist that this idea comes to us, not from the scholastic quiet of theological speculation, but stained with the blood of the battlefields of real life...I myself have learned it from observing the meaning of the lives of some suffering servants,—plain human beings,—who never cared for theology, but who incarnated in their own fashion enough of the spirit of their community."[32]

In creating this sketch, Royce could very well have had Du Bois in mind. Du Bois's response to the treason of lynching—through the staging of literary lynchings of a black Christ and his continued embrace of sacrifice for the social good—represents the sort of work of Royce's great mystic. Theophus Smith tells us that the strategy that Royce describes—of treating and healing wounds with small antidotal doses of the original poison—is an old African American tradition. Smith describes this sort of pragmatic engagement as "conjuring culture": "the 'trick' of turning victimization against the victimizers and to the benefits of the victims...reconfigur[ing] the embodied person herself or himself, who is configured by the culture as a victim or scapegoat, using the biblical forms and democratic traditions revered by the society and its institutions."[33]

Why, then, does Du Bois persist with a discourse of sacrifice? Because he can conjure *that* language. He knows what Carolyn Marvin and David Ingle's work confirms: "*Bodily* sacrifice is the totem core of American nationalism."[34] White America has sacrifice in its bones. Through rhetorical mastery, Du Bois uses the very terms of sacrifice—its language, lore, and traditions—first to lay claims of ownership to the goods of the system and, second, to indict and implicate that system by showing how it violates its own terms. In fact, the trick of Du Bois's conjuring with sacrifice is that he gains the first—the goods—by pursuing the second—showing how the system is not honoring its own values. Said slightly differently, Du Bois holds on to the language of sacrifice because he needs precisely that language to get white folks to see that they are violating their own sacred tenets. Smith describes this conjuring technique as "effect[ing] and enlist[ing] antagonists [read: white people] directly in the enactment of their own mimetic performances."[35] Unlike Girard, Du Bois does not want to abolish either the terms or the goods of the sacrificial system. Rather, he wants those terms to be expanded to include African Americans, and he wants this with no further violence. There is no passage in Du Bois's

writings that more supremely and sublimely expresses his mystical and conjuring powers than this one from the closing of *Souls:*

> Around us the history of the land has centred for thrice a hundred
> years; out of the nation's heart we have called all that was best to
> throttle and subdue all that was worst; fire and blood, prayer and
> sacrifice, have billowed over this people, and they have found peace
> only in the altars of the God of Right. Nor has our gift of the Spirit
> been merely passive. Actively we have woven ourselves with the very
> warp and woof of this nation,—we fought their battles, shared their
> sorrow, mingled our blood with theirs, and generation after genera-
> tion have pleaded with a headstrong, careless people to despise not
> Justice, Mercy, and Truth, lest the nation be smitten with a curse.
> Our song, our toil, our cheer, and warning have been given to this
> nation in blood-brotherhood. Are not these gifts worth the giving? Is
> not this work and striving? Would America have been America with-
> out her Negro people?[36]

What is exceptional about this passage is the way Du Bois, through the language of sacrifice, builds or enfolds African America into the larger American
project. Fire, blood, prayer, battle, and godly altars are, he knows, the language
in which white America understands its own project. In raising "all that was
worst," Du Bois engages with the utterly horrible practice of lynching. To be
sure, this is terribly dangerous ground. Nonetheless, he turns this history of
sacrifice into a set of claims for black America's birthrights. Moreover, these
birthrights are sonorous American values such as justice and truth. Du Bois's
use of sacrificial tropes signals to white America that black America speaks a
common sacred language—that of nation and its ideals of equality. Consider for
a moment what Du Bois is not saying: He is not saying that African American
sacrifices have been for the sake of God or the church or even the ideals of
justice and mercy alone. These ideals, in fact, make sense or truly matter to
Du Bois only insofar as they are evidenced in national form and experience.
For example, in a revealing line from the opening of *Souls,* Du Bois speaks of
black America as "the race thus sacrificed in its swaddling clothes on the altar
of national integrity."[37] He reminds America both white and black of the terms
of black America's contributions: They are national. Thus, we again ask why
Du Bois persists with a discourse of sacrifice. Because sacrifice, as he uses it,
evokes and upholds the idea of nation.

At the same time, in one crucial sentence Du Bois resists the bald triumphalism of American values. In calling white Americans "headstrong" and
"careless" and in suggesting that only black America keeps America from

God's curse and wrath, Du Bois implicates white America in the violation of all it holds sacred. America may claim to represent justice, mercy, and truth, but Du Bois makes it clear that it has in no way lived these values. In fact, while he suggests that the curse on the American nation has been forestalled—*"lest the nation be smitten with a curse"*—it seems more accurate to see this passage as Du Bois's *enacting* a sublime curse on the country. In the end, he has marshaled sacrifice, blood, and prayer in the name of black America against America itself.

Equally significant is Du Bois's insistence on speaking of black American sacrifice as *activity*, as accomplished enterprise, and as a form of liveliness. Sacrifice, Du Bois says explicitly, is "work and striving." In turn, he opposes sacrifice to servility and instead uses the idea of sacrifice to recuperate the idea of service: "Have we degraded service with menials? Abolish this mean spirit and implant sacrifice."[38] For Du Bois, the politics of service is the politics of social activism—engaged efforts at self- and communal betterment. Thus, in Du Bois's economy, aligning sacrifice with service combats the idea of African American victimhood. By turning sacrifice into an activity of political engagement, Du Bois rehabilitates it by bringing that original treason under his control.

In using sacrifice to introduce a type of national coherence, Du Bois's sacrificial discourse reinforces the central insights of theorists of sacrifice, Henri Hubert and Marcel Mauss: "The sacred things in relation to which sacrifice functions are social things. And this is enough to explain sacrifice...[which] is a social function because sacrifice is concerned with social matters."[39] Their account of sacrifice as motivated by and ministering to social desires represents a fundamental shift away from understanding sacrifice as concerned solely with the relationship between worshipper and whatever it is that the worshipper holds divine. With Hubert and Mauss, sacrifice becomes a salutary strategy for acquiring social goods such as security and status and even material resources such as food and wealth: "Abnegation and submission are not without their selfish aspect...This is because if he gives, it is partly in order to receive."[40] Sacrifice allows individuals to "confer upon each other, upon themselves, and upon those things they hold dear, the whole strength of society."[41] It is true that the "sacrifiers," or "the subject to whom the benefits of sacrifice accrue,"[42] must endure certain hardships. However, if "[t]he sacrifier gives up something of himself...he does not give himself. Prudently, he sets himself aside."[43] For current theorist of sacrifice Ivan Strenski, this insight is startling: It represents the difference between "'giving *of*' oneself" with an expectation of worldly return and demanding "a total annihilating surrender of the self, a 'giving *up*' of oneself."[44] In other words, what Strenski reads from Hubert and Mauss is a *moderate* and *modulated* sacrificial system that rejects extreme forms of bloodletting. Importantly, this way of thinking does not require the designation of a scapegoat. In Hubert and Mauss's terms, the sacrifiers moderate their own acts of sacrifice.

Du Bois's discourse of sacrifice represents the hope that it is possible to engage in the acquisitive social dynamics of sacrifice without being forced to the maximalist ends of annihilating either oneself or someone else. His explicit talk of "reasonable sacrifice"[45] or sacrifice "for that which our souls called sufficient"[46] suggests an alternative sacrificial system whose focus is on limiting (and even eliminating) degradation. In his chapter on Alexander Crummell and the sufferings of black people, Du Bois speaks in similar ways about sacrifice: "All this and more would they bear did they know that this were sacrifice and not a meaner thing."[47] Suffering turns "mean" and is, in effect, no longer an act of sacrifice when the sacrifice does not pay—when there is no return. In this moment Du Bois's Crummell rejects an economy of sacrifice in which it is believed that black suffering must either yield theological goods or end in death and instead insists that black sacrifice demands real-world repayment.[48] For Crummell, sacrifice serves as a bludgeon against passivity: "steeled by Sacrifice against Humiliation."[49] Sacrifice becomes an activity that produces the virtues of worldly engagement. This short passage is a distillation of the Gospel of Sacrifice.

Du Bois, of course, is all too familiar with the number of abuses that nations and their sacrificial discourses are responsible for. However, this language of reasonable sacrifice (sacrifice for "sufficiencies") presents sacrifice not as a mythic primordial blood rite but as an economy of worldly exchange and negotiation of rewards for service rendered. As the long passage I cited earlier makes clear, Du Bois conceives of African American abnegations and deprivations not as duties that can justifiably go unrequited but as investments that the nation is now expected to repay. His emphasis on black contributions of blood reinforces the idea that African Americans are already participants in America's sacrificial system. In doing so, he transforms African Americans from being forced to "give up" their selves as sacrificial victims into active sacrificial agents who "give of" their selves only to receive national benefits in return. It is also, I suggest, the difference between sacrificing for the sake of a pluralistic vision of social coherence and sacrificing to achieve social purity. Indeed, Du Bois's society requires sacrifice. Yet what he insists upon is that specific types of sacrificial discourse aspire to different types of society. He charts a nonviolent sacrificial and nationalist path and avoids the extremes of utter self-abnegation or utter bloodlust.

What are the benefits he expects to receive? At this point in his career, Du Bois rejected the option of urging black Americans to disown and flee the United States entirely and instead was intent on creating just conditions for them within the larger American nation: no more and no less than complete civil and political integration. He wanted the rights owed him and his people as American citizens. Political theorist Michael Dawson describes these years as Du Bois's "radically egalitarian" period, in which "a severe critique of racism in American society" was coupled with "an impassioned appeal for America to live up to the best of its values."[50]

It is certain that Du Bois's discourse of sacrifice pursues the sort of egalitarianism that Dawson describes. Plying sacrifice as a demand, Du Bois insists that white America recognize black America as embodiments and even authors of the rights and ideals enumerated in the nation's sacred civil documents. Black America has given its blood for what Du Bois calls American brotherhood; it is in part because of their sacrifices that he claims that "there are to-day no truer exponents of the pure human spirit of the Declaration of Independence than the American Negroes."[51] In this, he attempts to make the acquisitive or consolidating grammar of sacrifice pay for the purposes of conjoining black America to the American nation writ large.

However, there are other benefits, too. It is not enough to see Du Bois's claims for the distinctiveness of African Americans' contributions to the United States as attempts to build black America into the larger nation. His use of a discourse of sacrifice also emphasizes the unique position of black Americans within America, which needs to be understood as initiating a second nationalist discourse, the brand of black nationalism I spoke of in the previous chapter. It is rooted in a sense of peoplehood that comes from surviving communal struggles together. The result is a sense of black ownership of the nation's best ideals. In turn, these ideals cannot be conceived of without reference to those struggles and sacrifices; through sacrifice they become the *particular* property of black America. This line of thinking provides a new way to hear Du Bois's speaking of "the race thus sacrificed in swaddling clothes on the altar of national integrity."[52] On the one hand, his use of "integrity" is harshly sardonic; in light of American sacrifices, American integrity is a sham.[53] Still, I do not believe that Du Bois's reference to national integrity reflects only causticity. He is also speaking of black national integrity embodied in African Americans' sacrifices in the pursuit of Justice, Mercy, and Truth.

I am suggesting that Du Bois's discourse of sacrifice is aimed not solely at engaging and convincing white people to accept black Americans as part of the larger national discourse. Du Bois also uses his discourse of sacrifice to speak specifically to black people. He is using the dynamics of sacrifice to consolidate a sense of nationhood in order to create a sense of black peoplehood. Indeed, sacrifice is also the language of black America. For the sake of his people Du Bois uses the very same language with which he conjures against white oppression. For this reason I believe Smith defines African American conjuring too narrowly by restricting it to efforts to engage "antagonists." In using sacrifice to imagine a black national community, Du Bois conjures to effect transformations in the *protagonists,* that is, to help black America sustain a complex self-understanding of fighting not only for but also against the larger American nation.

Du Bois's uses of a nationalist discourse of sacrifice—at once to raise fundamental doubts about the regnant nationalist discourse and to build less malignant forms of American and black American solidarity—is the lasting mark of his system of sacrifice. Strenski sees what he calls a "brave" genius in the way Hubert and Mauss imply that "there can be no durable social life— much less a 'nation'—without sacrifice and the transcendent sanctions embodied in it."[54] He condenses Hubert and Mauss to a pithy formula and a human truth—"no sacrifice, no society."[55] He writes: "The persistence of discourses about sacrifice testifies perhaps more eloquently to the structural requisites that human social life places on us all. This is to say that the persistence of talk about sacrifice seems to mean that many believe that it is in the very nature of viable social life that sacrifice—in some description—will be required."[56]

This, to be sure, is treading on dangerous ground. Strenski seems to be offering an essentialist conclusion that humans at base require sacrifice— that bloodletting or some type of abnegation is genetically indispensable to social cohesion. Pushed to its extreme, Strenski's "no sacrifice, no society" suggests a deeper, fatalistic Nietzschean truth about the necessary brutalities in human cohesion.[57] Here we would do well to heed sacrifice theorist Nancy Jay's pointed cautionary words about the persistent dangers of sacrificial discourses: "When theory posits a collective subject, some people's subjectivity will be more collective than others', and when theory construes society as one and whole, some people are always going to be more 'social' than those whose voices, if heard, would damage the unity of the model."[58] As a result, those voices whose subjectivity is deemed not central to the whole can justifiably be quashed. This echoes Girard's conclusions—sacrifice of any sort traffics in its basest logic, which follows a slippery slope to the worst nativist and xenophobic abuses of those on the social margins.

Strenski's pithy formula, "no sacrifice, no society," forces us to think hard about whether we can have civil society without costs and demands, without distinctions between who is of the nation and who is not. Strenski clearly believes we cannot. On this view, certain abnegations and certain drawings of social boundaries are necessary not simply for social peace but also for social flourishing. Strenski, it can be argued, does not spend enough time thinking about ways of minimizing the damage done by the sacrifices and the us/them distinctions, which are part of national formations. Still, I am reminded here of Benedict Anderson's comments: "Indeed, nation-ness is the most universally legitimate value in the political life of our time."[59] Anderson is not an apologist for nationalism; indeed, his critical review of the nation is obvious to all. Nevertheless, on the strength of that same critical review he reminds us that the nation does not only produce ill but also gives form to higher aspirations: "In an age when it is so common for progressive, cosmopolitan intellectuals (particularly in Europe?) to insist on the near-pathological character of nationalism, its roots in fear and hatred of the Other, and its affinities with racism, it is useful to remind ourselves that nations inspire love, and often profoundly self-sacrificing love."[60]

I am far from equipped to sort through the structuralists' claims about the nature of sacrifice and the nation. I do not know whether sacrificial systems necessarily traffic in nationalist abuses. What I do know is that Du Bois's discourse of sacrifice represents an attempt to create a system of sacrifice that criticizes nationalist abuses while simultaneously insisting on the legitimacy of the nation. In taking on the virulence of American systems of sacrifice with a countersystem of sacrifice, Du Bois presents the promise of this most implausible and fragile of triangles—the one formed by sacrifice, nation, and love. This may be tying incompatibles together. In producing a discourse of sacrifice that is at once a scathing critique of America's regnant discourse of sacrifice and a critical embrace of the powers of solidarity in sacrifice, Du Bois, it might be said, wants to have his cake and eat it, too.[61]

In Du Bois's case, this combination produces a discourse of sacrifice that is rooted in democracy and dissent and gives voice to the oppressed and disenfranchised. His efforts are not simply to consolidate authority and community but also to question them. In this, his discourse of sacrifice is aimed at addressing the abuses that Girard and others see as necessarily inherent in systems of sacrifice. Du Bois's attempt to ply a rhetoric of sacrifice to engender democratic pluralism anticipates Marvin and Ingle's suggestion that "the sacrificial system of nationalism can be challenged only by those who embrace with still greater commitment alternative sacrificial systems to replace it."[62] Again, Anderson's words are helpful here: "How truly rare it is to find…nationalist products expressing fear and loathing."[63] The fear and loathing Anderson refers to is of the nation itself. How rare it is, he says, to find a nationalist discourse that is critical of the national project. How rare it is to find a discourse of sacrifice that is critical of sacrificial dynamics. Du Bois's discourse of sacrifice, I suggest, is that rare example of a nationalist project of fear and loathing. Consider again the moment I spoke of earlier, when Du Bois places a curse on white America for its refusal to recognize the sacrifices of black Americans. This decidedly nationalist moment holds out the hope of a capacious American solidarity, yet articulates that hope by means of indictment and the threat of malediction. The nationalist aspirations of Du Bois's discourse of sacrifice preempt a pernicious form of American nationalism by initiating a national moral reckoning. Du Bois's hope is that the stuff of stiff reckonings and criticism can give rise to a rhetoric of sacrifice of chastened nationalist desires. If we are led by the right sorts of leaders and if we refuse to listen to the sort of criticism that warns us against dreaming of transcending our all-too-human limitations, might we and the nation—through sacrifice—come to accomplish brave and virtuous ends beyond those we believed we were capable of?[64]

Treacherous Ground: Du Bois's Lynching Parables

All of Du Bois's lynching literature includes a black Christ figure; in all of them, that figure is lynched. Du Bois's literary lynchings represent elaborations of and glosses on the long African American religious tradition of imagining "a lynched black man as Christ on the Cross,"[65] never more succinctly captured than by Gwendolyn Brooks's observation that "the loveliest lynchee was our Lord."[66] By rehearsing, staging, and reliving African American lynchings in Christological terms, Du Bois presides, in Smith's terms, as a conjuror whose "imitation of Christ" functions as "'homeopathic' applications...designed to 'cure' violence in the form of racism at the level of social change."[67] The crucial question is how they effect this cure.

The answers here are not obvious. Earlier I suggest that Du Bois's lynching parables partake in the acquisitive dynamics of sacrifice. In this, they are homologous to the Gospel of Sacrifice. Yet, we also need to acknowledge the distinction between the lynching parables and the Gospel of Sacrifice. After all, the ethos of the Gospel of Sacrifice, in which certain abnegations produce collective improvements is decisively a model of "giving of," not one of "giving up." In the Gospel of Sacrifice, Du Bois encourages reflexive acts of sacrifice, which are *willingly* done by an agent and not *to* that person. The lynching parables stand in contrast; they are on their face stories about "giving up" the self. This should not, however, be mistaken for passivity. Though the black Christ is a victim, he is not a passive one. It is his agency, which takes the form of activist actions in the name of racial justice, that leads to his end. Nevertheless, the common end of stories such as "Jesus Christ in Texas," "The Gospel according to Mary Brown," "The Second Coming," and "The Son of God" is a dead, black Christ figure. Consider the Christ character, John, in "Of the Coming of John." Girding himself for an encounter with the white power structure of his small Southern town, John says, "Here is my duty...plain before me; perhaps they'll let me help settle the Negro problems there,—perhaps they won't. 'I will go in to the King, which is not according to the law; and if I perish, I perish.'"[68] Indeed, he does perish. The role that the death of the black Christ plays makes the lynching parables a challenging literature.

Here is where Du Bois's pragmatic religious naturalism is important. His parables show a hesitant and cautious regard for traditional soteriological questions such as Christ's saving and redeeming of the world from sin. This is the central truth of Du Bois's lynching parables. In none of his stories does Du Bois suggest that the black Christ's meaning resides in a divine economy; nor does he suggest that a connection exists between human and divine history. In truth, Du Bois's parables speak to this-worldly dynamics of human finitude, which foreground the politics of human community. For example, consider again the earlier lines from "Of the Coming of John." Du Bois's interest is not in how confronting injustice fulfills a divine teleology; his focus on death is not to sanctify suffering for the promise of eternal reward. John simply represents the courage and the very real mortal stakes involved in confronting racism. It is not, I believe, incidental that this last Du Bois quotation is from the Book of Esther, a text in which what is at stake is not eternity but the ability to survive laws that threaten extermination. The quote's emphasis on "perishing" speaks to the terms of human finitude, not the sanctification of death and suffering in the name of a divine economy.

Du Bois's lynching parables exhibit a distinctively earthly logic in which the death of the Christ figure goes no further than exposing what is sinful in the laws of the world. On these terms, the fact that the lynching parables culminate in a hanged Christ figure should not be interpreted as Du Bois's sanctification of death and suffering in terms of eternal reward.[69] Instead, as we will see, the deaths of the Christ figures in his lynching parables function to foreground the political and social issues for which the deaths were a price. The parables eschew theology and instead work as pieces of social criticism by disrupting modern life to heighten and plumb contemporary concerns. Thus, the story "Pontius Pilate" stands as a commentary on the way Southern Christianity was an accessory to lynching in the United States. Even in stories like "The Gospel according to Mary Brown," where classical questions of Jesus's suffering and his resurrection loom, Du Bois responds with religious naturalism. For Du Bois, the resurrection and black suffering become vehicles of remembrance of those lost, which in turn, become experiences that connect the lived past to the hoped-for future. Suffering does not save. Accounts of suffering, however, help us understand how to pay homage to ancestors, create tradition, and shape an ethics of social activism, which for Du Bois are critical to relieving present and future suffering without resorting to a supernatural design.[70] It is exactly here, in eschewing soteriology and in using suffering to build narratives of what amounts to natural piety that the lynching parables exhibit an active, acquisitive dynamic. In his lynching parables, Du Bois acquires modes of social and ethical criticism that are necessary for social change. Ideally, the lynching parables equip readers with crucial lenses for examining contemporary social and political concerns.

For example, the deep drama of "Pontius Pilate" is the complicity of white Christianity with Southern lynching. A Southern bishop brings before him two men: the white Barabbas, a "criminal and a drunkard—he has killed men before," and the black "Iscariot," who is "guilty" of preaching a message of race equality. The bishop exclaims: " 'Do you know what he wants?'—'He wants equality for Everybody—everybody, mind you...talking, sleeping, kissing, marrying...He is going to overthrow all the government...He blasphemed against the White Race.' "[71] Du Bois's depiction of the white bishop as both an engine and a vehicle of mob behavior corroborate Donald Mathews's masterful argument on the contributing role Christianity played in lynchings: "This silence about the meaning of religion in discussions of lynchings is strange because of the common knowledge that crucifixion, an act of violence, is the very core of the Christian paradigm that was so essential as a part of Southern culture. African Americans understood this; they understood that Christ, too, had been lynched."[72] Mathews does not say that Christianity is responsible for lynching: In fact, he explicitly makes it clear that Christianity "did not make white Christians lynch black people." Instead, his point is that the sacred order in the South (at least a prevalent type of sacred order preached from a good many pulpits) was one that emphasized a harsh and retributive form of justice as divinely sanctioned. Thus, in the prevailing religious ethos of the South, where God was conceived of as a "Supreme Hangman," "righteous retribution is one of the glories of the divine character." This dynamic comes to life in "Pontius Pilate." Behind the bishop we hear the roar of the white crowd amassing outside Pilate's door: "Something floated in by the window. It was a low, but monstrous sound and in it lay anger and blood."[73] What Du Bois depicts is the Southern confluence of religion and a generalized social norm of blood-lust, particularly for violations of Jim Crow.

Additionally, consider "Jesus Christ in Texas," which is a complex meditation on the possibility of white renunciation of racism. It is the only parable in which Du Bois's Jesus is not obviously black: "His face was olive, even yellow."[74] Christ's complexion allows him to move fairly freely and unrecognized as black among the story's whites. In turn, Du Bois uses this Christ figure to expose inveterate white racism, especially among those whites who keep it below the surface. In the story's central conversation, Jesus asks a poor white farming woman whether she loves her neighbor as herself. Her response is bald and frank: "'I try—' she began, then looked the way he was looking; down under the hill where lay a little, half-ruined cabin. 'They are niggers,' she said briefly. He looked at her. Suddenly a confusion came over her and she insisted, she knew not why. 'But they are niggers!'"[75] Through intimate conversations like these, Du Bois gives voice not to the hatred of the mob but to the hatred of single white folks, whose racism seems intractable. It is also, as Du Bois depicts it, utterly seamless with white culture. Whether at a dinner party or in a business meeting, deep racism coexists with an air of courtesy and gentility among whites.

What is ultimately distinctive about "Jesus Christ in Texas" is that the story ends with the changing of the white farmer woman's racial consciousness—though not before a Christ figure is lynched. In some sense she is responsible for his lynching. During their conversation, she finally sees the Christ in full light: "She saw his dark face and curly hair. She shrieked in angry terror."[76] A lynching begins in defense of her womanhood, and she is witness to the primal frenzy of the white mob, which also goes on to burn her innocent black neighbor's cabin. It is from that flame of fire, turned into "a great crimson cross," that the farmer woman has a vision of the Christ hanged, "riven and blood-stained, with thorn-crowned head and pierced hands." She makes the connection between the lynchee and Christ: "She knew," "'despised and rejected of men.'" Du Bois ends the story with a word of redemption: "This day thou shalt be with me in Paradise."[77] It is a version of Luke 23:43, where Jesus redeems the crucified thieves who were dying next to him on the cross.

Nonetheless, it is not clear whether the reader can take solace in the farmer woman's transformation. Her redemption hardly has systemic effects. Only she disgorges herself of her racism; society itself does not. Indeed, the lasting impression of the story is its depiction of the stubborn dynamics of racial healing. What is sobering is that the real transfiguration occurs only after the horrible lynching occurs; murder is almost required for a deeper realization. It is a theme Du Bois vividly returns to in his poem titled "The Prayers of God." He narrates from the perspective of a white man who is alone with God essentially for the first time: "Wait God, a little space. / It is so strange to talk with Thee—/ Alone!"[78] In the course of the conversation, it begins to dawn on him that the white man's justification for his pursuit of land, power, and riches—"For this we killed these lesser breeds / And civilized their dead / Raping red rubber, diamonds, cocoa, gold!"—have been an abomination and a blight. The white man even admits that "once, and in Thy Name, / I lynched a Nigger—...I saw him crackle there, on high, / I watched him wither!" Like the white farmer woman, this white narrator comes to realize that he had lynched his Lord: "Awake me, God! I sleep! / What was that awful word Thou saidst? / That black and riven thing—was it Thee? / That gasp—was it Thine? / This pain—is it Thine?"[79] These fantasies of white reform are dual edged. On the one hand, they implicate racist practices not simply as deeply immoral but also as deeply impious; here, too, we hear Mathews's argument about the supporting role of religion in lynching. On the other hand, internal self-reflectiveness seems to pale in the face of the larger problem; white society is saturated with this impiety. Both "Jesus Christ in Texas" and "The Prayers of God" point out their own propaedeutic limitations: They can provide only partial instruction.[80]

On they go, Du Bois's lynching parables, dealing with flashpoint contemporary concerns. "The Second Coming" portrays white sexual insecurities that fuel lynchings; "The Son of God" is a meditation on tensions within the black family due to slavery; "Of the Coming of John" is a lynching parable that, as chapter 2 explains, raises the tensions between tradition and the Enlightenment. In each, the Christ figure is lynched so as to remind us of the sorts of concerns we who remain need to work on. Henry Levinson's words about George Santayana's relationship to Christ make a nice fit for Du Bois: "So if Santayana's pragmatic naturalism abandons supernaturalism, metaphysical comfort, metaphysical disclosure, and the denial of death, it does not thereby abandon the idea of Christ in the Gospels of life lived under the Cross."[81] Du Bois, too, abandons all of these while conjuring a black Christ for us to emulate and to live for. The loveliest lynchee is, indeed, the Lord. His death is sanctified insofar as we struggle to embrace the social and political values and virtues for which he lived.

Conjoining the Gospel of Sacrifice and the Lynching Parables

In *Salvation at Stake* Brad Gregory tells us that Protestant martyrologists distinguished themselves from their Catholic counterparts precisely on whether Christ's sacrifice was repeatable.[82] Catholic theology tended to emphasize the iterability of Christ's sacrifice. The result was that the defining and central event for Catholic martyrs was their death; if in death they did not become Christ, their demise was certainly the most critical way in which they mirrored his life. Protestants, however, argued that Christ's death was unique and not repeatable. Protestant martyrs died not to emulate Christ's death but to example the ideals by which he lived his life.[83]

It is helpful to think of Du Bois's lynching parables as constituting a modern Protestant martyrology that honors the dead, preserves their memory, makes certain that they are the focus of later worship, and attempts to ensure that future sacrifices do not happen. There is a crucial hint that Du Bois was, in fact, quite aware of and familiar with the Protestant tradition of writing memorial accounts of those who have died in the name of religious virtue. In the chapter titled "On Alexander Crummell" in *Souls,* Du Bois has Crummell notice John Fox's seminal, sixteenth-century Protestant martyrology, *The Book of Martyrs,* on the bookshelf of the head bishop of Philadelphia.[84] Protestant martyrologists like Foxe sought to drive a wedge between Christ's original sacrifice and later deaths that resulted from unwavering attempts to live by Christian ideals. In his martyrology, Du Bois wants to honor the lynched dead and their original sacrifice, but in no way is he calling for continued dying either in their name or as an emulation of their sacrifice. Du Bois's lynching parables compose a literature devoted to ending the form of sacrifice the literature itself describes. On this reading, the lynching parables are actually not forms of "giving up"; they are forms of "giving of" in order that black Americans will not have to give up their bodies and souls again.

Here is where the lynching parables join the Gospel of Sacrifice. Despite their differences, they both express a determination to make the loss of the lynched pay in social and political terms that honor their lives. To be certain, they effect this in different ways. The lynching parables look back to previous sacrifices, to the idea of the black Christ who has already lost his life for white America's sins. Through this, Du Bois provides complex narratives on the nature of American racism. The lynching parables are, in this sense, diagnostic. To read them is to get a sense of the variety of America's racial ailments. At once, Du Bois profoundly commemorates the lynched dead while turning their lives into tools for exact social criticism. Du Bois's lynched black Christs are self-conscious agents for change, certainly victims of virulent violence, as well as empowered actors whose lives are rooted in the activities of worldly engagement.

The Gospel of Sacrifice looks forward to acts of social activism that are expected to pay real rewards. It is an engine by which to initiate a life's work, and it aspires to a day when loss of life is not the norm for acts of sacrifice. The Gospel of Sacrifice eagerly awaits the day when sacrifice is not a "meaner thing" but the result of self-directed acts by the black community done in the service of caring for one another. Sacrifice, on these terms, represents a deep Du Boisian spiritual striving. (Certainly Du Bois hopes against hope that

America writ large will embrace this ethos as well, but this is, alas, a hope not hopeful.)

Is it not the case that the forward-looking Gospel of Sacrifice cannot do without the deep social criticism of the lynching parables? Will not present-day acts of sacrifice work best when informed by the lives rendered and lost in the lynching parables? For in these parables Du Bois provides a set of narratives and ideals for directing the sorts of future sacrifices that are worth fighting for. On this view, the Gospel of Sacrifice is entrusted with the task of protecting and honoring the lives lost in the lynching parables. It is their spark that the Gospel of Sacrifice is charged with protecting. For Du Bois, the very idea of sacrifice is tied to notions of piety and remembrance. Sacrifice, even when it is forward looking, also looks to the past for other sacrifices to honor and even emulate. Du Bois's lynching parables can be understood as narratives of natural piety. As I said earlier, sacrifice and piety are intimates. One crucial way Du Bois makes sacrifice pay in both his lynching parables and the Gospel of Sacrifice is by using it as a reminder of the sources of his existence. Sacrifice is a virtue that reminds him of his duties and obligations to the black community, on which he depends.

Consider the way Du Bois uses the notion of sacrifice to write this prayer of pragmatic religious naturalistic piety:

> We thank Thee, O Lord, for the gift of Death—for the great silence
> that follows the jarring noises of the world—the rest is Peace. We
> who live to see the passing of that fine and simple Old Man, who has
> so often sat beside us here in this room, must not forget the legacy
> he leaves us or the Hope he still holds to us: we are richer for his
> sacrifice, truer for his honesty and better for his goodness. And his
> living leaves us firm in the faith that the Kingdom of Heaven will yet
> reign among men.[85]

To be sure, there is more than a touch of romanticism in this. However, we should not overlook the virtues that prayers like this cultivate—gratitude, reverence, and obligation, which are the virtues of natural piety. Clearly, in Du Bois's hands, these virtues need to be put to use and made to yield results. Consciousness of debts and of ancestors alone is not enough. Practices and social acts are needed to honor these trusts and sources of being. This is precisely what the combination of the lynching parables and the Gospel of Sacrifice effect.

Conclusion: Beyond Du Bois

Toward a Tradition of African American Pragmatic Religious Naturalism

How are we to take measure of African American voices, which on the one hand vociferously speak out against normative religious commitments—either to institutions or to traditional supernatural beliefs—and on the other hand invoke religious rhetoric, concepts, and stories in their moral, political, and literary imaginations? What sort of religious categories do we have to describe the religious sensibilities of Hurston's *Moses, Man of the Mountain,* a text that plays with and even disrupts the traditional African American archetype of the Exodus as a triumphant and progressive story of God's leading the slaves out of Egypt?[1] The same question about religious categories and sensibilities can be asked of James Baldwin's *Go Tell It on the Mountain* and *The Fire Next Time,* postmetaphysical texts both, in which religion is necessary reading for his kaleidoscopic interrogation of identity. Despite Baldwin's unrelenting hostility to religion in *The Fire Next Time,* how can we possibly think of his ultimate embrace of a love ethic as anything other than intimately related to Christian agape?[2] Texts like these confound normative categories of the secular and the religious, to my eye, and felicitously blur the lines between the two. If our accounts of the religious significance of these texts tell us only that they rejected religious convention, we have revealed only one thing: an impoverished understanding of the nature of religion in modernity. Moreover, if we are unwilling to attend to their unconventional renderings of religious moods, narratives, symbols, and insignia, then we have left the details of the texts themselves untouched and uninterpreted.

In writing this book on Du Bois I hope to provide the initial vocabulary to give this tradition of heterodox African American religious thought its due. That vocabulary derives from pragmatic religious naturalism. As I see it, Du Bois heads a tradition of black American pragmatic religious naturalist thinkers who are deeply engaged with religion and its resources but who question its metaphysical certainties and no longer understand it as a permanent source of truth. For Du Bois, religion is not about simply confirming stable sources of knowledge. What we learn from him is how religious vocabularies can be used to critically question living conditions, metaphysical certainties be damned. Thus, instead of doing political theology, in which God inspires the politics, Du Bois creates a politics of religion that is sensitive to history and contingency. Instead of explaining suffering as divinely inspired, he creates a black Christ in order to better analyze the nature and depict the tragic costs of suffering here and now. Furthermore, when it comes to black identity, religion becomes for Du Bois a way to reinforce the crucial importance of black solidarity while also insisting on the social fluidity of the sources of black selves. In all of this, a deep and rich intimacy with religious vocabularies—from preacher cadences to biblical text to religious forms of denunciation and reform—is absolutely required. Religion is the crucible in which all of this work takes place.

It is helpful to think of Du Bois's pragmatic religious naturalism as a form of what Albert Murray describes as blues improvisation. Flights of improvisation, Murray tells us, only seem radically spontaneous and transgressive; in truth, "the invention of creative processes lies not in the originality of the phrase as such, but in the way it is used in a frame of reference!" Said slightly differently: "As a very great trumpet player, whose soulfulness was never in question, used to say, "Man, if you ain't got the chops for the dots, ain't nothing happening."[3] That is, musicians can be inventive only by first knowing the traditional forms and meters and then working their innovations into these recognizable patterns.

Like the blues musician, Du Bois imitates, mimics, and even at times mocks traditional forms yet is all the while careful to respect the discipline, habits, and customs of the art form. What is to be avoided is disrespectful mimicry and mockery: "Far worse is casual mimicry . . . As for deliberately distorted mimicry, not only is it outright misrepresentation (and thus naked misidentification and misdefinition), but it is also undisguised defiance become downright mockery expressing contempt and even disdain."[4] What is needed for appropriate mimicry (might we call this natural piety) is "in a word, training," which is to say that one disregards and ignores traditional forms only at one's peril.[5] In turn, Du Bois's contrapuntal relationship with religion demands a real literacy with traditional patterns and forms. His religious voice must remain conversant with the faith of his fathers and mothers. Like any masterful improviser, Du Bois has the chops for the dots. This is to say, then, that pragmatic religious naturalists like Du Bois have gone and must continue to go to "church," where "church" represents some type of living connection or relationship to traditional religious ways. In mobilizing Christian vocabulary, Du Bois continues to use religion to provide a crucial narrative form for his conception of an ideal life, which is one of sacrifice, political activism for the sake of interests bigger than one's own, prophetic denunciation and reform, reading the Bible, and paying homage to the sources of his existence. It is true that the narrative this provides is not that of the traditional believer, which aims for a divine *telos*. Nevertheless, that Du Bois continues to use religion to provide life's narrative form represents an exemplary, traditional religious way.[6]

Let me present at greater length a further example of this sort of contrapuntal engagement with religion. Consider the utterly remarkable but entirely neglected religious experience that presides over the opening pages of Ralph Ellison's *Invisible Man*. The power of the text's epoch-making statement on invisibility has ironically rendered invisible the role that religion plays in the novel's opening struggle with how race is lived. For directly after the invisible man diagnoses and laments his state of invisibility to white people, he has a religious experience, the core of which consists of a stunning and remarkably complex call-and-response sermon on the nature of race and black identity. Within this religious setting, race is spoken of collaboratively to create a pragmatist's sense of black identity that is both strong enough to rely on for solidarity and dynamic enough to see race reflecting flexible social realities.

The scene goes like this: Invisible Man, high on reefer and listening to Armstrong's "What Did I Do to Be So Black and Blue" (a breathtakingly complex title in light of the account of race to come), first hears a slave spiritual being sung, and then he hears a preacher shout:

> "Brothers and sisters, my text this morning is 'Blackness of Blackness.'"
> "And a congregation of voices answered: 'That blackness is most black, brother, most black...'
> And the preacher says,
> "In the beginning...there was blackness."[7]

The preacher here is seemingly establishing a type of original or even essential blackness, which would appear to be epistemically foundational. The battle royal, Ellison might say, is on between the sorts of white folks whose foundational view of race renders the invisible man invisible and antipodal foundational views of race, which lead black folks to assert that blackness is both first and original and goes all the way down.

However, in a flash, the preacher's discourse swerves, and he begins to radically disrupt this racial ontology. In a stunning series of couplets, the preacher says:

> *"Now black is..."...*
> *"...an' black ain't..."...*
> *"Black will git you..."...*
> *"...an' black won't..."...*
> *"It do..."...*
> *"...an' it don't."*
> *"Black will make you..."...*
> *"...or black will un-make you."*

And then the Invisible Man narrates:

> *And at the point a voice of trombone timbre screamed at me, "Git out of here, you fool! Is you ready to commit treason?"*
> *And I tore myself away, hearing the old singer of spirituals moaning, "Go curse your God, boy, and die."*

With that final line, if it were not already clear, Ellison unmistakably signals that the religious realm of this sermon is far from the traditional. Treason—in the form of questioning, undoing, and redoing conventional loyalties to race, peoplehood, and God—is precisely what Ellison is preparing the invisible man to commit. This passage is in my view distinctly one of pragmatic religious naturalism for the way its religious bearing is, to cite Kenneth Burke again, "not about God, but rather, about the way we use our words about God on each other."[8] Furthermore, Ellison's intent here is to use his words about God not to talk about true belief but, as he says, for treason, which is to say to create a liminal space that unsettles and destabilizes racial essentialisms. In the ambivalence of his couplets—"black is and black ain't"—he urges us to ask ourselves what we really mean by black (or, by extension, white). Do we have or need control over these terms? Moreover, by phrasing definitions of race in terms of what they "do" or "make," Ellison is asking what the effects are of living according to this or that form of racial understanding. How is one's soul (and I mean "soul" in Ellison's sense as the "creative struggles against the realities of existence"[9]) made by the meaning of the terms one uses to describe racial identity?

The relationship Ellison sees between questions of what blackness is and what it does or makes embodies the key epistemological insight of pragmatism, which insists that the meaning of words or ideas is not located in some secure unchanging realm. Instead, they are forever disputed because meaning resides in the very rapidly changing world of human use. James famously captures the "pragmatic method...of settling metaphysical disputes" with this question: "What difference would it practically make to anyone if this notion rather than that notion were true?"[10] This line is one of the crucial antiessentialist linguistic turns of the twentieth century. By locating its meaning in what notions of race do, Ellison's destabilization of blackness in his *Invisible Man* sermon is the century's most profound literary statement of race pragmatically conceived.

Now, if Ellison follows pragmatic principles in construing race, he resolves the uncertainties he raises in ways that differ from those of the classical pragmatists. James asks questions pragmatically in order to *clarify* meaning by *reducing* ambiguity and uncertainty. If he had ever asked questions about race (which he did not), he would have wanted in pragmatic terms to narrow down and resolve the question of what black was or was not.

And this is exactly where Ellison takes pragmatism in new directions. His radical questions about race reveal that once the meaning of race is released, as it were, into the world, ambiguity and uncertainty about its meaning endlessly ramify. Ellison suggests that blackness—because it is and it is not and because it exists not as a metaphysical fact but as multiple social discourses with real-world effects—is not a dispute that, in the language of William James, can be settled. Instead, the *tertium quid* of Ellison's sermon *unsettles* race fundamentally and permanently. Ellison does this, however, not to eliminate race. He insists on race—*but in its unsettled form*.[11] Consider here the invisible man's response to the spiritual singer after she tells him to curse God and die: " 'I too have become acquainted with ambivalence,' I said. 'That's why I'm here.'"[12]

Living with ambivalence is, as any neurotic will tell you, not easy. Freud called it pathological. When it comes to living with the ambivalence of race, however—of facing up to the fact that this source of existence is profound and diaphanous—Ellison does not believe that either health or a profounder way of living results from its elimination or resolution. Nonetheless, by simultaneously insisting that race "makes" and "unmakes," Ellison brings to consciousness the way deep sources of identity are contingent, arbitrary, and perishable. This is the challenge of this passage on pragmatic religious naturalism. Ellison does not ask how we make sure that our terms of identity are firm enough to weather all encounters. Instead, he asks what sorts of lives we enter into when we learn that the terms that are most important to us and deserve our devotion are also irredeemably transient and accidental. What practices do we participate in? What sorts of loves do we feel?

Why is this a passage of pragmatic *religious* naturalism? Why cannot we simply say that Ellison is speaking pragmatically about race? What does religion have to do with it? To not account for religion is to ignore the obvious: Ellison chooses a religious setting and religious language in order to make this point about race. We need to ask, What is it about religion that makes it a particularly good language to help us become increasingly acquainted with this ambivalence? On my view, religion is rhetorically indispensable for these ends precisely because it represents the historical grounds of two things: certainty and deep human meaning. Ellison's use of God strives to disrupt this pairing: Too often certainty is considered synonymous with deep meaning. Ellison's use of God talk—with its willingness to commit treason, its impertinence, and its iconoclasm—attempts to replace certainty as the source of deep human meaning with indeterminacy and ambiguity. As such, Ellison turns religion into a productive source of the types of ambivalences that nurture and strengthen the soul's creative confrontation with the racial terms of its existence. Consider the impetuousness in this couplet of his: "Amazing grace, how sweet the sound / A bullfrog slapped my grandma down."[13] Then consider Ellison's description of what he sees it doing: "Well, yes, the irreverence toward religious ceremonies—this is an escape valve, of which there's a large body of lore... but this lore functions to release doubt, and to give it some sort of social expression. And doubt *strengthens*."[14] Here again we can see the type of respectful or appropriate mimicry and mockery that Murray speaks of. Ellison transforms the seriousness of "Amazing Grace," but he does so in a continuing pursuit of meaningful standing in an indeterminate world. This is serious work, work that religious vocabulary continues. It is no joke that, in Ellison's case, religion includes a heavy dose of the comic.

Ellison's pragmatic religious naturalism begins with an irreverent impulse, but when it leads to a doubt that strengthens, its results are a new reverence and devotion. By riffing on an African American tradition of God talk to undermine the certainties of racial identity, he introduces a new dispensation: a life's work of knowing that the tools that make for the deepest forms of human meaning—and for Ellison those are the very tools that make him black—are also, if held in the wrong way, the tools of one's undoing. He has used black religion to gain release from the drive for epistemic certainty about race, which throws him into a liminal space wherein lies the possibility of spiritual transformation rooted in a new appreciation of the finitude of race.

To be sure, Ellison and Du Bois are different types of pragmatic religious naturalists. Du Bois does not crack jokes or deploy comical irreverence;

of course, Ellison's prose never turns purple in romantic flights that stitch together all of humanity in rhapsodic harmony. What they share is a contested stance toward religion: Both Du Bois and Ellison are unable to do with it and unable to do without it. The pinch of this stance leads them to play fast and loose—or not at all—with theological conviction while relying deeply on religious narratives and symbols to envision the terms of human life, to give shape to their loves, and to curb the violence in us all. From their engagements with religion emerges a beautiful uncertainty in the way their writings, in particular, show that playing pragmatically with religion can help us all manage the uncertainty of race in America by turning terror into political practice, communal sacrifice, existential reflection, and a deep love for the African American sources of American existence. Thus far I have only briefly suggested that this tradition also lives in Ellison, Hurston, and Baldwin. In short, Du Bois and this tradition together demonstrate the way our racial selves become spiritualized insofar as they embrace the fast-moving unpredictability of racial signifiers.

Facing this sort of uncertainty is enough to make one want to curse God and die. However, the tradition of African American writers that begins with Du Bois turns such curses into a religious rebirth. Du Bois stands at the start and demands a new religious ideal and a reverent faith. Through pragmatic religious naturalism, he is born again into the conditions of human finitude, particularly those that attend to black American life. Without the supernatural, these conditions remain awe inspiring and allow for continued love for, solidarity with, and attachment to the complex vicissitudes of religious life. They also make for a radical and critical faith in which intelligence is paired with social consciousness and action. This is the lasting legacy of Du Bois's religious imagination: He turned his divine discontent into a religious state of being. He responded to his demand for a new religious ideal and reverent faith with a black faith of his own.

Now more than ever, America, with national and international battle lines drawn, would do well to hold its ears open to the sermons of black America's pragmatic religious naturalists. These types of sermons summon religious vocabulary to reveal and revel in the strength that comes from acknowledging the fragility of the bonds between race and nation. In committing treason and cursing God, the pragmatic naturalistic religious life continues to bring us home.

Notes

INTRODUCTION

1. W.E.B. Du Bois, "Careers Open to College-bred Negroes," in *Writings by W.E.B. Du Bois in Non-periodical Literature Edited by Others*, ed. Herbert Aptheker (Millwood, N.Y.: Kraus-Thomson, 1982), 9, emphasis mine. Reprinted from *Two Addresses Delivered by Alumni of Fisk University, in Connection with the Anniversary Exercises of Their Alma Mater, June 1898* (Nashville: Fisk University, 1898).

2. W.E.B. Du Bois, "The Future of Wilberforce University," *Journal of Negro Education* 9(4) (October 1940): 554.

3. Ibid., 564–565.

4. Barbara Savage's essay "W.E.B. Du Bois and 'the Negro Church'" represents the most nuanced account of Du Bois's relationship to the black church. Savage notes that, while Du Bois readily acknowledged the central role that religion and its institutions played in the creation of black political and social life, "Du Bois's overall stance toward black Christianity and the black church remained far from celebratory. Even when he acknowledged the centrality of the church to black life, including black political life, his greatest ideological consistency was seeing that fact not as a strength but as an impediment to be overcome or managed." See Barbara Savage, "W.E.B. Du Bois and 'The Negro Church,'" *Annals of the American Academy of Political and Social Science* 568(1) (2000): 236. Du Bois did not hesitate to call the black church leaders "pretentious" and "dishonest and immoral" (quoted in Savage, 237).

5. W.E.B. Du Bois, *The Souls of Black Folk* in W.E.B. Du Bois, *Writings*, ed. Nathan Huggins (New York: Library of America, 1986), 366. Hereafter cited as *SBF*.

6. W.E.B. Du Bois, "The Church and the Negro," in Aptheker, *Writings by W.E.B. Du Bois*, 269.

7. W.E.B. Du Bois, "Religion in the South" (1907), in *Du Bois on Religion*, ed. Phil Zuckerman (New York: AltaMira, 2000), 88. See also W.E.B. Du Bois, "Will the Church Remove the Color Line?" *Christian Century* 9 (December 1931): 1554–1556.

8. W.E.B. Du Bois, *The Autobiography of W.E.B. Du Bois: A Soliloquy on Viewing My Life from the Last Decade of Its First Century* (New York: International Publishers, 1991), 43.

9. Adolph Reed Jr., *W.E.B. Du Bois and American Political Thought: Fabianism and the Color Line* (New York: Oxford University Press, 1997), 5.

10. Cornel West, "Black Strivings in a Twilight Civilization," in *The Future of the Race*, ed. Henry Louis Gates Jr. and Cornel West (New York: Knopf, 1996), 60. It is interesting to note the difference in West's critical stance on Du Bois in "Black Strivings" and *The American Evasion of Philosophy: A Genealogy of Pragmatism* (Madison: University of Wisconsin Press,1989). In *Evasion*, Du Bois occupies a heroic position as a branch on West's genealogical tree of American pragmatism. In "Black Strivings," West takes Du Bois to task for his elitism, particularly in *Souls*, where West counts "eighteen references to 'black, backward, and ungraceful' folk" (58).

11. David Levering Lewis, *W.E.B. Du Bois: Biography of a Race, 1868–1919* (New York: Holt, 1993), 65–67.

12. David Levering Lewis, *W.E.B. Du Bois: The Fight for Equality and the American Century, 1919–1963* (New York: Holt, 2000), 22, 19.

13. Herbert Aptheker, "W.E.B. Du Bois and Religion: A Brief Reassessment," *Journal of Religious Thought* 39(1) (1982): 5. In this short essay Aptheker presents a smattering of Du Bois's views on religious matters such as God and immortality.

14. W.E.B. Du Bois, ed., *The Negro Church: Report of a Social Study Made under the Direction of Atlanta University, Together with the Proceedings of the Eighth Conference for the Study of the Negro Problems, Held at Atlanta University, May 26th, 1903* (Walnut Creek, Calif.: AltaMira, 2003), 207.

15. Ibid.

16. Du Bois, *SBF*, 505.

17. Ibid., 366, 438.

18. W.E.B. Du Bois, "Untitled," in *Creative Writings by W.E.B. Du Bois*, ed. Herbert Aptheker (Millwood, N.Y.: Kraus-Thomson, 1985), 41.

19. W.E.B. Du Bois, "Hymn to the Peoples," in *Darkwater: Voices from within the Veil* (Mineola, N.Y.: Dover, 1999), 161.

20. W.E.B. Du Bois, *The World of W.E.B. Du Bois: A Quotation Sourcebook*, ed. Meyer Weinberg (Westport, Conn.: Greenwood, 1992), 165. Original "To Virginia Shattuck, April 15, 1937, W.E.B. Du Bois Papers, University of Massachusetts, Amherst.

21. Du Bois, in Weinberg, *World of W.E.B. Du Bois*, 169. Original "To Sydney Strong," May 4, 1929, W.E.B. Du Bois Papers, University of Massachusetts, Amherst.

22. W.E.B. Du Bois, "Credo," in Weinberg, *World of W.E.B. Du Bois*, 166. Original "Credo," Feb. 28, 1939, microfilm reel no. 77, frame no. 726, W.E.B. Du Bois Papers, University of Massachusetts, Amherst.

23. Du Bois, in Weinberg, *World of W.E.B. Du Bois,* 170. Original "To Larry and Carol Hautz," Sept. 29, 1954, W.E.B. Du Bois Papers, University of Massachusetts, Amherst.

24. Du Bois, "Future of Wilberforce University," 565.

25. Isaiah 52:1.

26. In this sense, Du Bois's divine discontent bears resemblance to what—more than half a century later—Martin Luther King Jr. called "divine dissatisfaction":

> So, I conclude by saying again today that we have a task and let us go out with a "divine dissatisfaction." Let us be dissatisfied until America will no longer have a high blood pressure of creeds and an anemia of deeds. Let us be dissatisfied until the tragic walls that separate the outer city of wealth and comfort and the inner city of poverty and despair shall be crushed by the battering rams of the forces of justice. Let us be dissatisfied until those that live on the outskirts of hope are brought into the metropolis of daily security. Let us be dissatisfied until slums are cast into the junk heaps of history, and every family is living in a sanitary home.... Let us be dissatisfied. Let us be dissatisfied until every state capitol houses a governor who will do justly, who will love mercy and who will walk humbly with God.... Let us be dissatisfied. And men will recognize that out of one blood God made all men to dwell upon the face of the earth. Let us be dissatisfied until that day when nobody will shout "White Power!"—when nobody will shout "Black Power!"—but everybody will talk about God's power and human power." (Martin Luther King Jr., *A Testament of Hope: The Essential Writings and Speeches of Martin Luther King Jr.,* ed. James M. Washington [New York: HarperCollins, 1986], 251.)

27. Du Bois, *SBF,* 505.

28. Arnold Rampersad, *The Art and Imagination of W.E.B. Du Bois* (New York: Schocken, 1990), 86.

29. Arnold Rampersad, "Slavery and the Literary Imagination: Du Bois's *The Souls of Black Folk,*" in *Slavery and the Literary Imagination,* ed. Deborah H. McDowell and Arnold Rampersad (Baltimore: Johns Hopkins University Press, 1989), 296, emphasis mine.

30. Aptheker, "W.E.B. Du Bois and Religion," 7. Elsewhere, Aptheker points out Du Bois's hostility toward religious institutions: "The fact is that Du Bois disliked denomination religion and detested that 'Christianity,' which became an excuse for the status quo—whether slavery or racism or war: the religion, as he once put it, of J.P. Morgan rather than of Jesus Christ." See Herbert Aptheker, "Introduction," in W.E.B. Du Bois, *Prayers for Dark People,* ed. Herbert Aptheker (Amherst: University of Massachusetts Press, 1980), viii–viii.

31. There are other works as well that emphasize Du Bois and religion and are tremendously suggestive yet, again, do not provide sustained accounts. For example, Theophus H. Smith's *Conjuring Culture: Biblical Formations of Black America* (New York: Oxford University Press, 1994) characterizes Du Bois as a biblical conjuror, yet Smith does not provide a full conversation on Du Bois's biblical rhetoric.

32. Manning Marable, "The Black Faith of W.E.B. Du Bois: Sociocultural and Political Dimensions of Black Religion," *Southern Quarterly* 23(3) (Spring 1985): 15. The depth of Adolph Reed's animus against the religious Du Bois can perhaps be measured by his accusing Marable's essay of "racial vindication," Reed's term for the "hagiographical, sanitizing impulse...all too common in the study of Afro-American thought," which "especially prevails in Du Bois scholarship" (Reed, *W.E.B. Du Bois and American Political Thought,* 5).

33. Blum's ear for the religious Du Bois is superb and capacious. Moreover, his positioning of Du Bois as a proto–black liberation theologian yields a novel reading of *Souls* as a text of black theology that claims divine favor for black America: "Read in dialogue with the religious battle over the sacred status of blacks and whites, *Souls* stood as a spectacular intervention, an act of religious defiance and theological creation.... With *Souls,* Du Bois tried to tear apart the conflation of whiteness and godliness and, conversely, to connect blackness with the divine." See Edward J. Blum, *W.E.B. Du Bois: American Prophet* (Philadelphia: University of Pennsylvania Press, 2007), 63.

34. Ibid., 160.

35. I borrow this language from Mark Cladis's work on Rousseau: "A religious vocabulary enabled Rousseau to highlight the need to be attentive to social matter—traditions—beliefs, customs, ideals, symbols, and rituals—for the sake of establishing and sustaining a vibrant, progressive democratic society" (*Public Vision, Private Lives: Rousseau, Religion and 21st-century Democracy* [New York: Columbia University Press, 2003], xxv). In fact, Du Bois's engagements with religion can be seen along similar lines—though his interests are not simply in developing the larger American democracy but also in developing African American solidarity and survival.

36. Du Bois, "The Temptation in the Wilderness," in Aptheker, *Creative Writings,* 138.

37. Indeed, Du Bois stages his own "death of God" scene in *Darkwater,* based on Frederick Douglass's famous interaction with Sojourner Truth in a Boston public marketplace. Truth takes exception to what she sees as the riot and moral anarchy in Douglass's abolitionism: " 'Frederick, is God dead?' " Du Bois does not respond to Truth's question, and like Nietzsche he seems to want his readers to consider the possibility (*Darkwater,* 102).

38. Clifford Geertz, "Religion as a Cultural System," in *Interpretation of Culture: Selected Essays* (New York: Basic Books, 1973), 104. There is much I admire about Geertz's definition of religion, yet its shortcomings are readily apparent if we ask whether Du Bois's writings can be considered religious on Geertz's account. It seems to me that they cannot. There are three main reasons for this: (1) Geertz demands that religious symbols fit into a well-oiled, coherent, working-in-unison system of beliefs; (2) he insists that religions affirm or describe the way the world really is—religions must be metaphysical; and (3) he insists that religious beliefs occupy a space that is distinct from other types of cultural spaces such as politics, secular social practices, and structures of authority. Du Bois's religiosity flagrantly violates all three.

39. Du Bois, "Immortality," in *W.E.B. Du Bois: A Reader,* ed. David Levering Lewis (New York: Holt, 1995), 134.

40. W.E.B. Du Bois, "Don't Be Bitter!" from *The Crisis* (1914), in *The Seventh Son: The Thought and Writings of W.E.B. Du Bois,* vol. 2, ed. Julius Lester (New York: Vintage, 1971).

41. W.E.B. Du Bois, "The Joy of Living," in *Writings in Periodicals Edited by Others,* ed. Herbert Aptheker, vol. 1, 1891–1909 (Millwood, N.Y.: Kraus-Thomson, 1982), 219.

42. George Santayana, *Reason in Religion,* vol. 3, *The Life of Reason* (Mineola, N.Y.: Dover, 1982), 185.

43. See George Hutchinson, *The Harlem Renaissance in Black and White* (Cambridge, Mass.: Belknap Press of Harvard University Press, 1995), especially 35–50; Ross Posnock, *Color and Culture: Black Writers and the Making of the Modern Intellectual* (Cambridge, Mass.: Harvard University Press, 1998), chapters 2–5; Paul C. Taylor, "What's the Use of Calling Du Bois a Pragmatist?" *Metaphilosophy* 35(1–2) (January 2004): 99–114, and Paul C. Taylor, *Race: A Philosophical Introduction* (Cambridge, UK: Polity, 2003).

44. See Eddie S. Glaude Jr., *In a Shade of Blue: Pragmatism and the Politics of Black America* (Chicago: University of Chicago Press, 2007) and *Exodus! Religion, Race, and Nation in Early Nineteenth-century Black America* (Chicago: University of Chicago Press, 2000); Beth Eddy, *The Rites of Identity: The Religious Naturalism and Cultural Criticism of Kenneth Burke and Ralph Ellison* (Princeton, N.J.: Princeton University Press, 2003).

45. Du Bois writes, "I became a devoted follower of James at the time he was developing his pragmatic philosophy." W.E.B. Du Bois, *The Autobiography of W.E.B. Du Bois,* 133. He continues, "I revelled [sic] in the keen analysis of William James, Josiah Royce and young George Santayana. But it was James with his pragmatism and Albert Bushnell Hart with his research method, that turned me back from the lovely but sterile land of philosophic speculation, to the social sciences as the field for gathering and interpreting that body of fact which would apply to my program for the Negro" (148). Elsewhere Du Bois expresses gratitude for "land[ing] ... squarely in the arms of William James of Harvard, for which God be praised." Some of this, it would seem, is the result of James's convincing Du Bois to "turn aside" from studying philosophy. Du Bois quotes James: "If you must study philosophy you will; but if you can turn aside into something else, do so. It is hard to earn a living with philosophy." See W.E.B. Du Bois, *Dusk of Dawn: An Essay toward an Autobiography of a Race Concept* (New Brunswick, N.J.: Transaction, 1997), 33, 39.

46. On this I am in full agreement with the best critical dissenter on thinking of Du Bois as a pragmatist. Shamoon Zamir argues that "scholars have accepted [Du Bois's pragmatist] autobiographical statements too uncritically" (*Dark Voices: W.E.B. Du Bois and American Thought, 1888–1903* [Chicago: Chicago University Press, 1995], 11). Of course, Zamir believes this is the only leg that Du Bois and pragmatism claims have to stand on. Unlike Zamir, I believe that Du Bois's pragmatism can readily be found in his writings.

47. Taylor writes, "Declining to see Du Bois as a pragmatist not only obscures important aspects of his work and life but also reinforces our willingness to overlook important aspects of pragmatic thought and practice. Reading Du Bois pragmatically, then, is doubly illuminating. It reveals aspects both of Du Bois and pragmatism we might otherwise miss" (Taylor, "What's the Use of Calling Du Bois a Pragmatist?" 100).

48. Lewis, *W.E.B. Du Bois: The Fight for Equality,* 307.

49. Jeffrey Stout, "Commitments and Traditions in the Study of Religious Ethics," *Journal of Religious Ethics* 25(3) (1998): 51.

50. Stout, in any event, does not intend the list to be authoritative, and his essay represents his further hope that "readers who share my democratic commitments will be disposed, even on the basis of the hints dropped here, to join me in the scholarship that will be required" in developing it further (ibid., 53). My attempt to explain what Du Bois's variety of interests in religion says about religion's role in creating persuasive and compelling public narratives of American life represents my attempt to answer Stout's call.

51. Ibid., 52, emphases in original.

52. See Jonathan Z. Smith's essay, "Religion, Religions, Religious," in *Critical Terms for Religious Studies,* ed. Mark C. Taylor (Chicago: University of Chicago Press, 1998), 269–283. Russell McCutcheon's *Manufacturing Religion: The Discourse on Sui Generis Religion and The Politics of Nostalgia* (New York: Oxford University Press, 1997).

53. From an unpublished essay by Jeffrey Stout, "The Concept of Religion."

54. See Zora Neale Hurston, "Characteristics of Negro Expression," in *Folklore, Memoirs, and Other Writings,* ed. Cheryl A. Wall (New York: Library of America, 1995), 830–846.

55. Ludwig Wittgenstein, *Philosophical Investigations,* trans. G.E.M. Anscombe (Malden, Mass.: Blackwell, 1997), 32e.

56. Of course, someone—a fundamentalist—might respond that only the narrowest and fewest features count as legitimate family resemblances, and that same person might have three necessary features in mind. Instead of arguing about whether those three are the essential family resemblances, we might have a discussion about the cultural, social, and political factors that might lead the fundamentalist to insist on a narrow definition and the Wittgensteinian pluralist to allow for a larger variety of resemblances. In this, religion too becomes a discursive affair.

57. This is the beginning of a response to Timothy Fitzgerald's criticisms of "family resemblances." Fitzgerald argues that "the problem...is that on this view we have no way of knowing who are genuine members of the family and who are not. With human families, we at least have laws that specify the rules of descent and inheritance, and these have to be extremely precise in settling disputes." See Timothy Fitzgerald, *The Ideology of Religious Studies* (New York: Oxford University Press, 2000), 26. I believe Fitzgerald is taking a much too narrow view of how variably humans understand family. The laws and the constructions of family to which they apply are much less precise and much more diverse and elastic than he is willing to acknowledge. Besides, not being able to identify "genuine" members of the family

becomes a problem only if we want to identify them. I agree with him that using "family resemblances" does not allow us to distinguish genuine family members: I simply do not believe that we need to determine who they are. In fact, it seems much more interesting to think about what makes someone a family member when they do not possess normative familial markers.

58. The stripes of these recent scholars are remarkably varied. Pragmatist perspectives include James Edwards's *The Plain Sense of Things: The Fate of Religion in an Age of Normal Nihilism* (University Park: Pennsylvania State University Press, 1997). For a different postmodern perspective see John D. Caputo's *On Religion* (New York: Routledge, 2001); Michel Gauchet, *The Disenchantment of the World: A Political History of Religion,* trans. Oscar Burge (Princeton, N.J.: Princeton University Press, 1999); and Mark C. Taylor, *Erring: A Postmodern A/theology* (Chicago: University of Chicago Press, 1987). From anthropology and cultural studies, see Talal Asad, *Formations of the Secular: Christianity, Islam, Modernity* (Palo Alto, Calif.: Stanford University Press, 2003).

59. Blum, *W.E.B. Du Bois,* 11.

60. Kenneth Burke, *The Rhetoric of Religion: Studies in Logology* (Berkeley: University of California Press, 1970), v, emphasis in the original.

61. Ibid., vi. Also quoted in Eddy, *Rites of Identity,* 2. Eddy's work introduced me to Burke.

62. Sally McFague, *Metaphorical Theology: Models of God in Religious Language* (Philadelphia: Fortress Press, 1982), 15.

63. Ibid., 17.

CHAPTER I

1. Richard Wright, *The Outsider* (New York: HarperPerennial, 2003), 483.

2. W.E.B. Du Bois, *Dusk of Dawn: An Essay toward an Autobiography of a Race Concept* (New Brunswick, N.J.: Transaction, 1997), 153; emphasis mine.

3. W.E.B. Du Bois, *Dark Princess: A Romance* (Jackson: University Press of Mississippi, 1995), 19.

4. Ibid., 21.

5. Ibid., 25–26.

6. W.E.B. Du Bois, *The Gift of Black Folk: The Negroes in the Making of America* (New York: Oxford University Press, 2007), 117.

7. Du Bois, *Dark Princess,* 25.

8. W.E.B. Du Bois, *Prayers for Dark People,* ed. Herbert Aptheker (Amherst: University of Massachusetts Press, 1980), 62.

9. See Gayraud Wilmore, *Black Religion and Black Radicalism: An Interpretation of the Religious History of African Americans* (Maryknoll, N.Y.: Orbis, 1998).

10. Manning Marable, "The Black Faith of W.E.B. Du Bois: Sociocultural and Political Dimensions of Black Religion," *Southern Quarterly* 23(3) (Spring 1985): 24.

11. In my view, no such *single* category exists. The Christianity of David Walker is different from that of Nat Turner, which is different from Sojourner Truth's and

Alexander Crummell's. My point is not to deny the very idea of religious traditions, African American or otherwise. Continuities, resemblances, and historical relations are quite real; however, these do not make up a single narrative, a single version.

12. Edward J. Blum, *W.E.B. Du Bois: American Prophet* (Philadelphia: University of Pennsylvania Press, 2007), 180.

13. W.E.B. Du Bois, *W.E.B. Du Bois: A Reader,* ed. David Levering Lewis (New York: Holt, 1995), 134.

14. W.E.B. Du Bois, "Easter," in *Creative Writings by W.E.B. Du Bois,* ed. Herbert Aptheker (White Plains, N.Y.: Kraus-Thomson, 1985), 90.

15. Du Bois, "The Song of Smoke," in Aptheker, *Creative Writings by W.E.B. Du Bois,* 10.

16. Du Bois, "A Hymn to the Peoples," in *Darkwater: Voices from within the Veil* (Mineola, N.Y.: Dover, 1999), 161.

17. Eric Sundquist's observation inches closer to capturing the sort of tension I am striving for: "If black religion did not provide [Du Bois] a language, however, it did provide the central matrix of his reconstruction of African American culture" (Eric J. Sundquist, *To Wake the Nations: Race in the Making of American Literature* [Cambridge, Mass.: Harvard University Press, 1993], 459). It is certainly true that Du Bois did not speak in the vernacular of black religion, particularly black religion of the South. However, it is not the case that black religion did not provide him with any language. He clearly borrows the language of "soul," not to mention all the biblical language and narratives, from black religion. Moreover, what Sundquist fails to account for is the way that Du Bois reworks and wrestles with the matrix of black religion by rejecting the supernatural.

18. Consider, for example, Du Bois's honest acknowledgement that he began to identify strongly with other African Americans only when he traveled south at the age of eighteen to Fisk University: "My African racial feeling was then purely a matter of my own later learning and reaction; my recoil from the assumptions of the whites; my experiences in the South at Fisk (Du Bois, *Dusk of Dawn,* 115). My point is not to question Du Bois's "blackness"; rather, it is to note that Du Bois himself seeks to complicate blackness, in particular by sometimes acknowledging the distance between him and black folk. Like Shamoon Zamir, I believe the rhetorical question of the last lines of "The Forethought" to *Souls*—"Need I add that I who speak here am bone of the bone and flesh of the flesh of them that live within the Veil?" (W.E.B. Du Bois, *The Souls of Black Folk,* in *Writings,* ed. Nathan Huggins [New York: Library of America, 1986], 360; hereafter cited as *SBF*)—is multivalent, signaling both intimacy and distance from black folk. Why the need to "add" this? Zamir writes:

> Du Bois, right from the very start of *Souls*, problematizes his own status as a guide to the black world for the white reader and incorporates the exploration of the difference between himself and the vast majority of blacks as part of the central drama of *Souls*. If *Souls* is a journey into the world behind the veil for the white reader, it is also presented as a journey into unknown or half-known aspects of black life for Du Bois himself. (Shamoon Zamir,

Dark Voices: W.E.B. Du Bois and American Thought, 1883–1903 [Chicago: University of Chicago Press, 1995], 139).

19. Du Bois's efforts are not to execute a clean break from tradition but are the *clinamen* of the strong poet: "a corrective movement...which implies that the precursor poem went accurately up to a certain point, but then should have swerved, precisely in the direction that the new poem moves." Harold Bloom, *The Anxiety of Influence: A Theory of Poetry* (New York: Oxford University Press, 1973), 14.

20. Cited in Henry S. Levinson, *The Religious Investigations of William James* (Chapel Hill: University of North Carolina Press, 1981), 58. Hereafter cited as *William James.* Levinson writes the following of James's account of the religious demand: "Religious experience encompassed both the sense of *well-doing* that the moralist achieved and the sense of *well-being* that religious people demanded but moral activity could never guarantee." See Levinson, *William James*, 91; emphasis in the original.

21. Russell McCutcheon uses Daniel Dennett's epistemological metaphors of skyhooks to represent ahistorical sources of knowledge and cranes to represent histor- icist sources: "Naturalism...sees our efforts to know the world around us as the work of cranes. Naturalist efforts to study religion, we could say, take as their datum the intriguing fact that some humans, from time to time, invoke skyhooks. This is not to say that skyhooks are not in fact out there or in here somewhere, but it is to say that in the discourse of the university, where our claims to knowledge are not privileged but open to debate and scrutiny, all we have are cranes." See Russell McCutcheon, *Manufacturing Religion: The Discourse on Sui Generis Religion and the Politics of Nostalgia* (New York: Oxford University Press, 1997), x–xi.

22. George Hutchinson, *The Harlem Renaissance in Black and White* (Cambridge, Mass.: Belknap Press of Harvard University Press, 1995), 14. Louis Menand's Pulitzer Prize–winning *Metaphysical Club* is such an example. The irony is that Menand argues that pragmatism's distrust of scientific and idealist claims to truth are rooted in the way dogmatic claims about race and human essences led to the carnage of the American Civil War. In other words, on the account Menand gives, concerns of race spur pragmatism's development. Yet his account of pragma- tism does not substantively deal with the concerns of race. See Louis Menand, *The Metaphysical Club: A Story of Ideas in America* (New York: Farrar, Straus & Giroux, 2001), especially part one, 3–71. Bruce Kuklick's otherwise well-nuanced narra- tives of American philosophy also fits Hutchinson's description. See Bruce Kuklick, *The Rise of American Philosophy: Cambridge, Massachusetts, 1860–1930* (New Haven, Conn.: Yale University Press, 1977).

23. See Ellison's classic essay, "What America Would Be Like without Blacks," in *The Collected Essays of Ralph Ellison*, ed. John F. Callahan (New York: Modern Library, 1995), 577–584. Also, consider Ellison's 1973 response to a dashiki-clad Robert G. O'Meally, who asked Ellison, "Don't you think the Harlem Renaissance failed because we failed to create institutions to preserve our gains?" O'Meally recounts: "He drew on his cigar and calmly told me: 'No.' Just before being led toward the stage, he paused to look at me with steely eyes: 'We *do* have institutions,' he said.

'We have the Constitution and the Bill of Rights. *And we have Jazz'"* (Robert O'Meally, "Introduction: Jazz Shapes," in *Living with Music: Ralph Ellison's Jazz Writings,* ed. Robert O'Meally [New York: Modern Library, 2002], xi; emphasis in the original).

24. I am playing off Du Bois's construction in *Souls* to "catch the shadows of the color-line" (Du Bois, *SBF,* 488).

25. Ralph Waldo Emerson, *The Spiritual Emerson: Essential Writings,* ed. David M. Robinson (Boston: Beacon, 2004), 144; emphasis mine.

26. Du Bois, *SBF,* 359.

27. Ibid.

28. Ibid., 363.

29. Du Bois, *Dusk of Dawn,* 551, 776.

30. My emphasis on pragmatism as a critical theory about how to create problems—problematizing—represents a shift away from thinking of it as a method of problem solving. This phrase, "problem solving," has led to a key misunderstanding of pragmatism as a crude theory of instrumentalism, of taking the road of least resistance, and of truth being purely a matter of public acceptance. Without exception, the early pragmatists renounced this model. James realized that the title of his widely read book, *The Will to Believe,* was in part responsible for this impression. He came to regret the title precisely because it gave the false impression that pragmatism was a vulgar endorsement for the power of positive thinking: "All the critics, neglecting the essay, pounced on the title" (William James, *Pragmatism: A New Name for Some Old Ways of Thinking* [Cambridge, Mass.: Harvard University Press, 1975], 124); properly understood, James's "will to believe" represents his attempt to justify believing—"our right to believe" (in light of a universe that is radically full of problems and conflicts). It is not a model of belief that lends itself to renouncing life's stubborn difficulties:

> When you find a man living on the ragged edge of his consciousness, pent in to his sin and want and incompleteness, and consequently inconsolable, and then simply tell him that all is well with him, that he must stop his worry, break with his discontent, and give up his anxiety, you seem to him to come with pure absurdities...as if you proposed to assert cold-blooded falsehoods. "The will to believe" cannot be stretched as far as that. We can make ourselves more faithful to a belief of which we have the rudiments, but we cannot create a belief out of whole cloth when our perception actively assures us of its opposite. (William James: *The Varieties of Religious Experience* [New York: Penguin, 1982], 211–212; hereafter cited as *Varieties.*)

Charles Peirce's understanding of belief is essentially identical: "A man may go through, systematically keeping out of view all that might cause a change in his opinions, and if only he succeeds...I do not see what can be said against his doing so....But this method of fixing of belief, what may be called the method of tenacity, will be unable to hold its ground in practice. The social impulse is against it" (Charles S. Peirce, "Fixation of Belief," in *The Essential Peirce: Selected Philosophical Writings,* vol. 1, 1867–1893, ed. Nathan Houser and Christian Kloesel [Bloomington: Indiana University Press, 1992], 116). Here is an example of Dewey on the same topic: "But the idea that this causal factor can be changed by purely direct means, by an exercise of 'will' or 'thought' is illusory. A change of desire and purpose can itself be effected only indirectly, by a change in one's actual relation to environment" (John Dewey, *The Quest for Certainty*, in *John Dewey: The Later Works, 1925–1953*, vol. 4, 1929, ed. Jo Ann Boydston [Carbondale: Southern Illinois University Press, 1988], 186).

31. Dewey, *Quest for Certainty*, 81.

32. Ibid., 83.

33. James, *Pragmatism*, 32.

34. Zamir, *Dark Voices*, 11; emphasis mine. Robert Gooding-Williams, whose work I strongly disagree with but also find productively provocative, flatly rejects Cornel West's characterization of Du Bois's pragmatism: "Du Bois's voice cannot be unequivocally or even plausibly interpreted as that of a pragmatist, and so should be eliminated from West's narrative" (Robert Gooding-Williams, "Evading Narrative Myth, Evading Prophetic Pragmatism: Cornel West's *The American Evasion of Philosophy*," *Massachusetts Review* 33[4] [Winter 1991–1992]: 531). Other critical voices of Du Bois's pragmatism include eminent scholars Wilson Jeremiah Moses and David Levering Lewis, who also challenge the idea of Du Bois's pragmatism. Moses writes: "Nothing could be more incorrect [than] to view this young authoritarian mystic as an heir to the liberalism of Thomas Jefferson or the pragmatism of William James." See Wilson J. Moses, "W.E.B. Du Bois's 'The Conservation of Races' and Its Context: Idealism, Conservatism, and Hero Worship," *Massachusetts Review* 34(2) (Summer 1993): 289. Lewis's biography of Du Bois calls into question James's influence on Du Bois, claiming that "philosophical principles were less important to the instructor-student bond than the personality of the philosopher." As far as those principles go, Lewis sees Du Bois as something of an absolute idealist: "He was an idealist by temperament, always believing that it was possible, somehow, to get from the world's welter—observed phenomena—to the bedrock of principles—upper-case Truth." See David Levering Lewis, *W.E.B. Du Bois: Biography of a Race, 1868–1919* (New York: Holt, 1993), 89.

35. Very interestingly, underneath his severe and ungenerous reading of James, Zamir presents in bits and pieces a more nuanced account of Du Bois's relationship to James's work. Zamir writes that "James's defense of plurality, his sense of energy and openness of process" "had a liberating impact" on Du Bois: "It is not that James offers Du Bois nothing that can be recuperated as positive value. James's emphasis on contingency and striving in the real world plays a significant part.... James plants the germ of pragmatism in the young Du Bois that later flowers into a radical-liberal social analysis and activism" (Zamir, *Dark Voices*, 34, 24, 46, 73).

36. Gooding-Williams writes that pragmatism "has been largely oblivious to feminist, black, and third-world concerns" and claims that West's insistence on Du Bois "is best read as marking a huge rift between [West's] narrative of American pragmatism and the politics essential to prophetic pragmatism" (Gooding-Williams, "Evading Narrative Myth, Evading Prophetic Pragmatism," 530, 533). Zamir sees pragmatism as the crucial part of the "traditions of American philosophical and social thought [that] failed W.E.B. Du Bois" (Zamir, *Dark Voices*, 1). Larry Miller attempts a forceful case

for James's late-in-life political activism. However, he admits that, even in James's last years, "he directed most of his energy toward problems without obvious ethnic implications. He did enough during his last years to stimulate and influence major ethnic theorists, but he formulated no coherent theory of his own." Miller cites Du Bois as one of those theorists—"heroes"—who learned from James: "If he was not a hero of the twentieth-century campaign against ethnocentric scholarship, he was a hero to the heroes." See Larry C. Miller, "William James and Twentieth-century Ethnic Thought," *American Quarterly* 31(4) (Autumn 1979): 539, 553.

37. James Kloppenberg, *Uncertain Victory: Social Democracy and Progressivism in European and American Thought, 1870–1920* (New York: Oxford University Press, 1986), 195.

38. William James, "A World of Pure Experience," in *Essays in Radical Empiricism* (Cambridge, Mass.: Harvard University Press, 1976), 22, 23; emphasis in the original.

39. Kloppenberg, *Uncertain Victory*, 174. Here is Henry Levinson's vision of pragmatism as cultural criticism:

> Once we admit the pragmatists' acceptance of the contingent and historical character of existence, once we take into account their animus toward the metaphilosophical position that philosophy can be placed on the secure path of a rigorous science capable of breaking through historical variation and change, along with their rejection of foundationalism, scientism, representationalism, essentialism, and existential arrogance, it makes more sense to construe these pragmatists as trying to forge something that looks more like present-day cultural criticism than transcendental idealism, old-time epistemology, or Kant's critical philosophy. It makes more sense to describe them as fashioning a model of the way we hang together all the ways in which we hang things together—a synoptic picture of our intellectually active life—capacious enough to pay all the compliments due the arts and sciences along with every other sort of rational human activity (including religious ones), than it does to picture them constructing something as singular as a distinctive theory of knowledge (Henry Samuel Levinson, "Stuck between Debility and Demand: Religion and Enlightenment Traditions among the Pragmatists," in *Knowledge and Belief in America: Enlightenment Traditions and Modern Religious Thought*, ed. William M. Shea and Peter A. Huff [New York: Cambridge University Press, 1995], 276).

40. William James, "Does 'Consciousness' Exist?" in *Essays in Radical Empiricism*, 5; emphasis in the original.

41. William James, *The Principles of Psychology* (Cambridge, Mass.: Harvard University Press, 1983), 281, hereafter cited as *PP*.

42. James, "The Moral Philosopher and the Moral Life," in *The Will to Believe: and Other Essays in Popular Philosophy* (Mineola, N.Y.: Dover, 1956), 210.

43. Ibid., 239.

44. Du Bois, *SBF*, 502.

45. Ernest Allen is one of the few critics who sees the idea of "twoness" in Du Bois "emerging as an equally distinct but more positively laden notion.... Du Bois recognized negative as well as positive regions of duality in African-American life. What he wished to eliminate was not the two-fold character of African-American life, but rather its most alienating characteristics." See Ernest Allen Jr., "Ever Feeling One's Twoness: 'Double Ideals' and 'Double Consciousness,' in *The Souls of Black Folk,*" *Critique of Anthropology* 12(3) (1992): 262, 272. Oddly, Allen also renounces this very idea within the same essay. Double consciousness "with its positive connotations, the notion of 'second sight' as a gift has no parallel with the way in which Du Bois employs any of the other permutations of 'twoness' in *The Souls of Black Folk*. For Du Bois, manifestations of African-American 'twoness,' in the largest sense, posed more problems than possibilities at the turn of the century" (272). More typical are readings that see Du Bois as trying to imagine life without the terms of race. Stanley Brodwin's reading emphasizes this theme of transcendence: "Du Bois structured fourteen essays in the form of a neo-Hegelian dialectic whose stage of synthesis carried him—and by extension, all those who would follow—into a spiritual realm of historical and racial understanding that does not merely rend, but transcends the veil of color." See Stanley Brodwin, "The Veil Transcended: Form and Meaning in W.E.B. Du Bois' 'The Souls of Black Folk,'" *Journal of Black Studies* 2(3) (March 1972): 306. Also, Dickson Bruce follows these lines in his claim that Du Boisian double consciousness is of a piece with Emersonian Romanticism in seeing "social forces inhibiting genuine self-realization." See Dickson D. Bruce Jr., "W.E.B. Du Bois and the Idea of Double Consciousness," *American Literature* 64(2) (June 1992): 300.

46. Du Bois, *SBF*, 359.

47. Toni Morrison, "Home," in *The House That Race Built: Black Americans, U.S. Terrain,* ed. Wahneema Lubiano (New York: Pantheon, 1997), 12.

48. Du Bois, *SBF*, 368.

49. Ibid., 488; emphasis in the original.

50. Ibid.

51. Ibid., 431.

52. Ross Posnock, *Color and Culture: Black Writers and the Making of the Modern Intellectual* (Cambridge, Mass.: Harvard University Press, 1998), 117–118.

53. Ibid., 105. Du Bois himself was aware of the element of vagueness in *Souls*. In a 1904 review of *Souls,* Du Bois apologizes for "a penumbra of vagueness and half-veiled allusion which has made these and others especially impatient. How far this fault is in me and how far it is in the nature of the message I am not sure." See W.E.B. Du Bois, *Book Reviews by W.E.B. Du Bois,* ed. Herbert Aptheker (Millwood, N.Y.: KTO Press, 1977), 9.

54. Du Bois, *SBF*, 359.

55. My claim that Du Bois uses the veil as a tool of careful historical analysis runs counter to an essay that I admire greatly. Cynthia Schrager sees in Du Bois's use of the veil and double consciousness a mystical political protest against the medical materialism. For Schrager, the veil represents an embrace of the feminine mystical; on these terms, the veil and double consciousness are meant to obscure more

than clarify. See Cynthia D. Schrager, "Both Sides of the Veil: Race, Science, and Mysticism in W.E.B. Du Bois," *American Quarterly* 48(4) (1996): 551–586.

56. This reading contrasts sharply with Robert Gooding-William's claim that "Du Bois' master trope, 'the veil,' betokens an idealistic outlook that cannot speak adequately to our need to explain the institutional circumstances of human existence." See Robert Gooding-Williams, "Philosophy of History and Social Critique in *The Souls of Black Folk*," *Social Science Information* 26(1) (1987): 113.

57. Du Bois, *SBF*, 410.

58. John Dewey, *A Common Faith* (New Haven, Conn.: Yale University Press, 1962), 49.

59. Anthony Appiah, "The Uncompleted Argument: Du Bois and the Illusion of Race," in *"Race," Writing, and Difference*, ed. Henry Louis Gates Jr. (Chicago: University of Chicago Press, 1986), 21–37.

60. W.E.B. Du Bois, "The Conservation of Races," in *Writings*, 818, 822.

61. For an incisive refutation of Appiah and the best account of Du Bois's racial pragmatism, see Paul C. Taylor, "Appiah's Uncompleted Argument: W.E.B. Du Bois and the Reality of Race," *Social Theory and Practice* 26(1) (Spring 2000): 103–128. Taylor, in fact, reads Du Bois's "Conservation" and its seemingly ontological claims about blackness as a form of rhetorical play that stands as evidence of Du Bois's pragmatism:

> Du Bois was a pragmatist, which means in part that we should interpret his argument in light of at least certain Deweyan convictions: that judgments, even metaphysical judgments, are hypotheses offered in the context of specific situations; that such hypotheses are to be assessed for the extent to which they facilitate human efforts to cope with these situations; and that judgment hypotheses are motivated by and laden with the same values and interests that distinguish situations, values that are sometimes political. (111)

62. Du Bois, "Of Work and Wealth," in *Darkwater*, 56.

63. Du Bois, *Dusk of Dawn*, 133.

64. W.E.B. Du Bois, "The Name 'Negro'" in *The Seventh Son: The Thought and Writings of W.E.B. Du Bois*, vol. 2, ed. Julius Lester (New York: Vintage, 1971), 55. Barton, it should be noted, preferred to be identified solely as "American."

65. Ibid., 56.

66. James, *Pragmatism*, 102.

67. This account of Du Bois's pragmatism is deeply indebted to Eddie Glaude, who more than anyone has shown the ways in which pragmatic accounts of race have deep roots in African American renderings. His latest book, *In a Shade of Blue: Pragmatism and the Politics of Black America*, is a continuation of the tradition that he unearths in his first book, *Exodus!* In fact, Du Bois's letter to the young Barton reminds me of Glaude's reading in *Exodus!* of William Watkins's pragmatic construction of racial identity in his letter to the 1838 convention of the American Moral Reform Society (AMRS). Against the AMRS's position that race distinctions only reified the mind-set and politics of discrimination and thus should be abandoned,

Watkins writes: "In vain do we carp at some supposed inapplicability of a term as applied to a certain object, when imperious custom or common consent has established the relation between the sign and the word." Glaude points out that Watkins proceeds pragmatically: He is concerned with the social effects of race talk and not the ontological question of whether race *really* exists. Watkins preserves race talk, writes Glaude, because "[g]iven the social relations of the nation, race language provided a useful tool to single out and account for the distinctiveness of their oppression." See Eddie S. Glaude Jr., *Exodus! Religion, Race, and Nation in Early Nineteenth-century Black America* (Chicago: University of Chicago Press, 2000), 134–140, 145–159. Also see his "Pragmatism and Black Identity: An Alternative Approach," *Nepantla: Views from South* 2(2) (2001): 295–316.

68. W.E.B. Du Bois, "The Name Negro," 57. There is even a way that Du Bois's own stubborn refusal to give up the name "Negro" bears a Jamesian stamp. James writes: "Names are arbitrary, but once understood they must be kept to. We mustn't now call Abel 'Cain' or Cain 'Abel.' If we do, we ungear ourselves from the whole book of Genesis, and from all its connexions with the universe of speech and fact down to the present time" (James, *Pragmatism*, 103).

69. Du Bois's need for a "word that means Us" is a paradigmatic example of Eddie Glaude's understanding of Wilfred Sellars's concept of "we-intensions" as historically conditioned expressions of racial solidarity. See Glaude, *Exodus!* 15–16.

70. My claim that Du Bois's use of the word "Negro" looks both backward and forward borrows Jeffrey Stout's use of "retrospective" and "prospective" to classify the different criteria with which black nationalists construct community. See Jeffrey Stout, "Theses on Black Nationalism," in *Is It Nation Time? Contemporary Essays on Black Power and Black Nationalism*, ed. Eddie S. Glaude Jr. (Chicago: University of Chicago Press, 2002), 243.

71. James, "Philosophical Conceptions and Practical Results," in *Pragmatism*, 259.

72. James, "Is Life Worth Living?" in *Will to Believe*, 41.

73. In addition to the book on James, Levinson has written definitively on George Santayana in *Santayana, Pragmatism, and the Spiritual Life* (Chapel Hill: University of North Carolina Press, 1992); hereafter cited as *Santayana*. For a stirring account of pragmatic religious naturalism shaped by Levinson, see William Hart, "Cornel West: Between Rorty's Rock and Hauerwas's Hard Place," *American Journal of Theology and Philosophy* 19(2) (May 1998): 151–172.

74. Cited in Levinson, *William James*, 25.

75. W.E.B. Du Bois, "Exchange with George Vaughn: Spiritual 'Awakening,'" in *The Correspondence of W.E.B. Du Bois*, vol. 1, ed. Herbert Aptheker (Amherst: University of Massachusetts Press, 1978), 477–478.

76. George Santayana, *Reason in Religion*, vol. 3, *The Life of Reason* (Mineola, N.Y.: Dover, 1982), 12. In lines like this one, it is possible to hear the influence Santayana had on Clifford Geertz. It is often overlooked that Geertz begins his famous essay, "Religion as a Cultural System," with an epigraph from Santayana's *Reason in Religion*. For a brief mention of the connection between Geertz and Santayana see Levinson, *Santayana*, 102.

77. James, *Varieties*, 523. At the end of *Varieties*, James writes:

> Disregarding the over-beliefs, and confining ourselves to what is common
> and generic, we have *in the fact that the conscious person is continuous with a*
> *wider self through which saving experiences come*...If I now proceed to state
> my own hypothesis about the farther limits of this extension of our per-
> sonality...the world of our present consciousness is only one out of many
> worlds of consciousness that exist, and that those other worlds must contain
> experiences which have a meaning for our life also; and that although in
> the main their experiences and those of this world keep discrete, yet the two
> become continuous at certain points, and higher energies filter in. (515, 519;
> emphasis in the original)

James, it is important to see, does not go so far as to endorse a traditional monotheistic supernaturalism. He is decidedly uncertain about the forms and workings of
these other worlds of consciousness.

78. As Stanley Hauerwas observes of James, "Whether the God to whom prayer
is directed exists does not seem to bother James. What makes prayer authentic is not
the status or character of the one to whom one prays, but the subjectivity of the one
who is praying" (Stanley Hauerwas, *With the Grain of the Universe* [Grand Rapids,
Mich.: Brazos, 2001], 66).

79. Santayana, *Reason in Religion*, 190. Santayana's language reminds me
of Reverend Hickman's sermon, "The Valley of Dry Bones," in Ralph Ellison's
Juneteenth: "Amen, stirring, and right there in the midst of all our death and bur-
iedness, the voice of God spoke down the Word.../ Crying Do! I said, Do! Crying
Doooo—. These dry bones live? / I said, Do...I said Do, Son of Man, Doooooo!—
These dry bones live?" See *Juneteenth: A Novel*, ed. John F. Callahan (New York:
Random, 1999), 125–127.

80. Levinson, *Santayana*, 73.

81. James, *Pragmatism*, 125.

82. Levinson, *Santayana*, 97.

83. Ibid., 35.

84. Ibid., 34–35.

85. Santayana, *Reason in Religion*, 11, 30.

86. Dewey, *Common Faith*, 80.

87. James, *Pragmatism*, 23.

88. Ibid., 64.

89. James, "The Moral Philosopher and Moral Life," in *Will to Believe*, 195;
emphasis in the original. On a related note, it is worth pointing out that Zamir's
account of James's consciousness as "passive and self-absorbed introspection" and
perception "as a faculty of...registering objects" misrepresents the basics of James's
understanding of perception (Zamir, *Dark Voices*, 12). James understands perception not as a wholly passive process but as a form of experience actively shaped by
the senses: "We carve out everything, just as we carve out constellations to suit our
human purposes....We break the flux of sensible reality into things, then, at our

will" (James, *Pragmatism*, 122). Here is a longer representative passage from *The Principles of Psychology*: "Out of what is in itself an indistinguishable, swarming continuum, devoid of distinction or emphasis, our senses make for us, by attending to this notion and ignoring that, a world full of contrasts, of sharp accents...And then again, among the sensations we get from separate things, what happens? The mind selects again. It chooses certain of the sensations to represent the thing most truly, and considers the rest as its appearances, modified by the conditions of the moment" (James, *PP*, 274). James's understanding of perception is one of the clearest examples of the way pragmatism *joins* empiricism to rationalism: "Take our sensations. *That* they are is undoubtedly beyond our control; but *which* we attend to, note, and make emphatic in our conclusions depends on our interests" (James, *Pragmatism*, 118; emphasis in the original).

90. James, *Pragmatism*, 23.

91. Dewey, *Common Faith*, 70, 49. Here is a similar passage from James: "The whole universe of concrete objects, as we know them, swims...for all of us, in a wider and higher universe of abstract ideas, that lend it its significance...goodness, beauty, strength, significance, justice....Such ideas...form the back-ground for all our facts, the fountain-head of all the possibilities we conceive of" (James, *Varieties*, 99).

92. John Dewey, "The Need for a Recovery of Philosophy," in *John Dewey: The Middle Works, 1899–1924*, vol. 10, *1916–1917*, ed. Jo Ann Boydston (Carbondale: Southern Illinois University Press, 1980), 21.

93. Cited in Levinson, *Santayana*, 98.

94. James, *Pragmatism*, 137. Paul Taylor provides a similar reading of James's meliorism. Like me, he sees a type of Jamesian meliorism in Du Bois. See Paul C. Taylor, "What's the Use of Calling Du Bois a Pragmatist?" *Metaphilosophy* 35(1–2) (January 2004): 101–103.

95. James, "The Dilemma of Determinism," in *Will to Believe*, 171. Zamir ignores James's indictment of optimism in "The Dilemma of Determinism." He also gets James's use of the "gnosticism" backward. Zamir claims that James sees "gnosticism" as a form of pessimism (Zamir, *Dark Voices*, 36). However, for James, "gnosticism" represents a type of *optimism*; the gnostic guarantee that all is right with the universe "violates my sense of moral reality through and through...gnostical romanticism, wrenches my personal instincts in quite a violent a way...transforms life from a tragic reality into an insincere melodramatic exhibition, as foul or as tawdry as any one's diseased curiosity pleases to carry it out" (*Will to Believe*, 177). This should make it clear that James's sensibilities are far from blindly, naively, and foolishly optimistic.

96. James, *Pragmatism*, 141.

97. Ibid., 142–143; emphasis mine.

98. Ibid., 137.

99. James, *Varieties*, 4.

100. Ibid., 31.

101. Ibid., 74. This ambivalence of James to follow his own naturalism in *Varieties* is to my mind the most interesting drama of that text. In other texts such

as *Will to Believe* and *Pragmatism* James is committed to a naturalism that allows for social, cultural, and political factors. For example, in "The Will to Believe" James conceives of belief as shaped not only by private psychology but also by the interposition of social and historical factors: "When I say 'willing nature,'... I mean all such factors of belief as fear and hope, prejudice and passion, imitation and partisanship, the circumpressure of our caste and set" (*Will to Believe*, 9). Nonetheless, in the *Varieties,* James holds to (perhaps desperately) the hope of a vague supernaturalism that "still supposes that grace or the achievement of well-being is an event that occurs outside cultural life, indeed, on the margins of natural life" (Levinson, *Santayana*, 93). For an account of the way James's *Varieties* betrays his pragmatic naturalism, see Wayne Proudfoot's "Pragmatism and an 'Unseen Order' in *Varieties*," in *William James and a Science of Religions: Reexperiencing the Varieties of Religious Experience*, ed. Wayne Proudfoot (New York: Columbia University Press, 2004), 31–47.

102. Levinson, *Santayana*, 93.

103. Santayana, *Reason in Religion*, 47.

104. Ibid., 12, 8.

105. Levinson, *Santayana*, 214.

106. Dewey, *Common Faith*, 70.

107. Ibid., 23.

108. Ibid., 79. See also "Philosophy and Democracy," "Search for the Great Community," and "Creative Democracy—The Task before Us," in *The Essential Dewey*, vol. 1, *Pragmatism, Education, Democracy*, ed. Larry Hickman and Thomas Alexander (Bloomington: Indiana University Press, 1998), 71–78, 293–307, 340–343. It is Dewey's connecting faith and democracy that lead Cornel West to position him as the progenitor of West's "prophetic pragmatism." See Cornel West, *The Evasion of American Philosophy: A Genealogy of Pragmatism* (Madison: University of Wisconsin Press, 1989), 69–111, 211–239.

109. Levinson, *Santayana*, 259.

110. Ibid.; emphasis in the original.

111. Santayana, *Reason in Religion*, 33.

112. Ibid., 29.

113. Cited in Levinson, *Santayana*, 5.

114. Ibid., 42.

115. Du Bois, *Prayers for Dark People*, 53.

116. W.E.B. Du Bois, *Color and Democracy: Colonies and Peace* (New York: Harcourt, Brace, 1945), 137.

117. Du Bois, *W.E.B. Du Bois: A Reader*, 134.

118. On this I am in disagreement with Harold Bloom's reading of Du Bois's double consciousness, which Bloom very briefly glosses in *The American Religion* as an example of the apolitical gnostic mind-set that typifies American religiosity. He describes it as "the division in the self that is part of the African-American cultural legacy... which I think is the inevitable paradigm now for all similar American quests. Is the self to be made free of itself, or free of other selves? The goal is to be made free for God, however you interpret *that* freedom, but do you deny the self for

a community, past or present, or do you affirm the self by evading community?"
See Harold Bloom, *The American Religion: The Emergence of a Post-Christian Nation*
(New York: Simon & Schuster, 1992), 254. I find these observations a nonstarter
for talking about African American religious consciousness because the scale of its
generalizations is too big. Nonetheless, as I argue in the next chapter, we would do
well to hold on to the basic insight that Du Bois's double consciousness is rooted in
his account of African American religion.

119. W.E.B. Du Bois, "The Revelation of Saint Orgne the Damned," in
Writings, 1058.

120. Du Bois, *Color and Democracy*, 137.

121. W.E.B. Du Bois, *The Correspondence of W.E.B. Du Bois*, vol. 3, ed. Herbert
Aptheker (Amherst: University of Massachusetts Press, 1978), 394–396.

122. Du Bois, *Prayers for Dark People*, 62.

123. Ibid., 25.

124. Du Bois, "Careers Open to College-bred Negroes," in *Writings by W.E.B.
Du Bois in Non-periodical Literature Edited by Others*, ed. Herbert Aptheker (Millwood,
N.Y.: Kraus-Thomson, 1982), 4.

125. Du Bois, *Prayers for Dark People*, 71.

126. Du Bois, *SBF*, 426. Revisability is also at the heart of James's empiricism: "I say 'empiricism,' because it is content to regard its most assured conclusion
concerning matters of fact as hypotheses liable to modification in the course of future
experience" (James, "Preface," *Will to Believe*, vii).

127. Ibid., 505.

128. Robert Gooding-Williams fails to realize this in his reading of Du Bois as
a Hegelian idealist in his essay "Philosophy of History and Social Critique in *The
Souls of Black Folk*." In general, discussions of Du Bois, Hegel, and pragmatism are
marred by an almost dogmatic insistence on a fundamental dichotomy between
Hegel and pragmatism. Zamir and Gooding-Williams share a philosophical calculus
in which Hegelian influences on Du Bois become certain proof against Du Bois's
pragmatism. This is too simplistic; the relationship between pragmatism and Hegel
is more complex than basic opposition. Ross Posnock argues that, despite his dis-
missals of Hegel, James "preserved what he, like Dewey, found vital in Hegel—his
dialectical vision, his antidualist stress on concrete embodiment and on becoming" (Posnock, *Color and Culture*, 120). Modern pragmatists such as Richard Rorty,
Jeffrey Stout, and Robert Brandom incorporate a Hegelian expressivism in their own
pragmatism. Zamir's reading of the Hegelian Du Bois is interesting in this respect.
As I have said, Zamir mightily resists Du Bois's pragmatism. In turn, he aligns
Du Bois with Hegel. Still, he insists, against Gooding-Williams, that Du Bois rejects
Hegel's teleological view of history and the "all synthesizing monism of Absolute
Spirit.... Du Bois['s] emphasis is not on the singular *Geist* but on souls" (*Dark Voices*,
115). This is a tremendous insight. Zamir concludes that Du Bois "does not *adopt*
Hegel but *adapts* him to his own ends" (114; emphasis in the original). Yet, as Ross
Posnock points out, this style of "adapting" Hegel for his historicism and empha-
sis on social context, while putting aside his strong monism, can be understood as

doing philosophy in the spirit of James's pragmatism (Posnock, *Color and Culture*, 121, 319n15).

129. Du Bois, *SBF*, 492.

130. Ibid., 419.

131. W.E.B. Du Bois, "Don't Be Bitter," in *Seventh Son*, 180–181.

132. Du Bois, *SBF*, 370.

133. Du Bois, "Beauty and Death," in *Darkwater*, 144.

134. Ibid.

135. Du Bois, *SBF*, 507; emphasis mine.

136. Ibid., 510–511.

137. Cornel West, "Black Strivings in a Twilight Civilization," in *The Future of the Race*, ed. Henry Louis Gates Jr. and Cornel West (New York: Knopf, 1996), 63. Besides, who among us is not going to respond to a child's death with a theodical gesture or impulse? Emerson, perhaps, is the only one, and he seems exceedingly unhuman. On the death of his son he writes:

> In the death of my son, now more than two years ago, I seem to have lost a beautiful estate,—no more. I cannot get it nearer to me. If tomorrow I should be informed of the bankruptcy of my principal debtors, the loss of my property would be a great inconvenience to me, perhaps for many years; but it would leave me as it found me,—neither better nor worse. So it is with this calamity: it does not touch me: something which I fancied was part of me, which could not be torn away without tearing me, nor enlarged without enriching me, falls off from me, and leaves no scar. It was caducous. I grieve that grief can teach me nothing, nor carry me one step into real nature. (Ralph Waldo Emerson, "Experience," in *Ralph Waldo Emerson*, ed. Richard Poirier [New York: Oxford University Press, 1990], 218.)

A comparison of Emerson's and Du Bois's words on the deaths of their sons begs to be written.

138. Du Bois, *SBF*, 476.

139. Ibid., 504.

140. Ibid., 369.

141. Ibid., 438. These lines come from the famous passage in which Du Bois revels in the idea of reading European classics: "I sit with Shakespeare and he winces not. Across the color line I move arm in arm with Balzac and Dumas.... So, wed with Truth, I dwell above the Veil." It is a passage that on first look unequivocally seems to endorse a raceless, unified existence. Yet, if looked at more closely, the fantasy is framed by a politicized notion of black experience and its vicissitudes: "Herein the longing of black men must have respect: the rich and bitter depth of their experience, the unknown treasures of their inner life, the strange rendings of nature they have seen, may give the world new points of view and make their loving, living, and doing precious to all human hearts." To my mind, Zamir is the only other critic who reads Du Bois's utopian vision as rooted

in social realities:

> The transcendental vision of art edges toward idealism but should not be
> mistaken for an abdication of politics.... In the above passage there is an
> American epic vision of past cultures, asserting against American anti-
> intellectualism a permission to read the achievements of pre-American
> experience.... It also states a now unfashionable belief that in each era
> notions of truth and beauty may deserve renewed consideration as part
> of a politics of self-realization and cultural transformation. (Zamir, *Dark
> Voices*, 17)

142. Du Bois, *SBF*, 510.

143. Ibid., 449.

144. Ibid., 370.

145. Ibid., 437.

146. Ibid., 540.

147. Ibid., 414.

148. Ibid., 530.

149. Du Bois, "Of Beauty and Death," in *Darkwater*, 144.

150. W.E.B. Du Bois, "Resolutions," in *The Negro Church* (Walnut Creek, Calif.:
AltaMira, 2003), 208.

151. Du Bois, *Color and Democracy*, 142.

CHAPTER 2

1. This account of the genesis of *The Souls of Black Folk* largely follows David
Levering Lewis's account. See *W. E. B. Du Bois: Biography of a Race, 1868–1919* (New
York: Holt, 1993), 277–291. For the most sophisticated literary account of Du Bois's
revisions, see Robert Stepto, *From behind the Veil: A Study of Afro-American Narrative*
(Chicago: University of Illinois Press, 1991), 52–91. For readers' responses to *Souls*,
see Herbert Aptheker, *The Literary Legacy of W.E.B. Du Bois* (White Plains, N.Y.:
Kraus International, 1989), 41–86.

2. *Dusk of Dawn: An Essay toward an Autobiography of a Race Concept* (New
Brunswick, N.J.: Transaction, 1991), 80.

3. Few have been more eloquent about the impact of *Souls* than Lewis: "*The
Souls of Black Folk*...redefined the terms of a three-hundred-year interaction between
black and white people and influenced the cultural and political psychology of
peoples of African descent throughout the Western Hemisphere, as well as on the
continent of Africa. It was one of those events epochally dividing history into a before
and an after. Like fireworks going off in a cemetery, its fourteen essays were sound
and light enlivening the inert and the despairing. It was an electrifying manifesto,
mobilizing a people for bitter, prolonged struggle to win a place in history" (Lewis,
Biography of a Race, 277).

4. For example, consider Lewis's remarks on the coming together of *Souls*.
Note that he excludes religion from the conceptual categories he uses to describe the

new essays:

> The five new essays ranged from confessional to fictional; all were intensely literary, and the best of them—"Of the Wings of Atalanta," "Of the Sorrow Songs," and, debatably, "Of Alexander Crummell"—of surpassing emotional power and beauty, while "Of the Passing of the First-Born" and "Of the Coming of John" ran to bathos and crimson. Yet what is weak or less successful in *The Souls of Black Folk* is but relative demerit in an ensemble of transcendent intellectual passion and numinous prose. (ibid., 278)

5. Arnold Rampersad, "Slavery and the Literary Imagination: Du Bois's *The Souls of Black Folk*," in *Slavery and the Literary Imagination*, ed. Deborah H. McDowell and Arnold Rampersad (Baltimore: Johns Hopkins University Press, 1989), 120. Rampersad's claim that the chapter is "anti-Christian" centers on his reading of the story as "one in which the central mourner, as a black, can find no consolation" (ibid.). To my mind, it is precisely Du Bois's refusal of other-worldly salvation while making use of Christian language and form that is the distinguishing characteristic of his religious voice.

6. W.E.B. Du Bois, *The Souls of Black Folk*, in *Writings*, ed. Nathan Huggins (New York: Library of America, 1986), 347. Hereafter cited as *SBF*.

7. Ibid., 359.

8. The emphasis on "spiritual" is mine. Robert Stepto writes: " 'Of our Spiritual Strivings' is the single most important title revision, because it establishes the tone for the volume as a whole." See Stepto, *From behind the Veil*, 54.

9. Du Bois, *SBF*, 538.

10. Ibid., 504.

11. Ibid., 502.

12. Herbert Aptheker, "W.E.B. Du Bois and Religion: A Brief Reassessment," *Journal of Religious Thought* 39(1) (1982): 5–11.

13. Wayne Proudfoot, "Religion and Naturalism," unpublished essay.

14. Ibid.

15. Du Bois, *SBF*, 501–502.

16. Stepto, *From behind the Veil*, 57.

17. Ibid., 66, 57; emphasis mine.

18. It is worth noting that Bloom himself provides a strong misreading of Du Bois and double consciousness by seeing in it an apolitical gnostic notion of self. See Harold Bloom, *The Anxiety of Influence: A Theory of Poetry* (New York: Oxford University Press, 1973), chapter 1, n110.

19. All of the passages in this paragraph are from Du Bois, *SBF*, 502.

20. Ibid.

21. Ibid., 500.

22. Ibid., 500, 502.

23. Ibid., 503.

24. Ibid., 504.

25. Ibid., 495.

26. Eddie S. Glaude Jr., *Exodus! Religion, Race, and Nation in Early Nineteenth-century Black America* (Chicago: University of Chicago Press, 2000), 32.

27. Ibid., 33.

28. Ibid. Glaude suggests replacing Du Bois's "double life" with "structures of ambivalence," a notion he adapts from Raymond Williams's "structures of feeling." See Glaude, 174–175n46.

29. Du Bois, *SBF*, 499.

30. Ibid., 493–494.

31. Ibid.

32. Cornel West, "Black Strivings in a Twilight Civilization," in *The Future of the Race*, ed. Henry Louis Gates Jr. and Cornel West (New York: Knopf, 1996), 60.

33. Shamoon Zamir, "'The Sorrow Songs'/'Song of Myself': Du Bois, the Crisis of Leadership, and Prophetic Imagination," in W.E.B. Du Bois, *The Souls of Black Folk*, ed. Henry Louis Gates Jr. and Terri Hume Oliver (New York: Norton, 1999), 348.

34. JoAnne Marie Terrell, *Power in the Blood? The Cross in the African American Experience* (Maryknoll: Orbis, 1998), 51.

35. Du Bois, *SBF*, 495.

36. Ibid., 497.

37. Ibid.

38. Ibid., 497–498.

39. Ibid., 494.

40. Ibid., 538–539.

41. Ibid., 536.

42. Cynthia D. Schrager, "Both Sides of the Veil: Race, Science, and Mysticism in W.E.B. Du Bois," *American Quarterly* 48(4) (1996): 567–568.

43. Ibid., 556–557. This is not to deny Du Bois's dissatisfaction with social-scientific discourse. However, dissatisfaction does not mean complete abandonment of the field's empirical commitments.

44. Charles Long also tries to salvage Du Bois's description of the revival. He sees in it Du Bois's "discovery of community": "Here we are not speaking of fantasies but of community, a community listening to sounds and words of each other, and there is something fantastic about this experience, such must obviously be present, for this experience was the occasion of demonic dread for Du Bois—it is Du Bois's experience of the *products* of this ex-slave community." See Charles H. Long, *Significations: Signs, Symbols and Images in the Interpretation of Religion* (Philadelphia: Fortress, 1986), 169; emphasis in the original. To the degree that Long understands "products" as historically shaped artifacts of human efforts—this seems to be his direction when he asserts the "reflective moment of a historical kind in Du Bois...in the concrete manner of memory and historical imagination" (164)—I am in agreement. Yet, at other turns, his emphasis on Rudolf Otto's notion of *mysterium tremendum* casts a phenomenological shadow. Long goes on to claim that this same scene, in effect, denies the concrete and the historical: "He ponders the beauty and sorrow of his community, and these ruminations rush his consciousness back to the African

forest, to the sense of a *primordium* of history and imagination" (ibid.). For Long, the dread Du Bois feels derives from "the power and majesty of the divine, the belittling of the creature and the human project itself" (163). Yet I can find no evidence of Du Bois's undermining of the human project. As I see it, Du Bois moves from this initial experience to give an account of the all-too-human factors of race, politics, and history that are hidden in religious experience.

45. Du Bois, *SBF*, 504; emphasis mine.

46. Glaude, *Exodus!* 32.

47. Du Bois, *SBF*, 504.

48. Ibid., 503.

49. In the final chapter I reflect on the opening of Ralph Ellison's *Invisible Man* as a masterful portrayal of religion as a site of the ambiguities of race and identity.

50. Du Bois, *SBF*, 529.

51. Ibid., 529–530.

52. Moses has read "John" singularly as Du Bois's depicting religion as a "power to stifle growth and development" and as "only a primitive level of struggle toward full political consciousness." See Wilson Jeremiah Moses, *Black Messiahs and Uncle Toms: Social and Literary Manipulations of a Religious Myth* (University Park: Pennsylvania State University Press, 1993), 20, 246n22.

53. W.E.B. Du Bois, "An Eastern City," in *The Negro Church* (Walnut Creek, Calif.: AltaMira, 2003), 110.

54. Du Bois, *SBF*, 520. I thank Eddie Glaude for pointing out the similarities between the two chapters' endings.

55. Ibid., 538, 541.

56. W.E.B. Du Bois, *Prayers for Dark People*, ed. Herbert Aptheker (Amherst: University of Massachusetts Press, 1980), 60.

57. Dewey, *A Common Faith* (New Haven, Conn.: Yale University Press, 1962), 6.

58. See Charles Taylor's discussions of Plato and Augustine in *Sources of the Self: The Making of Modern Identity* (Cambridge, Mass.: Harvard University Press, 1989), 111–142.

59. Ibid., 487.

60. Ibid., 418, 366, 542.

61. Ralph Ellison, "What America Would Be Like without Blacks," in *The Collected Essays of Ralph Ellison*, ed. John Callahan (New York: Modern Library, 1995), 582.

62. Du Bois, *SBF*, 370.

63. W.E.B. Du Bois, "Exchange with George Vaughn: Spiritual 'Awakening,'" in *The Correspondence of W.E.B. Du Bois*, vol. 1, ed. Herbert Aptheker (Amherst: University of Massachusetts Press, 1978), 477–478.

64. Dwight Hopkins, "Social Justice Struggle," in *Spirituality and the Secular Quest*, ed. Peter H. Van Ness (New York: Crossroad, 1996), 362. See Ralph Luker, *The Social Gospel in Black and White: American Racial Reform, 1885–1912* (Chapel Hill: University of North Carolina Press, 1991). Luker's book focuses on correcting the misperception that white social gospel prophets were unconcerned with race matters. Thus, Luker does not deal extensively with Du Bois. He mentions the important

effect *Souls* had on white social gospel figures, but nowhere does he ever claim
Du Bois as part of the social gospel movement. Although Hopkins does not use the
language of religious naturalism to describe Du Bois's religious bearing, his account
of Du Bois's rejection of traditional supernaturalism fits well with my account. For
example, Hopkins writes:

> Du Bois did not recognize guidance by a divine person acting outside of,
> above, and on behalf of humanity, but he did recognize a force that, from
> his vantage point, engendered human initiative in the struggle for democ-
> racy and equality.... On the one hand, this force could not dominate 'all life
> and change' and was not the exact equivalent of the human community.
> On the other hand, unlike the traditional conceptions of a divine person or
> the Christian God, this force was not external to human relationships. The
> force was inseparably and inextricably intertwined with the human spiritual
> quest. ("Social Justice Struggle," 366)

65. Du Bois, *SBF,* 438.

66. Ibid., 545.

67. My understanding of Nietzschean genealogy follows Raymond Geuss's
tremendous essay, "Nietzsche and Genealogy," which emphasizes Nietzsche's focus
on excavating contingent contributors that overturn "pedigreed" historical accounts.
Nietzschean genealogies do not preserve traditional origins but "take over and
reinterpret existing forms of living and acting" (339). This is a helpful way to think of
Du Bois's *Souls.* See Raymond Geuss, "Nietzsche and Genealogy," in *Nietzsche,* ed. John
Richardson and Brian Leiter (New York: Oxford University Press, 2001), 322–340.

68. Santayana, *Reason in Religion,* vol. 3, *The Life of Reason* (Mineola, N.Y.: Dover,
1982), 193.

69. Du Bois, *SBF,* 395.

70. Dewey, *Common Faith,* 23.

71. Du Bois, *Prayers for Dark People,* 72; emphasis in the original.

72. Ibid., 65.

73. Du Bois, *SBF,* 537.

74. Ibid., 492.

75. Levinson, *Santayana,* 15.

76. Santayana, *Reason in Religion,* 43.

77. Ibid., 193.

78. Du Bois, *SBF,* 505.

CHAPTER 3

1. Friedrich Nietzsche, *The Gay Science,* trans. Walter Kaufmann (New York:
Vintage, 1974), 280, 283.

2. See Giles Fraser, *Redeeming Nietzsche: On the Piety of Unbelief* (London:
Routledge, 2000), 38–41. Also see Jeffrey Stout, *Ethics after Babel: The Languages of
Morals and Their Discontents* (Boston: Beacon, 1988), 168–176.

3. Jeffrey Stout, *Democracy and Tradition* (Princeton, N.J.: Princeton University Press, 2004), 20.

4. Ibid., 25.

5. Ibid., 29.

6. Stout makes this claim against figures like Alasdair MacIntyre and Stanley Hauerwas, whom he calls the "new traditionalists." In particular, see chapter 5 of *Democracy and Tradition*.

7. Ibid., 28.

8. W.E.B. Du Bois, "Careers Open to College-bred Negroes," in *Writings in Non-periodical Literature Edited by Others*, ed. Herbert Aptheker (Millwood, N.Y.: Kraus-Thomson, 1982), 9.

9. W.E.B. Du Bois, *Prayers for Dark People*, ed. Herbert Aptheker (Amherst: University of Massachusetts Press, 1980), 48.

10. W.E.B. Du Bois, "The Joy of Living," in *Writings in Periodicals Edited by Others*, ed. Herbert Aptheker, vol. 1, *1891–1909* (Millwood, N.Y.: Kraus-Thomson, 1982), 221.

11. Santayana, *Reason in Religion*, vol. 3, *The Life of Reason* (Mineola, N.Y.: Dover, 1982), 193.

12. Ibid., 179.

13. Ibid., 183.

14. Ibid., 179.

15. John Dewey, *A Common Faith* (New Haven, Conn.: Yale University Press, 1962), 87.

16. Stout, *Democracy and Tradition*, 20; emphasis in the original.

17. Dewey, *Common Faith*, 87.

18. Ibid.

19. Ibid., 53.

20. Santayana, *Reason in Religion*, 185.

21. Ibid.; emphasis mine.

22. W.E.B. Du Bois, *The Souls of Black Folk*, in *Writings*, ed. Nathan Huggins (New York: Library of America, 1986), 537; hereafter cited as *SBF*.

23. Ibid., 545.

24. See "Jacob and Esau," the commencement address Du Bois gave at Talladega College on June 4, 1944, in *W. E. B. Du Bois Speaks: Speeches and Essays, 1920–1963*, ed. Philip Foner (New York: Pathfinder, 1970), 137–149.

25. W.E.B. Du Bois, "Credo," in *Darkwater: Voices from within the Veil* (Mineola, N.Y.: Dover, 1999), 2.

26. Du Bois, *SBF*, 545.

27. Wilson Jeremiah Moses, "W.E.B. Du Bois's 'The Conservation of Races' and Its Context: Idealism, Conservatism, and Hero Worship," *Massachusetts Review* 34(2) (Summer 1993): 278.

Moses writes: "It is a beautiful and moving chapter, but those who seek a factual treatment of Crummell's life have often been misled by Du Bois's romanticizing and hero worship" (277); "The thing that is most striking about Du Bois's

characterizations of Crummell is its vagueness, and its dreamy, romantic quality....Crummell's ambition, irascibility, and sardonicism do not impinge on the
author's imagination" (278); "Crummell was not a man of the people. His sometimes strident black nationalism was not complemented by any appreciation for the
folkways of the black American masses. Crummell's elitist ideology was inseparable from his religious opinions. Indeed, he viewed slave culture as degraded and
useless, consisting of nothing more than systematic introduction into licentious-
ness and irresponsibility" (279).

28. Eric Sundquist, *To Wake the Nations: Race in the Making of American
Literature* (Cambridge, Mass.: Harvard University Press, 1993), 516–517.

29. Robert Gooding-Williams, "Du Bois's Counter-Sublime," in *The Souls of
Black Folk: Authoritative Text, Contexts, Criticism*, ed. Henry Louis Gates Jr. and Terri
Hume Oliver (New York: Norton Critical Edition, 1999), 245–246. Using Kant's
understanding of the sublime, literary critic Harold Bloom's notion of the counter-
sublime, and Freudian idiom, Gooding-Williams suggests that Crummell functioned
for Du Bois as a transcendent ideal to model and to overcome: "Where Crummell's
I was…there my *I* is, more closely mixed with *it*" (260; emphasis in the original).

30. Du Bois, *SBF*, 515.

31. Ibid., 516.

32. Ibid., 517.

33. Ibid.

34. Ibid., 517–518.

35. Ibid., 519.

36. Ibid.

37. Ibid., 520.

38. Santayana, *Reason in Religion*, 185; emphasis mine.

39. Stout, *Democracy and Tradition*, 30; emphasis in the original.

40. W.E.B. Du Bois, "The Revelation of Saint Orgne the Damned," in Huggins,
Writings, 1048.

41. Ibid., 1069.

42. Ibid., 1066.

43. Ibid.

44. Ibid.

45. Ibid., 1063.

46. Ibid., 1050.

47. Ibid., 1061.

48. Du Bois's sympathetic critique of liberalism is typical. He always prized the
idea of individual will; however, he did not believe that people sit outside the social
forces that surround them:

As I now look back, I see in the crusade waged by the National Association
for the Advancement of Colored People from 1910 to 1930, one of the
finest efforts of liberalism to achieve human emancipation; and much
was accomplished. But the essential difficulty with the liberalism of the

twentieth century was not to realize the fundamental change brought about by the world-wide organization of work and trade and commerce." (W.E.B. Du Bois, *Dusk of Dawn: An Essay toward an Autobiography of a Race Concept* [New Brunswick, N.J.: Transaction, 1997], 288–289.)

49. Du Bois, "Revelation of Saint Orgne the Damned," 1063.

50. Ibid., 1059, 1057, 1054. "The Wheel in a Wheel" is a reference to Ezekiel 1:16. See chapter 4 for the way Du Bois uses this metaphor to express a type of black nationalism.

51. Ibid., 1069–1070.

52. Ibid., 1069.

53. Du Bois, *Prayers for Dark People*, 25.

CHAPTER 4

1. W.E.B. Du Bois, *The Souls of Black Folk* in *Writings*, ed. Nathan Huggins (New York: Library of America, 1986), 547; emphasis in the original; hereafter cited as *SBF.*

2. Sacvan Bercovitch describes these steps as the prophet's "lamenting a declension" that was followed "thence forward, with prophetic assurance, toward a resolution that incorporates (as it transforms) both the promise and the condemnation" (Sacvan Bercovitch, *The American Jeremiad* [Madison: University of Wisconsin Press, 1978], 180, 16). Also see David Howard-Pitney's pithy summary of the three-step process of "the rhetorical structure" of Bercovitch's jeremiad: "citing the *promise,* criticism of present *declension,* or retrogression from the promise, and a resolving *prophecy* that society will shortly complete its mission and redeem the promise" (David Howard-Pitney, *The Afro-American Jeremiad: Appeals for Justice in America* [Philadelphia: Temple University Press, 1990], 8; emphasis in the original).

3. Du Bois, *SBF,* 406.

4. Bercovitch, *American Jeremiad,* 6–10.

5. However, Bercovitch does acknowledge that some black Americans castigate the United States to reject it entirely. He calls this "the anti-jeremiad: the denunciation of all ideals, sacred and secular, on the grounds that America is a lie" (Bercovitch, *American Jeremiad,* 191). Think here of Malcolm X's denunciation of America in "The Ballot or the Bullet": "No, I'm not an American. I'm one of the 22 million black people who are the victims of Americanism. One of the 22 million black people who are the victims of democracy, nothing but disguised hypocrisy. So, I'm not standing here speaking to you as an American, or a patriot, or a flag-saluter, or a flag-waver—no, not I....I don't see any American dream; I see an American nightmare" (Malcolm X, "The Ballot or the Bullet," in *Malcolm X Speaks: Selected Speeches and Statements,* ed. George Breitman [New York: Pathfinder, 1989], 26).

6. Wilson J. Moses, *Black Messiahs and Uncle Toms: Social and Literary Manipulations of a Religious Myth* (University Park: Pennsylvania State University Press, 1993)· 38. Howard-Pitney's account of the African American jeremiad, as I have already suggested, follows a similar line of thought.

7. Eddie S. Glaude Jr., *Exodus! Religion, Race, and Nation in Early Nineteenth-century Black America* (Chicago: University of Chicago Press, 2000), 53.

8. Ibid., 35.

9. Ibid., 33. On this same point Glaude also writes: "[African Americans] were Christian but with a difference. American but not quite. Ambivalence marked their relation to a tradition within which they were ensconced and in tension" (ibid.).

10. W.E.B. Du Bois, "The Philosophy of Mr. Dole," in Huggins, *Writings*, 1154. The original appeared in *The Crisis*, May 1914. Du Bois is responding to Charles F. Dole's letter to the editor, "A Question of Policy," in which Dole objects to the *Crisis*'s capitalization of "Negro" and its holding President Wilson accountable for lynchings.

11. Bercovitch, *American Jeremiad*, 166.

12. Sacvan Bercovitch, *The Rites of Assent: Transformations in the Symbolic Construction of America* (New York: Routledge, 1993), 47.

13. Bercovitch, *American Jeremiad*, 174.

14. Ibid., 191.

15. Du Bois, "Of Work and Wealth," in *Darkwater: Voices from within the Veil* (Mineola, N.Y.: Dover, 1999), 59.

16. Du Bois, *SBF*, 434.

17. "A Negro Nation within the Nation" is the title of a Du Bois essay written in 1935. See *W. E. B. Du Bois: A Reader*, ed. David Levering Lewis (New York: Holt, 1995), 563–570. On the origin of the African American construction of a "nation within a nation," Philip Foner writes: "As early as 1852, Martin R. Delany in the appendix to his book, *The Condition, Elevation, Emigration, and Destiny of the Colored People of the United States*, wrote 'We are a nation within a nation;—as the Poles in Russia, the Hungarians in Austria, the Welsh, Irish, and Scotch in the British dominions.'" See *W. E. B. Du Bois Speaks: Speeches and Addresses, 1920–1963*, ed. Philip S. Foner (New York: Pathfinder, 1970), 333.

18. Du Bois, *SBF*, 475.

19. Du Bois, "Souls of White Folk," in *Darkwater*, 19, 20, 28.

20. W.E.B. Du Bois, "The Niagara Movement: Address to the Country," in *W. E. B. Du Bois: A Reader*, 367.

21. Thomas Jefferson, "Query XVIII," *Notes on the State of Virginia* (Raleigh, N.C.: Alex Catalogue), in Columbia University eBook Collection (database online), Apr. 15, 2003, http://www.netlibrary.com/ebook_info.asp?product_id=1085927&piclist=19799,20141,20155,40357.

22. For example, Stephen Haynes's *Noah's Curse* details the strands of American Christianity for which enslaving Africans constituted religious piety. Though Haynes does not mention the American jeremiad, his account of Benjamin Palmer's 1858 address, "Our Historic Mission," explains that the American exceptionalism of the jeremiad was adopted to argue that slavery was essential to the nation's providential mission. See Stephen R. Haynes, *Noah's Curse: The Biblical Justification of American Slavery* (New York: Oxford University Press, 2002), 128–130.

23. Du Bois's rendering of ideology resonates with Marx and Nietzsche, both of whom locate ideology in social experience. Hannah Arendt's work in *On Revolution*

is quite valuable for helping us to see the particular irony and even folly in disregarding social practice in American politics. Arendt's understanding of the formative American political experience is that it privileges the act of creating covenants, agreements, and partnerships over the content of the laws by means of which they are made. For Arendt, the American political experience is based on "[n]o theory, theological or political or philosophical" but on the way "these men...become obsessed with the notion of compact and prompted them again and again 'to promise and bind' themselves to another" (Hannah Arendt, *On Revolution* [New York: Penguin, 1990], 173). Her point is that American politics is rooted not only in "ideas and principles untested by reality" (120) but also in "the discussions, the deliberations, and the making of decisions" (119). She calls this "the grammar of action...it is an event not a theory" (175, 172). In a very real way, the idea of consensus Arendt would lead us to, *pace* Bercovitch, understands who is included in the consensus as fundamental to the consensus itself. I wish to thank Deak Nabers for discussing these points with me.

24. W.E.B. Du Bois, "Awake, America!" *Crisis* (September 1917), in *The Emerging Thought of W. E. B. Du Bois* (New York: Simon & Schuster, 1972), 252.

25. David Walker, *David Walker's Appeal to Coloured Citizens of the World, but in Particular, and Very Expressly, to Those of the United States of America* (New York: Hill and Wang, 19951), 70.

26. Ibid., 69–70.

27. Du Bois, "Awake, America!" 252–253.

28. Du Bois, *SBF*, 423.

29. Du Bois, "The Niagara Movement: Address to the Country," in *W. E. B. Du Bois: A Reader*, 369.

30. Du Bois, *Darkwater*, 9.

31. Ibid., 14.

32. Ibid., 84.

33. Cited in Wilson J. Moses, "W. E. B. Du Bois's 'The Conservation of Races' and Its Context: Idealism, Conservatism, and Hero Worship," *Massachusetts Review* 34(2) (Summer 1993): 281. Moses cites the original, *"The Nation's Problem," a speech delivered before the Bethel Literary Society in Washington, D.C., December 16, 1889,* reprinted in *Negro Social and Political Thought, 1850–1920: Representative Texts*, ed. Howard Brotz (New York: Basic Books, 1966), 319. David Blight affirms Moses's reading by presenting Douglass as a Jeremiah who "embraced virtually every aspect of America's mythology of mission....Nothing else in his life stimulated such an outpouring of his own brand of American nationalism as the crisis of the union." See David W. Blight, *Frederick Douglass' Civil War: Keeping Faith in Jubilee* (Baton Rouge: Louisiana State University Press), 111–112.

34. Philip S. Foner, in *W. E. B. Du Bois Speaks: Speeches and Addresses, 1920–1963*, ed. Philip S. Foner (New York: Pathfinder, 1970), 333.

35. For a comprehensive social scientific account of Black Nationalism see Michael C. Dawson, *Black Visions: The Roots of Contemporary African-American Political Ideologies* (Chicago: University of Chicago Press, 2001), esp. chapter 3.

36. For an example of a black nationalism that emphasizes black America as a coexistent nation within the United States, see Tommie Shelby's account of Martin Delany's black nationalism in "Two Conceptions of Black Nationalism: Martin Delany on the Meaning of Black Political Solidarity," *Political Theory* 31(5) (October 2003): 664–692.

37. Eddie S. Glaude Jr., *Exodus! Religion, Race, and Nation in Early Nineteenth-century Black America* (Chicago: University of Chicago Press, 2000), 16. For recent accounts of black nationalism that emphasize Glaude's pragmatic understanding of nation and blackness, see *Is It Nation Time? Contemporary Essays on Black Power and Black Nationalism,* ed. Eddie S. Glaude Jr. (Chicago: University of Chicago Press, 2002).

38. Wilson Jeremiah Moses, *The Golden Age of Black Nationalism, 1850–1925* (New York: Oxford University Press. 1978), 20; emphasis in the original. This sounds a good deal like the "simplest expression of black nationalism" from the anthology *Black Nationalism in America*—"that black people organize themselves on the basis of their common color and oppressed condition to move in some way to alleviate their situation" (*Exodus!* 10)—that Glaude relies on. Moses, however, insists that black nationalists base this sense of cohesion on an assertion of ontological racial differ-ence. Glaude's black nationalism is based in his pragmatism.

39. I borrow this sense of peoplehood from Jeffrey Stout's account of the black nationalism of Ralph Ellison and James Baldwin. See Stout's "Theses on Black Nation-alism," in *Is It Nation Time? Contemporary Essays on Black Power and Black Nationalism,* ed. Eddie S. Glaude Jr. (Chicago: University of Chicago Press, 2002), 244.

40. Benedict Anderson, *Imagined Communities: Reflections on the Origin and Spread of Nationalism* (New York: Verso, 1993), 12.

41. I am aware that this account of the nation is slightly at odds with Anderson's famous definition of the nation: "It is an imagined political community—imagined as both inherently limited and sovereign" (ibid., 6). Of course, there is a good deal of synonymy, too: My particular type of black nationhood is both imagined and limited in Anderson's sense. What is not apparent is whether it is also political and sover-eign. These discrepancies can be resolved if we understand political and sovereign not as a separatist, insular demand for representation but as a pluralistic demand for participation. That is, the black nationalism of Du Bois's jeremiads, though it does not imagine a geographically separate black nation, has a strong, politically sovereign edge in its demands for full political participation.

42. See Richard Cullen Rath, "Echo and Narcissus: The Afrocentric Pragmatism of W. E. B. Du Bois," *Journal of American History* 84(2) (September 1997): 461–495.

43. My main objection to Moses's account of the black jeremiad is that he never makes a full reckoning with its black nationalist impulses. Moses has no real account of a black nationalism that can coexist with the African American jeremiad's concerns for the redeeming of America. This, I think, explains why Moses frames Du Bois's black nationalism in internationalist pan-African terms and cannot see a vibrant form of black nationalism—that sense of peoplehood that black people feel—in Du Bois's jeremiads.

44. Du Bois, *SBF*, 418.

45. "As I looked at the living creatures, I saw a wheel on the earth besides the living creatures, one for each of the four of them. As for the appearance of the wheels and their construction: their appearance was like the gleaming of beryl; and the four had the same form, their construction being something like a wheel within a wheel."—Ezekiel 1:15–16, *The New Oxford Annotated Bible*, NRSV, ed. Bruce Metzger and Roland E. Murphy (New York: Oxford University Press, 1991).

46. Du Bois, *SBF*, 438.

47. Ibid., 545.

48. Even in moments when Du Bois consolidates black peoplehood under the romantic flag of Ethiopia, I still hear his call to history and not to a mythic racial essentialism. For example, he writes: "The shadow of a mighty Negro past flits through the tale of Ethiopia the Shadowy and of Egypt the Sphinx. Through history, the powers of single black men flash here and there like falling stars, and die sometimes before the world has rightly gauged their brightness" (ibid., 365). Yes, there is a flamboyance of rhetoric here, but I do not see what Moses calls Du Bois's "flamboyant Ethiopian millennialism" (Moses, *Black Messiahs and Uncle Toms*, 140), which sees blacks and whites as "separate varieties of humanity with distinct destinies competing for honor in the eyes of history and the world" (Wilson J. Moses, "The Poetics of Ethiopianism: W. E. B. Du Bois and Literary Black Nationalism," American Literature 47[3] [November 1975]: 415). This seems vastly overstated.

49. Moses, "W. E. B. Du Bois's 'The Conservation of Races' and Its Context," 284–285.

50. Moses, *Black Messiahs*, 46.

51. Walker, *David Walker's Appeal*, 28; emphasis in the original.

52. Ibid., 2; quoted in Glaude, *Exodus!* 35.

53. Glaude, *Exodus!* 35.

54. Du Bois, *SBF*, 401.

55. Ibid., 418.

56. Ibid., 437.

57. Ibid., 395.

58. See Du Bois, *The Gift of Black Folk*, (New York: Oxford University Press, 2007), chapters 4 and 9.

59. Du Bois, *Darkwater*, 92, 161, 31.

60. Moses, *Black Messiahs and Uncle Toms*, 172.

61. Moses, "W. E. B. Du Bois's 'The Conservation of Races' and Its Context," 284.

62. Michael Walzer, *Exodus and Revolution* (New York: Basic Books, 1985), 116.

63. Ibid., 119.

64. Glaude, *Exodus!* 146.

65. Du Bois, *SBF*, 423.

66. Ibid., 419.

67. Ibid., 424.

68. Ibid., 387.

69. Ibid., 434.

70. Ibid., 438.

71. Ibid., 514.

72. Ibid., 488.

73. Ibid., 462.

74. Du Bois, *Darkwater*, 86.

75. Ibid., 146.

76. Ibid., 147; emphasis mine.

77. Ibid., 42.

78. Ibid., 91.

79. Ibid., 122.

80. Ibid., 120.

81. I borrow and adapt this distinction between the "promise to American life" and the "promise of American life" from Martin Marty. See "Two Kinds of Civil Religion," in *American Civil Religion*, ed. Russell E. Richey and Donald G. Jones (New York: Harper and Row, 1974), 139–154.

82. Du Bois, "The Crisis," in *The Emerging Thought of W. E. B. Du Bois*, 402. Du Bois's jeremiads might be considered examples of what Robert Bellah envisions as the American civil religion: "not the worship of the American nation but an understanding of the American experience in the light of ultimate and universal reality." See Robert Bellah's classic essay, "Civil Religion in America," in Richey and Jones, *American Civil Religion*, 40. Bellah is far too optimistic in distinguishing American civil religion from the worship of the American nation. In fact, in any number of historical examples, the American civil religion appears to be nothing but the worship of the American nation. We might do better in thinking of American civil religion as composed of different strands that deeply oppose each other in crucial ways.

83. Du Bois, "Criteria of Negro Art," in Huggins, *Writings*, 994–995.

84. W.E.B. Du Bois, "Philosophy of Mr. Dole," in Huggins, *Writings*, 1158.

85. Du Bois, *SBF*, 547; emphasis in the original.

CHAPTER 5

1. W.E.B. Du Bois, "A Litany at Atlanta," in *Darkwater* (Mineola, N.Y.: Dover, 1999), 15.

2. W.E.B. Du Bois, "The Son of God," in *Du Bois on Religion*, ed. Phil Zuckerman (Walnut Creek, Calif.: AltaMira, 2000), 185.

3. Ibid.

4. Du Bois's insistence in his parables that Christ is black makes him an all-too-neglected predecessor of Albert Cleage and James H. Cone, who six decades later constructed a theological revolution based on this claim. See Albert B. Cleage Jr., *The Black Messiah* (Trenton, NJ: Africa World Press, 1989) and Cone's series of works on black liberation theology, such as *God of the Oppressed* (Maryknoll, NY: Orbis Books, 1997)and *A Black Theology of Liberation* (Maryknoll, NY: Orbis Books, 1990).

5. Trudier Harris's *Exorcising Blackness: Historical and Literary Lynching and Burning Rituals* (Bloomington: Indiana University Press, 1984), 187. This is the

most complete study of African American literary works that depict lynchings. Yet, in her exposition of the black male authors in this tradition, Harris does not mention Du Bois: "Works which fit into this category are those by James Weldon Johnson...Claude McKay, Ralph Ellison, Walter White, Langston Hughes, Paul Laurence Dunbar, James Baldwin, and Richard Wright" (184).

6. W.E.B. Du Bois, *The Souls of Black Folk*, in *Writings*, ed. Nathan Huggins (New York: Library of America, 1986), 420. All subsequent references to *The Souls of Black Folk* are cited as *SBF*. A few critics have paid attention to the "Gospel of Sacrifice" in Du Bois's discourse. See Susan Mizruchi, *The Science of Sacrifice: American Literature and Modern Social Theory* (Princeton, N.J.: Princeton University Press, 1998), "Chapter Four: Du Bois's Gospel of Sacrifice," 269–366. As Keith Beyerman writes of Du Bois's emphasis on sacrifice, "This essential religious view, the idea that those who would find themselves must lose themselves, helps to explain one aspect of his career." See Keith Beyerman, *Seizing the Word: History, Art, and Self in the Work of W. E. B. Du Bois* (Athens: University of Georgia Press, 1994), 5. Beyerman's work seems to have gone somewhat unnoticed. It should be noticed, however. His portrayal of Du Bois as critically "a profoundly conservative author" who does not "seek to supplant patriarchal culture but to denounce its false fathers" captures the Burkean tendencies in Du Bois (11).

7. W.E.B. Du Bois, *John Brown* (Armonk, N.Y.: Sharpe, 1997), 83.

8. Du Bois, "The Problem of Amusement," in *Du Bois on Religion*, 24–25.

9. W.E.B. Du Bois, "Of Beauty and Death," in *Darkwater* (Mineola, N.Y.: Dover, 1999), 132.

10. Over almost a sixty-year period from 1882 to 1939, an African American was lynched about every fourth day. My calculations are based on the data in Orlando Patterson, "Feasts of Blood: 'Race,' Religion, and Human Sacrifice in the Postbellum South," in *Rituals of Blood: Consequences of Slavery in Two American Centuries* (New York: Basic Books, 1998), 175. Patterson draws on "The Lynching Records at Tuskegee Institute."

11. Ralph Ellison, "Introduction" to *Invisible Man* (New York: Vintage, 1990), xv.

12. Consider the applicability to American racism in Girard's insight that "society is seeking to deflect upon a relatively indifferent victim, a 'sacrificeable' victim, the violence that would otherwise be vented on its own members, the people it most desires to protect"; "in some societies whole categories of human beings are systematically reserved for sacrificial purposes in order to protect other categories" (4, 8); or his insistence that the scapegoat needs to be both part of and separate from the sacrificing community:

> We should not conclude, however, that the surrogate victim is simply foreign to the community....He partakes of all possible differences within the community, particularly the difference between within and without....ritual victims tend to be drawn from categories that are neither outside nor inside the community, but marginal to it: slaves, children, livestock. This marginal quality is crucial to the proper functioning of the sacrifice. (271)

Girard's further insight that "sacrifice is primarily an act of violence without risk of vengeance" (13) speaks to both the power differential and cowardice underpinning American lynching. See René Girard, *Violence and the Sacred*, trans. Patrick Gregory (Baltimore: Johns Hopkins University Press, 1977).

13. Donald Mathews provides the most detailed account to date of the way in which lynchings functioned as religious dramas that relied on and were supported by Christian moral theology in the South. He notes the resistance of whites to acknowledging this connection: "This silence about the meaning of religion in discussions of lynchings is strange because of the common knowledge that crucifixion, an act of violence, is the very core of the Christian paradigm that was so essential a part of Southern culture." Mathews breaks that silence by reconstructing the way in which preachers of the time portrayed God as a "Supreme Hangman" for whom "punishment" and "righteous retributions" were crucial elements of "the glories of His divine character." He argues that this retributive theology, this "sacralization of punishment," made for an excellent fit with the social order of the South by framing and reinforcing its complex system of racial discrimination. In these terms, punishment was a sacred category, flexible enough to turn acts of cruelty sacerdotal. For Mathews, "the pervasive drama of salvation preached from pulpits throughout the region" "did not make white Christians lynch black people," but it did create "the pervasive ambience of society...perhaps its ruling ideology—the pattern of ideas that normal people are supposed to believe," which "could allow—when fused with whites' racial antipathy, patriarchal prerogative, sexual apprehension, and economic tenuousness— public violence against a black man." See Donald Mathews, "The Southern Rite of Human Sacrifice," *Journal of Southern Religion* 3 (2000), Association for the Study of Southern Religion (Nov. 15, 2002), http://jsr.as.wvu.edu/mathews.htm. Other voices on this topic include Anthony Pinn: "Lynchers—many of whom were not only church members but church leaders—felt their actions had religious justification and that the process of lynching contained the ethos of church ritual and the religious re-creation of a cosmic order." Anthony B. Pinn, *Terror and Triumph: The Nature of Black Religion* (Minneapolis: Fortress, 2003), 77; Theophus Smith asks, "What can account for lynchings as quasi-religious ceremonies, particularly in the context of a tradition like Christianity, which so highly emphasizes its love ethic?" (Theophus Smith, *Conjuring Culture: Biblical Formations of Black America* [New York: Oxford University Press, 1993], 97). Smith's is an excellent question, although he does not do much to answer it. Also see Orlando Patterson's claim in *Rituals of Blood* that "[t]here is abundant evidence that a significant minority of these thousands of killings were sacrificial murders, possessing all the ritual, communal, and in many cases, religious characteristics of classic human sacrifice" (Patterson, *Rituals of Blood*, 173).

14. For example, for Anthony Pinn, suffering is a surd: "*Suffering Has No Redemptive Qualities*" (Anthony Pinn, *Why, Lord? Suffering and Evil in Black Theology* [New York: Continuum, 1995], 157; emphasis in the original). He rejects any accounts in which "suffering strengthens African Americans, so to speak, for divine plans...suffering in the here-and-now allows for the ultimate fulfillment of a divine teleological design" (16).

15. Joanne Marie Terrell, *Power in the Blood? The Cross in the African American Experience* (Maryknoll, N.Y.: Orbis, 1998), 17; emphasis in the original. Wilson Moses's work also bears on this conversation. Moses traces the myth of the Uncle Tom to the racist idea of the "black race's innate propensity for Christian heroism. It was because the African race possessed the traits of patience, long suffering, and forgiveness that they would ultimately become a messianic redeemer race" (xii). In typical contrarian fashion, Moses goes on to argue that ideas of racial superiority employed by black nationalists actually have their roots in the Uncle Tom myth:

> For black nationalists, both the Uncle Tom and the Nat Turner models persisted as functional myths. Uncle Tom images were constantly present in the writings of black nationalists...who argued that Africans were natural Christians endowed by nature with inborn traits of Christian civilization...Uncle Tom represented a variety of racial superiority...the Uncle Tom myth was important as a means of impressing white and black alike with the ineradicable humanity of the slave...The myth contributed to the messianic vision of a millennial African civilization that would serve as a shining example of human fulfillment in an ideal nation state." (Wilson Jeremiah Moses, *Black Messiahs and Uncle Toms: Social and Literary Manipulations of a Religious Myth* [University Park: Pennsylvania State University Press, 1993], 60–66.)

16. Moses, *Black Messiahs and Uncle Toms*, 68.

17. The exception was the "Close Ranks" affair. "Close Ranks" was the name of the July 1918 *Crisis* editorial in which Du Bois urged fellow African Americans to "forget our special grievances and close our ranks shoulder to shoulder with our white fellow citizens" in support of the war. See "Close Ranks," in *W. E. B. Du Bois: A Reader,* ed. David Levering Lewis (New York: Holt, 1995), 697. For a stark contrast, consider these lines from the poem "The Riddle of Sphinx," written essentially contemporaneously: "The white world's vermin and filth: / All the dirt of London, / All the scum of New York; / Valiant spoilers of women / And conquerors of unarmed men...I hate them, Oh! / I hate them well, / I hate them, Christ! / As I hate hell! / If I were God, / I'd sound their knell / This day!" ("The Riddle of the Sphinx," in *Darkwater*, 30–31).

18. Du Bois, *SBF*, 499.

19. Mizruchi, *Science of Sacrifice*, 354.

20. W.E.B. Du Bois, "The Joy of Living," in *Writings in Periodicals Edited by Others*, ed. Herbert Aptheker, vol. 1, *1891–1909* (Millwood, N.Y.: Kraus-Thomson, 1982), 220.

21. James Weldon Johnson, "The Dilemma of the Negro Author," *American Mercury* 15 (1928): 477.

22. Girard, *Violence and the Sacred*, 4, 271.

23. See book 2 in René Girard, *Things Hidden Since the Foundation of the World,* trans. Stephen Bann and Michael Metteer (Stanford, Calif.: Stanford University Press, 1987). This text is divided into three "books" with multiple chapters in each.

24. Ibid., 210. Girard looks to usher in a new age when "mankind no longer has to base harmonious relationships on blood sacrifices, ridiculous fables of a violent deity, and the whole range of mythological cultural formation" (183). Against thousands of years of Christian doctrine, Girard argues that seeing Jesus's death as a sacrifice for human sin constitutes a fundamental misreading of the Gospels. He insists that Jesus is murdered, not sacrificed (180–181). Moreover, by realizing and making this distinction explicit, Girard allows readers to leave the apparatuses of sacrifice behind. Ivan Strenski, a critic of Girard, maintains that this type of reading shows that Girard's "real significance is as a Christian theologian and *moraliste*." See Strenski's "At Home with René Girard: Eucharistic Sacrifice, the 'French School' and Joseph De Maistre," in his *Religion in Relation: Method, Application, and Moral Location* (London: Macmillan, 1993), 202.

25. Girard, *Violence and the Sacred*, 300.

26. Burton Mack, "Introduction: Religion and Ritual," in *Violent Origins: Ritual Killing and Cultural Formation*, ed. Robert G. Hamerton-Kelly (Stanford, Calif.: Stanford University Press, 1987), 22.

27. Talal Asad, "Religion, Nation-State, Secularism," in *Nation and Religion: Perspectives on Europe and Asia*, ed. Peter van der Veer and Hartmut Lehmann (Princeton, N.J.: Princeton University Press, 1999), 180; emphasis in the original.

28. He continues: "And yet hiding and concealing this barbarism by every resource of American silence we are sitting in council at Geneva and Peking and trying to make the world believe we are a civilized nation" (W.E.B. Du Bois, "Lynchings," *Crisis* (August 1927), in *Writings*, 1219).

29. In thundering tones Du Bois called for violent resistance to lynch mobs: "In the last analysis lynching of Negroes is going to stop in the South when the cowardly mob is faced by effective guns in the hands of the people determined to sell their souls dearly." This conclusion came in the 1916 *Crisis* editorial "Cowardice," which severely castigated blacks of Gainesville, Florida, for not actively intervening in a lynching: "No people who behave with the absolute cowardice shown by these colored people can hope to have the sympathy or help of the civilized folk. The men and women . . . should have fought in self-defense to the last ditch if they had killed every white man in the county and themselves been killed." See "Cowardice," in *The Seventh Son: The Thought and Writings of W. E. B. Du Bois*, vol. 2, ed. Julius Lester (New York: Vintage, 1971), 14.

30. Josiah Royce, *The Problem of Christianity* (Chicago: University of Chicago Press, 1968), 183.

31. Ibid., 183–184; emphasis mine.

32. Ibid., 182, 193.

33. Smith, *Conjuring Culture*, 100. Also see Theophus Smith, "The Spirituality of African American Traditions," in *Christian Spirituality: Post-Reformation and Modern*, ed. Louis Dupré and Don E. Saliers (New York: Crossroad, 1989), 372–414.

34. Marvin and Ingle continue: "Group solidarity, or sentiment, flows from the value of this sacrifice . . . It must possess and consume, it must *eat* its worshippers to live." See Carolyn Marvin and David W. Ingle, *Blood Sacrifice and the Nation: Totem*

Rituals and the American Flag (New York: Cambridge University Press, 1999), 4; emphasis in the original. The bloodletting they refer to involves lives lost during military conflict; the soundness of their point is dramatically manifested in texts such as Lincoln's *Gettysburg Address* and Horace Bushnell's "Our Obligations to Our Dead," which insist that the nation can be built only from blood-drenched ground. However, when it comes to lynching, Marvin and Ingle are surprisingly silent.

35. Smith, *Conjuring Culture,* 187.

36. Du Bois, *SBF,* 545.

37. Ibid., 389.

38. Du Bois, "The Immortal Child," in *Darkwater,* 125.

39. Henri Hubert and Marcel Mauss, *Sacrifice: Its Nature and Functions,* trans. W. D. Halls (Chicago: University of Chicago Press, 1964), 101–102. Hubert and Mauss drew on the work of Emile Durkheim: "In summing up, then, it may be said that nearly all the great social institutions have been born in religion...it is obviously necessary that the religious life be the eminent form and, as it were, the concentrated expression of the whole collective life. If religion has given birth to all that is essential in society, it is because the idea of society is the soul of religion." See *The Elementary Forms of Religious Life,* trans. Karen E. Fields (New York: The Free Press, 1995), 421.

40. Hubert and Mauss, *Sacrifice,* 100.

41. Ibid., 102.

42. Ibid., 100.

43. Ibid.

44. Ivan Strenski, *Contesting Sacrifice: Religion, Nationalism, and Social Thought in France* (Chicago: University of Chicago Press, 2002), 4; emphasis in the original.

45. Du Bois, "The Immortal Child," in *Darkwater,* 119.

46. Du Bois, "Of Beauty and Death," in *Darkwater,* 130.

47. Du Bois, *SBF,* 518.

48. Though Crummell is not a lynched Christ figure, he does brush up against the threat of lynching. Recall from chapter 3 Crummell's rejection of the white bishop's offer of a segregated congregation. However, as the bishop waits for Crummell's response, Du Bois writes: "The Bishop cleared his throat suggestively" (518). Is it too much to think that the threat of lynching lies latent? It is a line that reminds me of the sound of Billie Holliday clearing her throat before she sang "Strange Fruit" in the Los Angeles Philharmonic Auditorium on Feb. 12, 1945. See *The Jazz Singers* (Washington, D.C.: Smithsonian Collection of Recordings, 1998) (disc 3), produced by Bruce Talbot and Robert G. O'Meally.

49. Du Bois, *SBF,* 519.

50. Michael C. Dawson, *Black Visions: The Roots of Contemporary African-American Political Ideologies* (Chicago: University of Chicago Press, 2001), 15–16.

51. Du Bois, *SBF,* 370.

52. Ibid., 389.

53. As Susan Mizruchi says of this line: "The flimsiness of this altar is obviously a joke at national expense. America neither has the political integrity nor the spiritual gravity essential to sacrifice" (*Science of Sacrifice,* 76).

54. Strenski, *Contesting Sacrifice,* 178–179.

55. Ibid., 160.

56. Ibid., 6. It can be argued that Durkheim was of this mind: "There is no moral act that does not imply a sacrifice, for, as Kant has shown, the law of duty cannot be obeyed without humiliating our individual, or, as he calls it, our 'empirical' sensitivity." Cited in Mathews, "Southern Rite of Human Sacrifice."

57. Nietzsche writes: "Man could never do without blood, torture, and sacrifices when he felt the need to create a memory for himself; the most dreadful sacrifices and pledges...the most repulsive mutilations (castration, for example), the cruelest rites of all the religious cults (and all religions are at the deepest level systems of cruelties)— all this has its origins in the instinct that realized that pain is the most powerful aid to mnemonics." See Friedrich Nietzsche, *On the Genealogy of Morals,* trans. Walter Kaufmann (New York: Vintage, 1989), 61. Nietzsche, of course, sees none of these mutilations as unnecessary or as pathological. We should not be similarly inclined.

58. Nancy Jay, *Throughout Your Generations Forever: Sacrifice, Religion, and Paternity* (Chicago: University of Chicago Press, 1992), 145.

59. Benedict Anderson, *Imagined Communities: Reflections on the Origin and Spread of Nationalism* (New York: Verso, 1991), 3.

60. Ibid., 141.

61. William James's essay "The Moral Equivalent of War" (1910) also sought to make these same incompatibles cohere. James bemoaned the lack of "the blood-tax...anything that one feels honored by belonging to" in American liberalism; at the same time he rejected as "nonsense" the "fatalistic view" that only through the worst excesses and abuses of war can a sense of national mission be made. See William James, "The Moral Equivalent of War," in *Essays on Faith and Morals* (New York: Longman, Green, 1949), 322. James continues: "For I know that war-making is due to definite motives and subject to prudential checks and reasonable criticism, just like any other form of enterprise" (322).

62. Marvin and Ingle, *Blood Sacrifice and the Nation,* 8.

63. Anderson, *Imagined Communities,* 141.

64. This is how David L. Chappell's book *A Stone of Hope: Prophetic Religion and the Death of Jim Crow* (Chapel Hill: University of North Caroline Press, 2003) conceives of the civil rights movement of the 1950s and '60s.

65. Mathews, "Southern Rite of Human Sacrifice."

66. Quoted in Harris, *Exorcising Blackness,* 77. Harris's *Exorcising Blackness* emphasizes that black American intellectuals saw lynchings as a murderous social ritual, but she does not deeply consider the religious dimensions of the ritual. Also quoted in Mathews, "Southern Rite of Human Sacrifice."

67. Smith, *Conjuring Culture,* 183–184. Though Smith "propose[s] a reevaluation of [Du Bois's] literary craft as that of a conjuration performer," he oddly does not mention any of Du Bois's Christ-lynching parables as examples of the "*imitatio Christi*" tradition in African American literary conjure (132).

68. Du Bois, *SBF,* 528. Du Bois is quoting directly from the biblical book of Esther 4:16.

69. In this vein, Du Bois's uses of the Christ figure are not calls to return to a biblical order; nor are they typologies, as Smith claims, "employed in synergy with a Deity who cooperates in the concrete historical realization of such figures" (Smith, *Conjuring Culture*, 254). Instead, Du Bois's Christ parables use the Bible as a tool for invoking sharp reactions in readers in order to help them see the pressing concerns of the day and not to connect history to Providence. In this, his uses of the Christ figure more resemble Robert Alter's account of "modernist" uses of the Bible, which both question the nature of Divine rule and yet "proceed from the assumption that the Bible can provide...a resonant structure of motifs, themes, and symbols to probe the meaning of the contemporary world." Robert Alter, *Canon and Creativity: Modern Writing and the Authority of Scripture* (New Haven, Conn.: Yale University Press, 2000), 96.

70. This is an important theodical strain in Du Bois. For example, questions about suffering on the death of Burghardt help give birth to a naturalized notion of redemption to be achieved within America's political landscape. In a brief reading of "On the Death of the First Born," Paul Gilroy claims that the "suffering" involved in the boy's death "has no redemptive moment" (Paul Gilroy, *The Black Atlantic: Modernity and Double Consciousness* [Cambridge, Mass.: Harvard University Press, 1993], 139). Gilroy is right insofar as he means that Du Bois rejects supernatural redemption. Nonetheless, Du Bois, as I mention earlier, holds out the goals of "liberty" and "freedom" as worthy, even redemptive pursuits.

71. Du Bois, "Pontius Pilate," in *Du Bois on Religion*, 158.

72. Mathews, "Southern Rite of Human Sacrifice." Mathews's reading includes an examination of Lillian Smith's *Killers of the Dream* for the way in which she makes an explicit connection between God's love and white skin, as well as of a "a strange and compelling little book" by a white pastor, Edwin Talliaferro Wellford, called *The Lynching of Jesus* (1905)—an antilynching pamphlet that clearly links Christ to lynched African Americans as a way of trying to get white readers to see lynching as a form of unjust oppression. For Mathews, the religious nature of Wellford's anti-lynching argument only reinforces the way in which religion was a crucial part of the vocabulary of lynching.

73. Du Bois, "Pontius Pilate," 158.

74. Du Bois, "Jesus Christ in Texas," in *Darkwater*, 73.

75. Ibid., 76.

76. Ibid.

77. Ibid., 77.

78. Du Bois, "The Prayers of God," in *Darkwater*, 146.

79. Ibid., 147.

80. On Sept. 8, 1936, A. L. McCamy was lynched in Dalton, Georgia. On September 9, as part of its antilynching campaign, the New York office of the NAACP flew from its Fifth Avenue window a flag that read, "A Man Was Lynched Yesterday" ("Flag Recording Lynching Is Flown on Fifth Avenue," *New York Times* [Sept. 9, 1936]). Thus began a very public practice of confronting the white American public (or at least passersby in New York City) with this national scourge. What are the

semiotics of this flag? What does it say about the way black and white people communicated about lynching? How effective was it in raising white consciousness about the national scourge? Answering these and other questions is obviously beyond the scope of this project, but they seem too crucial not to ask.

81. Henry Samuel Levinson, *Santayana, Pragmatism, and the Spiritual Life* (Chapel Hill: University of North Carolina Press, 1992), 234–245.

82. This account is drawn from Brad S. Gregory, *Salvation at Stake: Christian Martyrdom in Early Modern Europe* (Cambridge, Mass.: Harvard University Press, 1999), especially 1–8, 50–61, 139–164.

83. This resembles Darby Kathleen Ray's description of the Abelardian understanding of Christ's sacrifice: "It is not simply the *fact* that Jesus lived and died that is redemptive, according to the Abelardian model, but the *way* in which he did these things—the specific behaviors and attitudes that he exhibited in the process of living and dying." See *Deceiving the Devil: Atonement, Abuse, and Ransom* (Cleveland, OH: Pilgrim, 1998), 14; emphasis in the original. The basic Abelardian exchange is that in return for Christ having died for us, we are required to fulfill certain responsibilities (e.g., living by Christ-like virtues).

84. Robert Gooding-Williams is the only critic I have found who notices this detail. See his "Du Bois's Counter-Sublime," in *The Souls of Black Folk*, ed. Henry Louis Gates Jr. and Terri Hume Oliver (New York: Norton Critical Edition, 1999), 246–250.

85. W.E.B. Du Bois, *Prayers for Dark People*, ed. Herbert Aptheker (Amherst: University of Massachusetts Press, 1980), 25.

CONCLUSION

1. For a succinct account of the archetypal role of the Exodus in African American religious traditions, see Albert Raboteau's "African-Americans, Exodus, and the American Israel," in *Fire in the Bones* (Boston: Beacon, 1995), 17–36. Theophus Smith's essay on African American uses of Exodus is brilliant in his suggestion that the tradition is a dialectical one. Smith points out that Henry Highland Garnet's "Address to the Slaves of the United States of America" (1843) uses the Exodus to *resist* the classical archetype of God delivering African Americans to freedom. Smith asks whether this is "evidence of [Garnet's] advancement of, or alienation from, a vigorous and compelling tradition?" (318). See Theophus H. Smith, "Exodus," in *African American Religious Thought: An Anthology*, ed. Cornel West and Eddie S. Glaude Jr. (Louisville, Ky.: Westminster John Knox Press, 2003). Also see Allen Dwight Callahan's wonderfully comprehensive chapter, "Exodus," in *The Talking Book: African Americans and the Bible* (New Haven, Conn.: Yale University Press, 2006), 83–137.

2. Eddie Glaude also sees Baldwin as riveted by love, though to my mind Glaude does not connect Baldwin's love explicitly enough to religious sources. See Eddie S. Glaude, *In a Shade of Blue: Pragmatism and the Politics of Black America* (Chicago: University of Chicago Press, 2007), 11–16.

3. Albert Murray, *Stomping the Blues* (Cambridge, Mass.: Da Capo, 2000), 96, 98.

4. Ibid., 10.

5. Ibid., 98.

6. I am thinking here of the work of Alaisdair MacIntyre and Stanley Hauerwas, both of whom insist upon the necessary narrative nature of Christian life and ethics. For them Christian life is a full-bodied practice and not a set of rules to follow; full-bodied practices take shape and gain coherence only as part of larger narratives. Of course, neither would think there is anything particularly religious about a narrative if it does not include participating with the monotheistic God.

7. All citations of the sermon are from Ralph Ellison, *Invisible Man* (New York: Vintage, 1995), 9–10; emphasis in the original.

8. Kenneth Burke, *The Rhetoric of Religion: Studies in Logology* (Berkeley: University of California Press, 1970), vi.

9. Ellison, "What Would America Be Like without Blacks," in *The Collected Essays of Ralph Ellison*, ed. John Callahan (New York: Modern Library, 1995), 582.

10. William James, *Pragmatism: A New Name for Some Old Ways of Thinking* (Cambridge, Mass.: Harvard University Press, 1975), 28.

11. In concluding his essay on Sammy Davis Jr., Gerald Early similarly sees the Ellison passage I am concerned with as a statement of and for the ambiguity of race: "But Davis gave us an incredibly rich and strange embodiment of something Ralph Ellison had one of his characters say in the prologue of his novel *Invisible Man:* 'Black is…and Black ain't.'" See Gerald L. Early, *This Is Where I Came In: Black America in the 1960s* (Lincoln: University of Nebraska Press, 2003), 66.

12. Ellison, *Invisible Man*, 10; emphasis in the original.

13. Ralph Ellison, "My Strength Comes from Louis Armstrong" (interview by Robert O'Meally, 1976), in *Living with Music: Ralph Ellison's Jazz Writings*, ed. Robert O'Meally (New York: Modern Library, 2001), 279; emphasis in the original.

14. Ibid.

Index